TASK FORCE HOGAN

★ ★ ★ ★ ★

TASK FORCE
HOGAN

★ ★ ★ ★ ★

THE WORLD WAR II TANK BATTALION THAT
SPEARHEADED THE LIBERATION OF EUROPE

WILLIAM R. HOGAN

WM

WILLIAM MORROW
An Imprint of HarperCollinsPublishers

HarperCollins books may be purchased for educational, business, or sales promotional use. For information, please email the Special Markets Department at SPsales@harpercollins.com.

FIRST EDITION

Designed by Bonni Leon-Berman
Map by Nick Springer. Copyright © 2023 Springer Cartographics.

Images in the photo insert are courtesy of the author, except:
Page 1: (top and bottom) courtesy of the US Army Signal Corps; (middle left) courtesy of Jan Mundo / the family of Louis Spigelman; (middle right) courtesy of Will Saia. Page 2: (top) courtesy of the National Archives, photo no. 208-MO-11A-31079; (middle top) courtesy of the National Archives, photo no. 192513; (middle bottom) courtesy of James E. Grimes. Page 3: (top) courtesy of the Tank Museum of Brussels; (middle and bottom left) courtesy of Henri Rogister; (bottom right) courtesy of the National Archives, photo no. 111-SC-195914. Page 4: (top) courtesy of the National Archives, photo no. 111-SC-197822; (middle left) courtesy of the National Archives, photo no. 198386; (middle right) courtesy of the family of Lee Porter; (bottom) courtesy of the US Army Signal Corps. Page 5: (top) courtesy of the National Archives, photo no. 111-SC-334034; (middle) courtesy of the US Army Signal Corps; (bottom left) courtesy of the family of John Barclay; (bottom right) courtesy of the Sitzes family. Page 6: (top left) courtesy of the Elissondo family. Page 7: (top) John Florea / The LIFE Picture Collection / Shutterstock; (middle) courtesy of the US Army Signal Corps; (bottom) courtesy of the National Archives, photo no. 111-SC-282447. Page 8: (top) courtesy of the US Army Signal Corps

Library of Congress Cataloging-in-Publication Data

Names: Hogan, William R., author.
Title: Task Force Hogan : the World War II tank battalion that spearheaded the liberation of Europe / William R. Hogan.
Description: First edition. | New York, NY : William Morrow, an Imprint of HarperCollins Publishers, [2023] | Includes bibliographical references and index.
Identifiers: LCCN 2023024271 (print) | LCCN 2023024272 (ebook) | ISBN 9780063272026 (hardcover) | ISBN 9780063272040 (ebook)
Subjects: LCSH: United States. Army. Armored regiment 33rd—History. | Hogan, Samuel Mason, 1915-2005. | United States. Army. Task Force Hogan. | World War, 1939-1945—Campaigns—Western Front. | World War, 1939-1945—Regimental histories—United States. | United States. Army. Armored Division, 3rd.
Classification: LCC D769.3055 33rd H64 2023 (print) | LCC D769.3055 33rd (ebook) | DDC 940.54/1273—dc23/eng/20230627
LC record available at https://lccn.loc.gov/2023024271
LC ebook record available at https://lccn.loc.gov/2023024272

ISBN 978-0-06-327202-6

23 24 25 26 27 LBC 5 4 3 2 1

The majority of the dialogue and conversations in this narrative nonfiction book are not meant to be a word-for-word transcript. Rather, the author leaned on recollections of conversations with his father and knowledge of his personality, values, and manner of speech to re-create what dialogue that occurred over eighty years ago might have sounded like. In this, he also used his more than twenty years of experience in the US Army to re-create what is the common language of soldiers. Of course, with most of the eyewitnesses long deceased, the author relied on varying levels of conjecture to fill in the remaining gaps. Every effort was made to make the book as factually accurate as possible, including diligent research, personal interviews, and the inclusion of information from the personal records of the people involved in the story.

The views expressed in this publication are those of the author and do not necessarily reflect the official policy or position of the Department of Defense or the US government, and the public release clearance of this publication by the Department of Defense does not imply Department of Defense endorsement.

CONTENTS

ENGLISH CHANNEL

1°W

OMAHA BEACH

CAEN

NORTH SEA

HILL 91 "HAUTS VENTS"
PONT-HÉBERT
SAINT LÔ

NORMANDY
FRANCE

49°N

FALAISE

FALAISE
POCKET

CHÉRENCÉ-
LE-ROUSSEL

ÉCOUCHÉ

MORTAIN

0   10 Miles
0   10 Kms

AMSTERDA

ENGLAND

51°N

BELGIU

BRUSSELS

NAM

WEYMOUTH

MONS

SOLRE-LE-CHÂTEAU

50°N

ENGLISH
CHANNEL

THON

AISNE

LE HAVRE

PONT-HÉBERT
OMAHA BEACH
CAEN

MARNE

49°N

SAINT LÔ

CHÉRENCÉ-LE-ROUSSEL

FALAISE
ÉCOUCHÉ

PARIS

MORTAIN

SEINE

MELUN

2°W   1°W   0°

THE ROUTE OF
TASK FORCE HOGAN

GERMAN OFFENSIVES

KEY RIVER CROSSINGS

0   20   40   80 Miles
0   20 40   80 Kms

48°N

FRANCE

47°N

MAP BY NICK SPRINGER
COPYRIGHT © MMXXIII SPRINGER CARTOGRAPHICS

1°E   2°E   3°E   4°E

TASK FORCE HOGAN

1

★ ★ ★ ★ ★

FIRST BLOOD
ON HILL 91

JULY 10–15, 1944

Sam Hogan wiped the sweat off his brow. His leather tanker's-helmet liner was saturated, and the perspiration stung his blue eyes. Racing in all directions, his mind was a frenzy of thoughts and recollections. He tried to check off in his head some of the myriad "must-dos" learned over countless classes and field exercises preparing for this very day. *Use the folds in the terrain to protect your tanks and men from hidden enemy cannon.* He squinted to fight the burning and to narrow his vision in the vain hope of sighting the hidden enemy. *An enemy waiting in ambush will likely see you before you see them.*

More words of the *Armored Force Field Manual,* the bible of US tankers, echoed in his head: *Painstaking and meticulous attention to detail may mean the difference between success and failure of an operation and life and death of the individual.*

Time slowed to a crawl. Adrenaline put his body on high alert and made him aware of everything. His hands were slippery as he clenched field glasses to his chest. Churning acid flooded his stomach. A loud rhythmic beating, his heartbeat, amplified by the snug-fitting football-style crash helmet, pounded in his eardrums. He took a deep, slow breath in an attempt to slow his heart rate and calm his nerves.

Standing with his head and shoulders outside the hatch of his command tank, the twenty-eight-year-old army lieutenant colonel took one last look through his field glasses and swallowed hard. Somewhere across the fertile patchwork of chocolate-brown fields and loam-green hedgerows were the German positions—heavy tanks, antitank guns, and dug-in infantry waiting to repel the recently arrived invaders. Sam could smell his own sweat mixed with fuel fumes—hot, smoggy air escaping up through the commander's hatch into the relatively cooler summer air.

Ahead in the rolling Norman fields stood the forward elements of Field Marshal Erwin Rommel's Army Group B. Led by veterans of the Russian front, fitted with state-of-the-art equipment—camouflage uniforms, Mark V Panther tanks, and handheld antitank rockets, forerunners of the modern rocket-propelled grenades (RPGs) and Javelin missiles.

Initial reports from the other US battalion commanders were that even the Sherman medium tank was hopelessly underarmored and undergunned compared to the German Panzerkampfwagen tanks—or "panzers." As a result, Sam's light tanks were only good for reconnaissance missions, to guard command posts, and to screen his battalion's flanks. This dismal fact effectively cut his offensive armor strength by a third before a shot was even fired.

As his Third Battalion cautiously treaded forward, he spotted the burnt-out, collapsed hulk of a US light tank, destroyed during the previous day's assault by the Thirty-second Armored Regiment—a sister unit to his own Thirty-third Armored Regiment within the Third Armored Division. Some infantry and US tanks had taken the hill ahead before being driven back, with heavy casualties. The dark, ashy patch was mute testimony to a white-hot inferno of fuel and tank ammunition.

Try as he might, Sam couldn't spot the guns that had destroyed the American tanks the day before. Every clump of twisted, bombed-out shrubbery, every earthen wall, every gnarled tree root could be hiding a well-camouflaged antitank cannon. One position, a darker shade of brown than its surroundings, an angled shape in the shadows, suggested a half-hidden man-made silhouette, perhaps a PAK-43 antitank gun—a low-to-the-ground, long-tubed, high-velocity cannon with killer optics.

Inside Hogan's M4 Sherman command tank, four other soldiers shared the cramped interior with their commander. The gunner, Technician 5 Clement Pierre "Clem" Elissondo—a hard-charging émigré to California from the Basque region of France—and the loader, Corporal Edward Ball, sat next to Sam's legs as he stood peering through the commander's hatch. Below and in front of them in the tank's hull was Corporal Addison Darbison. Amid this deadly landscape, Addison worried that his younger brother William might soon follow his example and enlist in the tank corps instead of a safer, "rear echelon" specialty. He scanned the field through a tiny periscope in the stuffy confines of his hull position and spotted the same burnt-out tank husk Sam had seen a moment ago. He prayed his brother would remain safely back from the front lines in a support outfit.

On Darbison's right, separated by the loud metallic gearbox, was the assistant driver and bow gunner, Private Robert Begany.[1] The men sat at their stations, focused and still but for the beads of sweat running profusely over brow and cheek. Some muttered soft prayers. Some ran through the mental checklist of what they'd need to do if their tank was hit.

The armored fist of Sam's command deployed around him in a giant arc almost two kilometers across. He couldn't see them all—they sat in the middle of Normandy's bocage-hedgerow country. Solid walls of packed earth and dense trees enclosed each farmer's field. This was broken terrain and couldn't have been more perfectly designed as a scourge for advancing tanks.

To his left and right, two companies of Sherman medium tanks—G and H, each composed of fifteen tanks with five crewmen per tank—were in attack formation with the River Vire protecting their left flank. Infantrymen—foot soldiers—rode on the backs of the rearmost tanks, ready to jump off and attack any German tank-hunter teams. Missing was the C Company of light M3 Stuart tanks—they were a few kilometers back guarding a flank.

Behind Sam in the assembly area—the spot from which they had first prepared for the attack, well out of enemy artillery range—were his support elements. Supply troops waited to bring up ammunition and fuel, medics anxiously prepared for an influx of their comrades suffering from grievous wounds, and staff officers tracked every detail of the upcoming battle. Between the tanks and the supply units were Sam's indirect-fire assets: mortars, five-foot-tall tubes mounted in the back of open-topped, front-wheeled, rear-tracked, lightly armored M3 half-tracks. These, along with the snub-nosed M8 assault guns, were poised to unleash hell in the form of explosive rounds that could rain down in high arcs upon the enemy.

On July 10, after a series of nighttime marches under radio silence and through traffic jams in the narrow and muddy country roads, amid a constant haranguing from higher brass to "get forward" and "get bloodied," Sam found his battalion in its current predicament. These orders from the higher-ups went against Sam's ethos of "fight smart, not hard." Sam feared needlessly wasting lives in frontal attacks. But it was well-nigh impossible to find an open flank on an enemy that was to his front and sides with his back to the English Channel.

The battalion's mission was to capture Hill 91, so named for its elevation in meters on a military map. To the locals, the hill was Hauts Vents—"High Winds." Hauts Vents overlooked a small village, Pont-Hébert, named for its bridge, where—God willing—a forced crossing of the River Vire would place the allies on the road to Saint-Lô and off the Normandy perimeter. The quaint little town, with its stone bridge and idyllic two-story, redbrick, half-timbered homes, straddled both sides of the river.

Thankfully, French villagers had evacuated to nearby salt mines before US artillery destroyed the imposing Gothic brick church steeple that'd been used by the Germans to call in artillery strikes on the approaching Americans. The stone bridge was heavily damaged as well. And now, more metal and fire were headed to the hapless little town.

Sam stood with his knees bent, chest-deep inside the turret of his command tank, and fumbled briefly for the switch to the throat microphone connected to his tanker's helmet. Sam was hyperalert—his eyes darted around the tunnel vision of focus. He was conscious of the summer heat, and the stench of tank exhaust stung his nostrils, suddenly more pungent, but a slight breeze picked up from the English Channel and blew cool against the moisture on his exposed neck. He looked at his watch—11:15 A.M.—said a quick, silent prayer to himself, and gave the order to advance.

"Guidons, guidons, this is Blue Six—MOVE OUT!"

The transmission crackled and hissed over radios down to the company commanders and then to their respective tank and infantry platoons. In a haze of gasoline exhaust, with shimmering heat rising off the top rear decks as their Detroit engines churned, the Sherman tanks lunged forward. Sam watched the two tank companies move as enormous masses of steel, lumbering up the green fields and spreading wide swatches of mud. The tank treads left impressions in the soft earth that pointed like arrows toward the uncertainty of the German line.

SAM HOGAN WAS ONE OF the youngest lieutenant colonels in the US Army. He was a lean six feet tall, with an aquiline nose, strong chin, and piercing blue eyes. A West Pointer, he was firm in personality and convictions; but to armchair generals and colonels pressuring him to move his people forward from the safety of a command post ten kilometers behind him, he could be irreverent and understatedly sarcastic. On the way into this first battle, in response to hectoring from the one-star general over the radio to "get up there" through a sea of muddy road and backed-up traffic, Sam responded, "You're coming in broken, over," then squelched him off.

But Hogan's "war face"—all business, steely-eyed, with thin, downward-sloping lips—could and did relax into an easy, disarming, dimpled grin that betrayed his sense of humor and his kindness to others. He was buoyant and optimistic in spirit yet strong and unyielding in principles.

Back in the United States during training, he was always there to welcome the new draftees off the train with a smile and a firm hand-shake. "Welcome! We're glad to have you on the team." Whether they were former bankers or poor sharecroppers from the Rio Grande Valley, he treated everyone with equality, dignity, and respect.

At gunnery practice in England, he pressed his tank crew hard until their tasks became second nature. Unlike the majority of the other tank crews, his needed to be even sharper, because Sam had to focus on lead-ing the entire unit as well as his own command tank. "Gunner! Enemy tank, eleven o clock, eight hundred meters!" There were multiple targets to engage. Gunner Clem Elissondo quickly turned the powered turret but overshot it in his haste. He returned to the spot and put the optics on the cutout target. "Sir, I see him!" The loader meanwhile made the 75-mm cannon ready with a high-explosive (HE) round, replying, "HE up!" The command went out to fire as Clem stomped on the trigger pad below him, shouting, "On the way!" as everyone made sure they avoided the violent recoil of the cannon.

A hit! But the initial overshoot had cost them valuable time, and the stopwatch had run out. "We missed the last target" was all Sam had to say. His soldiers hated to disappoint him. Afterward, the usu-ally über-confident Elissondo was glum. Sam reassured him: "Keep at it, Clem. Next time you'll hit the bull's-eye."

Throughout their training, Sam, and his commanders by his exam-ple, never skipped out on sharing a hardship or task that the soldiers endured. That caring leadership earned him the love of his soldiers from the beginning.

Now the young lieutenant colonel from rural Texas found himself re-sponsible for the lives, welfare, and mission accomplishment of five hun-dred soldiers moving swiftly on fifty-four tanks and dozens of wheeled vehicles toward the front line.

Off the landing beaches, they had removed waterproof covers on their tank's hatches and armament, received extra ammunition from di-vision, and sent out small patrols to probe the line and ease some of the green troops' jitters. It was time to find out what he and his men were made of.

The beautiful early-afternoon sun cast a soft, peach-tinted glow on the pastoral landscape of rolling hills that sloped up to the ridge overlooking Pont-Hébert. Around them were fields of green apple orchards framed by thick hedgerows and tall firs. The formation straddled a sunken road. Golden dandelions and purple wildflowers lined the country path, sprinkled here and there on the green grass like fallen stars from a twilight sky.

But as the tanks climbed, the battle line came into view. The stench hit first, then the sight of bloated bodies. Dead cows littered the landscape, their legs sticking stiffly up in the air in grotesque rigor mortis. The black-and-white animals rotted in the summer heat. These bovines, famous for the delectable milk and cheese they produced during happier times, had fallen victim to artillery fire. As the tanks advanced farther, they encountered the first clumps of human bodies, some clad in German gray, others in US olive drab. A few of the ones in gray were flattened and ground into the earth by tank treads—picturesque French farmland soiled by Dantean horrors.

Sam's left flank was supposed to be held by elements of the 119th Infantry Regiment of the US Thirtieth Infantry Division—composed of North Carolinians, its nickname was "Old Hickory" in tribute to Andrew Jackson, who was known for his toughness and willingness to suffer hardships next to his soldiers[2]—but that flank had been left unguarded.

There had been poor coordination between the two units, plus some bad blood over the giant traffic jams in the narrow country lanes as the Americans had tried to surge forward through what resembled a funnel of roadways that led to the enemy line. The day before, the Thirtieth Infantry Division commander, Major General Leland Hobbs, had berated Sam's immediate commander, Brigadier General John J. Bohn, in the clear over the regimental radio net: "Get your tanks on Vents by 1700 or you're fired!"[3]

That pressure rolled on down the chain of command. Every soldier felt it. The hill had been briefly occupied on the previous day by six tanks from Lieutenant Colonel Roswell "Rosie" King's First Battalion,

Thirty-third Armored Regiment, before being mistakenly bombed by US artillery. The greenhorn Americans had succumbed to the fog and friction of war, combined with the rookie jitters, and then were driven off by powerful forces of the German Panzer Lehr Division. The result was Hobbs's making good on his promise to fire Bohn, with Rosie King's tanks pulling back to lick their wounds. This left Sam's battalion up to bat. The top of the ridge was within three hundred meters.

"Red Platoon is taking hits of shrapnel—over." Radio silence, broken by unseasoned tank crews. That pinging, metal-on-metal sound on their Sherman hulls and turrets was not artillery fragments. It was only the spent metallic links that held together the long belts of machine gun ammunition aboard the American P-47 fighter-bomber aircraft. The links rained down like hail as they flew above the formation and fired on German targets close to the tankers' front.

The sounds of real artillery and sniper fire grew closer and closer. A sharp crack here, the dull thud of a howitzer round leaving its tube there—the sounds of war closed in and rose in frequency. Then the cracks of rifle fire began, a sharp crescendo into sustained bursts punctuated by loud rips of machine gun fire as the front tanks made contact and returned fire.

Sam scanned the horizon, sweeping from left to right, then back toward the center. He decided it was time to button up—he popped down and closed the tank's hatch above him. Artillery bursts were exploding ahead, and a sliver of flying metal to the forehead or neck would take a soldier out permanently.

The group of tanks moved southwest now; the steep terrain and hedgerows meant the sunken road was their only way up. The old roads were so narrow that the Shermans' hulls avoided the muddy walls saddled with overgrowth by mere inches. It was impossible to turn the tanks around or retreat. It dawned on each tank crew member looking out: this terrain was an ambusher's dream.

As the advance continued, the terrain ahead became steeper and steeper. Once onto the northern ridgeline of Hill 91, the plan was to stay off the little country roads as much as possible. But well-sighted

German antitank cannons had badly mauled Rosie King's tanks the day before. They must have been hiding in the hedgerows that overlooked the entire length of the road on its approach south.

Furthering their hardships, artillery fire covered all crossroads along the likely avenues of approach to Pont-Hébert. Days before, the Germans had painstakingly aimed—in artillery parlance, "registered"— their artillery cannons from ten kilometers back. The heavy rounds were now landing and exploding just where they wanted them to. Once registered, all the enemy artillery needed to do was adjust their guns' elevation and direction toward the predesignated firing coordinates—day or night, rain or shine. Even without forward observers' "eyes-on," they could easily drop their deadly explosives on the advancing Americans.

Going cross-country presented challenges, too, as the hedgerows constricted formations and channeled them toward antitank-gun kill zones nearer to German infantry armed with deadly Panzerfaust ("armored fist" in German) antitank rockets or the US bazookas' bigger and deadlier counterpart, the Panzerschreck ("terror of armor").

The Panzerfaust—the direct ancestor of today's handheld antitank rockets, like the ubiquitous RPG—was a nasty little weapon that anyone could fire with little training. The mass-produced, disposable rocket had a sixty-meter range that was ideal for close combat and produced deadly effects inside American tanks. Its charge punched through a tank's hull, creating a large hole in up to two hundred millimeters of armor. On impact, the warhead—about the size and shape of a football—collapsed in on itself, injecting a mass of molten metal through the hole, picking up additional fragmentation ("spalling") from the tank's interior hull, and showering those white-hot shards of metal on the soldiers within.

The wedge of tanks rumbled forward. Sam saw—then, seconds later, heard—the US artillery strike the hedgerows about two kilometers in front of his forwardmost tanks. A group of three P-47 Thunderbolts screamed overhead; their tail fins glistened in the sun as they searched for targets. As the hilltop came closer into view, Sam saw the smoking wrecks of several of Rosie King's Sherman tanks: dark, dead stains of soot and burned ground against the barren hilltop.

He worried that the sloping terrain bordered by hedgerows was channeling the twenty-one Shermans off the sunken road like a giant funnel right into a trap. He observed that, as the tank formation climbed the slope, they were becoming visible to more hedgerows to their left, near the village called Belle Lande—which, according to intelligence, was supposed to be in the hands of General Hobbs's troops. But suddenly, from the little village, dark German tanks and cannons surged forward to firing positions. Their intel from division had been wrong. Their flank was not just open—it was in enemy hands.

Sam roared a command to pour fire into those positions at their ten o'clock, but it was too late. The tree line three hundred meters to his front exploded with flashes of bright light, immediately followed by the solid lightning of green tracer rounds—projectiles impregnated with a burning substance making them shine brightly, even in daylight—fixed for a moment in the distance as they zoomed directly toward the US formation like shooting stars.

The telltale *RRRRRIP* of the MG42 machine gun, with its twelve-hundred-round-per-minute firing rate, rang out between concussive blasts of cannon. The tracer rounds helped the enemy gunners hit home with their streams of bullets.

A cacophony of noise erupted from the company and battalion radio nets—tank, platoon, and company commanders screaming out the direction of the muzzle flashes and calling for suppressive fire to take out the 75- and 88-mm antitank guns that fired at them.

Out of the corner of his periscope, Sam saw an incoming antitank round smash the hull of one G Company Sherman. It jolted to a sudden stop, and acrid black smoke poured from the gunner's, driver's, and commander's hatches. Sam held his breath and saw one crewman escape the stricken vehicle. Five slow seconds passed, but through the smoke, Sam saw two more soldiers jump out as the ammunition ignited. Then a roaring eight-foot-high column of orange fire shot straight up through the open hatches. Sam blinked his eyes and tried to refocus on the battle raging before him—rather than on the two tankers who he knew remained on board.

Sam looked ahead at the tree line and barked at his gunner, "Anti-tank gun eleven o'clock. Load HE."

Loader Edward Ball responded over the intercom, "HE up!"

"Fire!"

The tank rocked back as the 75-mm round screamed away in a flash of smoky orange. Cordite filled the crew's lungs and obscured the view out of their periscopes. Through his periscope, Sam saw an explosion of dust and tree branches mixed with smoke kicked up from the clump of trees ahead. Too much going on to see if they had hit the mark. He switched his comms to the Fires net—the radio frequency used solely for talking with the operators of his artillery and mortars, and the observers directing their fire. Sure enough, his artillery liaison was already calling in artillery on the positions in front. Their hard training was paying off.

He switched back onto the battalion net. "George Six, How Six, move your platoons through the objective—get defilade on your left flank!" Defilade—putting a hillside or fold of the earth between your tank and the enemy's guns—was their only hope. Sam knew there was no way to attempt a flanking movement. Those damn hedgerows and the bend in the river ahead channeled them in. The battalion was taking fire from two sides, and both of the companies were engaged: antitank guns to their front and German tanks to their left.

They would just have to charge through to the top of the hill.

In front and below Sam's legs, Clem Elissondo poured fire from his turret-mounted machine gun, all the while yelling curses in a mix of English and French. Chaos reigned. The tanks on the right hopelessly fired at the hedges, hoping to hit camouflaged antitank guns that they couldn't clearly see. They continued to fire main gun shells and coaxial .30-caliber machine gun fire, poured round after round into where tank commanders thought they'd seen a muzzle flash. Anything to suppress this ambush.

Several tankers identified German tanks and fired on them. But their hearts sank into their stomachs as they saw their main gun rounds hit home, then slice up toward the sky in a ricochet off the German tanks' heavy, sloping armor. Frustrated curses echoed through the comms.

Two more US tanks stopped in their tracks and spewed smoke and fire as the German 75-mm high-velocity rounds penetrated the Sherman frontal and side armor through and through. But there was no way back, no retreat. Sam's two tank companies continued their advance.

Sam never heard the round that hit his tank—it traveled faster than sound. He felt a sharp crunch of metal on metal, saw a flash, and felt a jolt. They were hit. Tunnel vision. A ringing in the ears. A deep consciousness of time as it slowed to a crawl.

Through a haze of smoke and adrenaline, Sam looked on as an orange glow in front and below him surged from the driver's position. Unbearable heat built up in an instant inside the cramped turret and hull. Sam saw the round's path—right through the driver's position on the left side of the hull. In just a few short moments, smoke darkened everything. Sam's lungs burned, but he managed to yell out the order over the intercom.

"BAIL OUT!"

Nobody needed additional encouragement. Sam saw the soldier below him, Clem Elissondo, ejecting himself quickly out of the gunner's hatch. Sam pulled the locking lever, struggled to lift his own heavy hatch, and after a moment of wrestling with the mechanism, feeling like his pants were about to catch on fire, he was greeted by blue sky. He jumped out in two swift bounds from the commander's hatch, then rolled off the back of the tank. One soldier who'd witnessed Sam's escape observed later, "Colonel, you jumping out of that tank reminded me of when you peel a banana three-quarters of the way down and then squeeze."

With one sudden roar and a fireball soaring nearly a dozen feet out of the tank's open hatches like the afterburner of a jet, the stricken Sherman's remaining on-board ammunition exploded all at once. The bright orange turned to black sooty smoke as the inside was consumed.

"Where is Darbison?!" Sam was accounting for his crew but came up short looking for the tank's driver. Clem Elissondo, slightly injured, hoped that Darbison had crawled out of the bottom escape hatch, but nobody had seen him, and nobody could get anywhere near the blazing

Sherman. The group needed to find cover quickly or get into another armored vehicle before a machine gun round or chunk of artillery shrapnel whizzing by found its mark. Their grim hope was that the impact of the round against the driver's side had meant a quick and painless death for the young Oklahoman.

Sam's second-in-command, Captain Carl Cramer, stayed on radio and directed the tactical movements of the companies during the five minutes it took Sam to jump onto another Sherman. It felt like an eternity: the formation moved past him as a tank with bumper number H-4 ground to a halt. He climbed the road wheels up to the tank's hull, then took a step up on the turret, hesitating for the briefest moment.

In this moment, Hogan considered the fiery death he'd just escaped in the tank that now smoldered fifty meters behind them. He considered Darbison's sacrifice. His ears were still ringing as he took one look inside the dark, dank, lime-green interior of this fresh tank.

Sam then looked ahead to the hilltop objective erupting with dust, fire, and smoke. The young colonel knew that, even in this brief moment, he had already hesitated too much. He had to get in and keep driving on. If anyone saw him hesitate it could destroy morale. How could he ask his tankers to saddle up and ride into battle again if he couldn't do so himself? They'd need to do it again and again, even after surviving hits to their tanks, if they were to win this war. Airbursts rang out behind his ears as shell fragments pinged harmlessly against the Sherman's hull.

Well, if a bullet or a shard has your name on it, it's gonna get you no matter what, Sam thought as he suppressed mental images of German antitank rounds slicing through both sides of the armored hull. He willed his long limbs into the confined space, dropped in, adjusted the hard metal seat, connected his helmet mike to the intercom, and once again breathed that hot, musty air.

"Driver, get this thing going and catch up with the formation." He gave the gunner, Sergeant Guidrey, a hearty slap on the back. The Sherman lurched forward as Tech 5 Ronald Davison stepped on the gas from the cramped confines of his compartment in the hull.

H Company was somehow holding its own on the exposed left flank, though now out of sight as they hugged the reverse slope of Hill 91 to avoid being in the sights of the German tanks. Sam had complete confidence in the commander. Captain John R. Barclay was a consummate, caring professional with serious tactical chops.

Months earlier, he had become a minor celebrity among the Third Armored Division officers. Back in England, during the buildup and while still a lieutenant, he was picked to demonstrate Sherman tank gunnery to visiting VIPs. A widely circulated morale-building photograph showed a serious, brow-furrowed Lieutenant Barclay as he pointed out targets over a map board, binoculars draped around his neck, steel helmet cinched down, chin strap secured. To his right was Supreme Allied Commander General Dwight Eisenhower, who looked on while appearing to be quite cold. To Barclay's left was none other than Field Marshal Bernard Montgomery, who also looked like he was freezing under his double-badged black beret. Barclay, clad only in tanker coveralls and helmet, was the picture of professionalism, casually pointing to targets for his tank, looking much tougher than the frigid VIPs. He'd had no time to let his fifteen minutes of fame get to his head. He trained his H Company tankers hard and ensured all their needs were met so that they'd have the best possible chance to come home to their families.

Now, undergoing their baptism of fire, Barclay and his tankers performed deeds that would make their command proud. A Sherman led by Sergeant Dean Balderson charged down the left side of the hill to protect the battalion's flank from any German attack coming from Pont-Hébert across the river. As the tank crossed a small apple orchard, the Sherman's gunner, Corporal "Swede" Anderson, spotted three Mark IV panzers. Their turrets turned in the direction of the US attack, ready to take out the battalion's Shermans as they crested the hill, silhouetted perfectly against the blue summer sky.

Balderson called out the direction:

"Gunner, enemy tank eleven o'clock."

"Fire!"

A high-explosive 75-mm round rocked out of the barrel and screamed toward the enemy tank. The Americans held their breath, worried that their rounds would once again ping uselessly off the heavy German armor. But, in an explosion of fire and smoke, the first round set the panzer's ammunition on fire. Before the other two tanks could react, Balderson ordered loader Bill Wilson to get another HE round in the breech.

"Fire!"

The second Mark IV was on fire within three minutes of the first. The third panzer began turning its turret toward the advancing Sherman.

"Gunner: load AP!" Wilson screamed.

"Ready!"

"Fire!" Balderson yelled. Swede Anderson craned his neck and yelled, "On the way!" He set his eye on the gunner's periscope to look for the dreaded ricochet off the panzer's tough frontal armor, but the AP did its job and the third tank exploded in sparks and smoke. Balderson and his crew hooted and hollered in short-lived exuberance and adrenaline release—their luck in this situation was lost on no one.[4] If the three enemy tanks had been Mark V Panthers, the result might have been different.

Back in the center of the staggered line of tanks, artillery screamed in from behind. The two companies attempted to stay in wedge formation as the falling shells churned clods of dark brown mud fifteen feet in the air. The fact that this was "friendly" artillery made it no less dangerous—it was coming in from the division assembly area a few kilometers back at Saint-Jean-de-Daye. "Incoming!!" echoed in frantic calls over the company nets and shouts over the din of engines. Sam quickly switched to the regimental net. "Ozone Three-Seven, this is Blue Six, check fire, check fire!" Repeated radio calls to cease fire were ignored until Sam got on the horn and barked at the US artillery, "Lift fire for fifteen minutes!" The immediate pause confirmed that, yes, in fact those were "friendly" rounds kicking up dirt and steel behind them. As if the German mortars and direct fire weren't enough. No time to stew, though, the barrage had lifted and there was more to deal with out front.

The pause allowed for a renewed push. Ground pounders of the Thirty-sixth Infantry Regiment under Colonel Dorrance Roysdon—the fired General Bohn's former second-in-command and now the senior commander—surged ahead from their cover in a sunken road, which anchored the axis of advance. Sam heard Roysdon call out commands as the infantry moved forward in five-second rushes toward the gray shapes milling about in the hedgerows before them. "I'm up! They see me! I'm down!" The little mnemonic learned in training, whispered under their breath or recited mentally, helped them time their rushes—just enough time to move and get back down before a German got you in his sights and pulled the trigger.

Sam called out his remaining tanks, forming a skirmish line to shield the foot soldiers and support them by withering fire of 75-mm cannons and bow- and turret-mounted machine guns. Bow gunners fired off ammunition until the overheated barrels smoked. US artillery whizzed overhead and detonated timed fuses at treetop level—the German infantry was showered with molten steel that traveled at five hundred feet per second. The US tanks and infantry gained momentum, but explosions beside and behind him told Sam that the Germans were not to be pushed off easily.

From the stale confines of the turret, Sam pressed his grimy forehead to the periscope and turned—all around him was smoke, dust, and fire. Of the twenty-one tanks that had rolled out that morning, only ten remained. They lurched forward and spewed small puffs of machine gun fire, punctuated by the occasional loud explosions and recoil of the main gun.

Screw it, he thought, I have to get a better look. He popped the hatch and peered out, instantly deafened by the din of battle. To his left and down the hill, at least one camouflaged position in Belle Lande was engulfed in smoke. His front line of tanks and accompanying infantry had clawed their way to the first line of positions about halfway up the slope. This appeared to be the military crest of the hill, the first spot from which they could observe all of the ground below. The position would command both sides of the river and any bridge that crossed it.

Another flash came surging from a German assault gun, this time to Sam's ten o'clock. The high velocity 75-mm round shot low and fast in a flash of white. The high-quality German optics scored an easy hit on the front mantle of a tank in the center of H Company. It was Barclay's command tank.

"Antitank gun, ten o'clock!" sounded inside the remaining tanks. No sound was coming from Barclay's stricken tank. Lieutenant Ed Wray, H Company's second-in-command, did not hesitate for a moment. He directed his own tank to shift fire toward the enemy gun and pumped two high-explosive rounds into it until flames leapt out of the crew compartment. Back on the battalion net, he radioed, "Blue Six, this is How Seven, How Six is hit, and I've taken command." Sam acknowledged, a relieved look mixed with a little pride crossing his soot-covered face. They had rehearsed this many times in exercises. A salty old sergeant or captain, a veteran of the Great War, would interrupt the tank maneuvers with the bark: "L-T, your commander is dead; you're in charge. Drive on with the mission." Again, the hard training was paying off in combat.

Inside tank number H-6, Barclay's Sherman, the armor-piercing round passed through the mantle and out the other side. The impact sent shards of the lining of the tank in all directions. John bled from cuts to his neck and arms but made sure everyone was out before he crawled out the top hatch and rolled off the back, over the hot engine compartment, and onto the muddy ground. An armored ambulance pulled up and evacuated the bleeding and concussed crew members to the battalion aid station two kilometers back off the hill. The little open-top, half-tracked ambulance ground gears and tore up the soft ground with its tracks as it quickly got out of the kill zone.

The advance continued another fifty meters, when German mortars and artillery suddenly opened up on the formation. The artillery rounds—thirty-six pounds of metal and high explosive with a blast radius of fifty meters—caused the accompanying infantry to dive for cover in the sunken road and the clumps of hedgerows on either side. This slowed the US advance enough for two German assault guns and a dozen armored infantrymen to reoccupy the crest. Unlike the short-barreled, slow-firing US assault guns, the German assault guns, or Sturmgeschütz, made effective tank destroyers with their high-velocity 75-mm cannons. Just the long gun's muzzle brake at the tip was almost the length of the entire US gun tube.

The US attack was spending itself out on the slope too quickly. The combination of uphill movement, constricting terrain, and both friendly and enemy fire were taking their toll. Colonel Roysdon and Sam exchanged knowing glances; they both knew that the best thing to do was to keep driving forward, away from the area pinpointed by the German artillery forward observers.

Roysdon, tommy gun in hand, rallied the infantrymen with shouts at the top of his lungs. Sam stood in the turret and waved ahead what few tanks remained. The line re-formed quickly, grimly determined looks on the clammy, mud-caked faces of the infantry. In an instant, both GIs and tanks laid down a wall of lead at the line of hedgerows and bushes where the German infantry had ducked for cover.[5]

Supported by their own mortars, the American tanks and infantry pushed ahead hard another fifty meters. After five hours of hard back-and-forth fighting, the sunset cast a soft orange glow on a scene of chaos and devastation. The German defense petered out as US artillery and return fire destroyed antitank guns. The unit to the Third Battalion's left pushed ahead into Belle Lande, cleared the village, and secured the line up to the Vire and Pont-Hébert. One final push got the remaining tanks on the hill and onto the objective.

And just like that, the initial push was over. Thirteen Germans were now prisoners.

But the battle was far from finished. The Germans wanted the hill back at all hazards.

Sam directed Captain Cramer and Lieutenant Wray via radio to spread out their remaining tanks on the reverse slope of the hilltop and use the terrain to hide their vulnerable under armor. He dismounted, going to each tank and talking to the tank commander and any of the crew that weren't in the middle of cross loading ammunition or digging fighting positions. A line of infantry occupied foxholes in front of and behind the tanks. The defense was set.

Sam got on the radio and checked on Major William "Stewart" Walker's handling of the wounded to the battalion aid station three kilometers back at the bottom of the long hill. His hardworking medics, led by Captain Louis "Doc" Spigelman, had their work cut out for them. They stabilized young boys with horrific burns and puncture wounds, tended to the wounded with expert care, all the while reassuring and encouraging them, *Trooper, you're going to make it, just lie back and relax.* John Barclay's wounds were bad enough to require evacuation to a field hospital closer to the beachhead. As for their warhorses, Sam didn't have to tell Walker that after his first task, the companies needed more ammunition and fuel in expectation of the next advance—or a brutal German counterattack.

The Germans were masters of the counterattack. The shrewd military commanders of the German forces were keen to exploit an enemy that had just pushed them off their position. The first few minutes before troops can dig in, they are vulnerable as they search the empty fighting positions, take care of their wounded, redistribute ammunition among themselves, and generally become familiar with the area they've just captured. This was the time for the Germans to gather whatever they had and hit back hard. Ingrained in them was an almost reflexive instinct to aggressively counterattack, from their officers and sergeants all the way down to their rank-and-file soldiers.

Just like a boxer counterpunching. Get hit? Hit back—as hard as you can.

But the Americans were well trained, too, and company commanders and platoon leaders gathered in anticipation of this incoming counterpunch. A harsh mix of adrenaline and fatigue glowed in their eyes, ringed by dark circles of soot and grime from time spent behind gunsights encircled by clouds of dust and gunpowder smoke. Despite the tension, excited conversations broke out. The tankers spread the word that the Sherman's 75-mm AP rounds were ricocheting off the thick frontal armor of the German panzers, especially the Mark V Panther.

They had yet to encounter the even heavier panzers armed with deadly 88-mm cannons and also named after hunting felines, the Mark VI Tiger and King Tiger. The vaunted "88" was originally an antiaircraft cannon first put to use against tanks by Rommel in North Africa.

Attached to a carriage as large as a farm tractor or mounted on a tank, the 88's barrel—almost as long and as thick as a utility pole—gave it range and muzzle velocity high enough to shoot down bombers at altitude. It could slice a Sherman through and through. That heart-stopping experience was yet to come.

The awe-inspiring capability of the Tiger tank had been solidified three weeks earlier and thirty-five miles east at Villers-Bocage. A handful of Tiger tanks under Captain Michael Wittman held off the entire British Twenty-second Armored Brigade of sixty Sherman, Cromwell, and Stuart tanks. In only fifteen minutes, Wittman's Tigers destroyed over thirty British vehicles, including twenty-three tanks. The tankers had heard the stories, and now they knew with fearful certainty what they were up against.[6]

The American AP rounds were ineffective against the Panthers they encountered. Captain Carl Cramer, of G Company, made a recommendation: "My guys are having good results firing HE rounds at the tanks. The round won't penetrate but concussion stuns the crew inside, shatters the onboard optics, and jams their turret mechanisms."[7]

Sam nodded. "That's good, but plan your artillery fire to take out their escorting infantry. Expect their artillery to fire in preparation—infantry should shelter under our tanks in their foxholes. We have to hold this hill. We're the only thing protecting the Thirtieth Division's exposed flank." His commanders saluted, then sprinted back to their company sectors.

There was no time to stop and think. No time to wonder if they would get reinforced quickly enough to hold out. Time oscillated: either compressed or dragged out, depending on the effect of stress or of waiting. He could feel an adrenaline dump coming—the crash after the emotional intensity of battle—and needed to shake himself out it. He thought about Barclay and hoped that he would survive his wounds. He was also thankful that the hard-charging Ed Wray was there to take over. His company needed his leadership now, as the sun disappeared over their hard-won hilltop.

A few hours later, out of the impending dusk, the distant sound of enemy tank treads squeaked in from the west, and the infamous Panzer Lehr Division came into view. Officers and sergeants of the German Armor Training Center, arguably the German army's most tactically proficient soldiers, led this unit. The Panzer Lehr's commander, General Fritz Bayerlein, was about to throw his 901st and 902nd Panzer Grenadiers at the American positions with twenty tanks. Their armored infantry rumbled to battle on half-tracks instead of on foot.

No rest for the weary.

Deadly blasts of fire and counterfire burst forth in the night and spoiled the relative peace on the captured hill. German artillery had a direct line of sight on the US positions and fired on them in a desperate tactic. In no time, the American force was on the receiving end of every type of artillery fire. Sam ordered his radio operator over the deafening sounds exploding around them: "Tell Division we're taking heavy artillery fire, they're hitting us with everything but Hitler's mustache. We need air support and artillery counterfire!"

The German artillerymen were experts—they used air bursts to take out infantry who sat in their foxholes and point-detonated high explosives to damage or destroy US vehicles. These cunning tactics separated or killed the infantry, thereby leaving the tanks vulnerable to antitank rockets and unable to hold their ground. US half-track crews and infantry dug holes obsessively to find a level of protection against this "steel rain." These brutal tactics taught the survivors to "dig in deep" as soon as they arrived at a new position.

On the US side, the battalion mortars—three half-tracks each mounting an 81-mm tube in the open bay—fired back furiously. Star cluster rounds burning white hot with phosphorus illuminated the river valley below for the tankers. Sergeants John Grimes of Missouri and Robert Cordell of Texas ran themselves ragged. They counterfired in response to the German fire, then repositioned their tracks within the tight perimeter in order to dodge the Germans' return barrage. Attempting to take cover in a trench, Grimes's half-track received a large shrapnel hole through its quarter inch of side armor. The crew mounted back up and were able to shrug off the blown-out front tire thanks to run-flat inner tubes, and repositioned yet again to fire another three-round volley of 81-mm HE rounds back at the Germans.

The German tanks surged across the river and up the slope, but their infantry straggled far behind after receiving the first volleys of US mortar and artillery fire. Perched on their tanks, Sam, Ed Wray, and Carl Cramer helped call in a massive artillery mission from a battalion of 105-mm howitzers in support. The converged sheaf of high-explosive shells threw off tracks and knocked out optics on the platoon of German Mark IV tanks and assault guns. Shermans aiming down the hill set two more ablaze. The massive cannons firing back and forth lit up the river valley and the German positions like a full moonlit night.

US artillery in direct support of their divisions fired furiously. Bean counters would later tally nine thousand rounds fired by the Thirtieth Division Artillery and six thousand fired by the Third Armored Division cannon cockers on July 11 alone.[8]

Sam Hogan was all for it. There's no such thing as excessive expenditure of ammunition if it saves the lives of your troops.

The US riposte stopped the German attack in its tracks. The survivors pulled back to positions five hundred yards to the south. Shell-shocked German prisoners expressed fear and admiration for the US artillery.[9]

The following morning came cloaked with intermittent rain. The defensive line stayed down as artillery whistled in. To defecate, infantrymen rotated their bodies out of their foxholes, did their business, then rolled back into their holes, covering the mess with a few spadefuls of dirt to keep the smell and flies at bay. Officers and sergeants stayed busy distributing what little water resupply had made it up the hill, as well as ammunition and petroleum and oil for the tanks. All of these tasks were performed during the day in sprints, conducted in between the volleys of artillery fired by the Germans. It would've been better to resupply at night, but the Germans had a say in the matter.

The rain breaking offered no relief as the US position was strafed from the cloudy skies. The culprit this time was the army's own P-47s—foiled by the low visibility, they unwittingly fired on the US soldiers. Air Liaison Captain Ted Cardon called them off with an angry transmission on his UHF radio, but not before six soldiers among Roysdon's infantry were wounded. Many exhibited symptoms of "combat exhaustion," but there was little Doc Spigelman and his medics could do—every man was needed.

The enemy took advantage of the chaos to launch another probe and attempt to find a weak spot in the US line. Furious fire from the wedge of Hogan's tanks halted the attack, but not before an antitank cannon hidden in the hedges took out another command tank. Once again, Sam heard nothing before the loud crunch of metal defeating metal. Not again! he thought in the split second before yelling "Everybody out!" In seconds that felt like minutes, Sam and his crew bailed out through their respective hatches as smoke filled the rapidly heating interior. Everyone emerged from their respective hatches—except one. The armor-piercing round had gone straight through the driver's position, killing Tech 5 Ronald Davison instantly.

Sam dusted himself off and mounted another tank. This was not a spare, but the enlisted tank commander was happy to take a break helping at the aid station. Sam plugged his helmet into the intercom and let out a sigh. *What next?*

However, day two on the hill passed with both sides exchanging fire at long distance as they licked their wounds and prepared for another day of combat.

Like clockwork, on July 13 an artillery preparation heralded another charge of German assault guns. Infantry surged out of the hedgerows and along the road leading up to Hill 91 from the south. Ed Wray called in mortar fire and directed his H Company tanks to take out the assault guns. From his command tank in the center, Sam alerted Cramer to prepare to shift two tanks over to the right flank to bolster Ed's four Shermans. One assault gun shrugged off the US mortar fire, stopping long enough to send two 75-mm rounds whizzing at the US positions. A request for P-47 air support to stop the attack was denied, as there were no fighter-bombers in the area. Frustrating, as the day before they had been firing on their own troops with no problems.

Sam could hear Ed Wray directing the fire—indefatigably encouraging his tankers and infantry. As the German formation approached the slope of Hill 91, their attack slowed. US mortar rounds exploded over their heads in black puffs of smoke and shrapnel. This was another benefit of the battalion's own mortars—they could fire in any weather, night or day. The Germans faced a line of Sherman tanks looking down at them and, with only two assault guns left, they finally abandoned the attack and sprinted off to the cover of the hedgerows to either side.

But on the right flank, Carl Cramer's G Company Shermans were in a fight for their lives as German infantry surged up the hill under cover of the hedgerows. Enemy mortar fire pinned down the defending US infantry in their foxholes, which allowed several figures in camouflage smocks and "coal-bucket" helmets to fire their Panzerfaust rockets. One Sherman went up in flames as the warhead ignited the onboard fuel tank. The crew managed to bail out before the inferno consumed them, and they rolled on the churned up soil to extinguish the flames that scorched their backs. Cramer turned his turret toward the tree line and hosed it down with .30-caliber machine gun fire. This finally bought them some silence from the German patrol.

Back in the center of the defensive line, radio calls back to Division yielded little good news. To the west, Mark V Panther tanks of the 901st Panzer Grenadier Regiment dueled with the tank destroyer battalions of the Thirtieth Infantry Division. The Germans also rushed forward the Third Fallschirmjager (Parachute) Division to prevent the Americans from crossing the Vire and capturing Saint-Lô. Sam's men knew they had to hold on for a few more hours, but how many was anyone's guess—and the enemy always had a say in the matter.

By day three on the hilltop, everyone was coated in dust and debris.

The soldiers operated on a mix of epinephrine, cigarettes, murky canteen water doused with coffee, and the occasional can of quickly eaten Spam and dehydrated crackers. They nervously and obsessively checked downhill and looked to the sky above for incoming fire. The hours of darkness provided little respite except for the added difficulty of aiming for the German gunners. The US soldiers took turns to sleep, thirty minutes on, thirty minutes off. Those on guard clutched their weapons firmly as sounds of enemy diesel engines and yelled commands in guttural German drifted up to Hill 91 in the cool Norman breeze.

On July 15 at 3:00 P.M., as the exhausted and hungry soldiers on Hill 91 were about to give up hope of being relieved, a dust-covered .30-caliber machine gun position on the western picket of the hilltop position received the friendly passage-of-lines password from an American patrol. Sam's depleted and exhausted troops were to be relieved by soldiers from the Old Hickory division.

New soldiers took over foxholes and fresh tanks moved up into the track prints of the previous occupants. Each sergeant and officer showed his replacement where the sectors of fire were and what to watch out for from the Germans. Still alert, though fading, Third Armored Division tankers and infantry backtracked down the hill toward an assembly area whose coordinates were radioed in by higher headquarters.

A short, bleary-eyed march north led them to their battalion area. After the previous seventy-two hours, Lieutenant Jake Sitzes's smiling face was a sight for sore eyes. Jake was a young maverick platoon leader in C Company. Before the attack, Jake's light tanks had been detached to guard the right flank as they passed through the forward lines. There they stayed during the battle for Hill 91, but they had not remained idle. Jake, his commander, Captain Ben Creamer, and the rest of C Company had laid out a battalion camp with baths and breakfast ready for the exhausted and dirty tankers from their sister companies. After a bath and hot breakfast of fried Spam and eggs (blessedly fresh instead of the usual powdered variety), Sam was filled with renewed hope that maybe he could survive the war.

The Third Battalion, Thirty-third Armored Regiment of the Third

Armored Division had largely survived its baptism of brutal, close-up combat. But Sam considered the casualties. Seven killed in action. He knew the names and faces of every one of the killed and wounded. He had met most of these men during the Thirty-third Regiment's initial training in the bayou around Camp Polk, Louisiana, in 1941. They got to know each other as only men who sleep, eat, and fight together can—from the early days of training in Louisiana all the way to Europe. Corporal Addison Darbison, the driver of Sam's destroyed tank, was one of several missing in action. He was likely dead after the hit by an 88-mm round through the hull. His body was never found.

Also missing in action were two members of H Company. Their tank was one of the first hit on the morning of July 11. An antitank round hit the rear of the Sherman's turret, immediately setting it ablaze. In the turret were the gunner, Tech 5 Robert Scheelk, and the tank commander, Sergeant Frank Matthews—they had been killed instantly. Loader Private Irving Fried managed to get out, but later died of his wounds. Only the driver, Private Harry T. Masram, escaped the inferno.[10]

It was obvious the Germans had been targeting the tanks containing the commanders. The battalion lost all six of them. H Company's commander, Captain John R. Barclay, had survived, but nobody knew if his shrapnel and burn wounds would heal enough for him to return. He was an officer who knew his tactics and knew how to take care of his men and machines. The losses were heavy but were not in vain. The Americans had stopped a major German counterthrust dead in its tracks and helped render the Panzer Lehr Division ineffective.

Sam lay down within earshot of his command post. He was exhausted but couldn't sleep. The adrenaline dump meant his body was spent but his mind still raced. Their first battle was over. Tomorrow was another day—but he had never expected to lose so many, including one of his company commanders, on their first combat action. How many more battles awaited his outfit? How many more men would have to die? He was too wound up to sleep.

He thought back to his momentary hesitation in battle. What if soldiers had seen him hesitate to mount up into the turret of another Sherman after getting one shot out from under him? Word would have spread, and the entire unit's morale could be in jeopardy because of his one moment of indecision.

Think pleasant thoughts, he reminded himself. You've got to get some sleep. His mind began to wander to thoughts of sunny days riding his horse along the Rio Grande. His parents, Dodge and Mary, on the farm in Texas and the warm smile of his wife, Belle. He recalled happy days during his graduation from West Point, the sunbeams dancing on Belle's auburn hair with Trophy Point and the meandering Hudson as a backdrop.

He thought back to West Point and long cold nights in gray barracks. Sam had always felt grateful and indebted for the first-rate free education funded with US-taxpayer dollars. The discipline and the hard winters had prepared him to lead men in the worst of conditions. The academy had given him an opportunity to move out of rural south Texas and make something of himself.

Then his mind flashed back to the sight of that green lightning coming at him out of an enemy gun at three thousand feet per second.

The debt is paid, he thought. He drifted into the dreamless slumber of complete exhaustion.

2

★ ★ ★ ★ ★

PREPARING TO
UNLEASH HELL

JULY 16–31, 1944

The morning after the battle at Hill 91 began in a beautiful salmon-colored sunrise turning into a clear, blue-sky morning. A beautiful morning that didn't do justice to the soldiers who'd died the day before and didn't foreshadow the bloodier days that lay ahead. For a frontline leader in World War II, mid-July 1944 was like the start of a race of unknown length and duration—and one where you were commanded to sprint.

There were only a few honorable ways out of this race before its finish: death, severe wounds, or "getting fired." In the case of firings—different from being relieved of command for cowardice or ineptitude—a higher commander deemed a subordinate "not aggressive enough." You were fired and the next leader in the chain moved up to your hot seat. A combat officer worth his salt feared this fate almost as much as death, because it meant delivering his troops into the unknown hands of an unproven commander.

But it was better not to dwell on those things and take events a day at a time. There was much to do. Sam rose early and had an eye-opening shave with cold canteen water out of his steel helmet. He went for a short drive in his "peep." In contrast to the more numerous foot-borne infantry divisions, fully motorized tank divisions had a wide inventory of tracked and wheeled vehicles. Small 4x4 cars used for scouting, towing antitank cannons, or the transportation of officers across their widely dispersed units came in several varieties. One was a half-ton armored command car with leather seats called the general-purpose car—"GP," or "jeep." Another was the ubiquitous little unarmored quarter-ton car that is today known as the jeep, but in 1942 tank units called it a "peep" to distinguish it from its armored counterpart. Sam preferred the speed and maneuverability of the peep, though its springs played havoc on a man's skeleton after hours of cross-country driving. Peeps were also far more numerous and didn't advertise to the enemy *Shoot me first! I'm a vehicle full of commanding officers!* as the GP "jeep" did. Private First Class Charles F. Gast was Sam's peep driver. He was a quick-witted kid from Sandusky, Ohio, with a brother, Richard, serving in the Pacific at New Guinea.

The oldest of the Gast brothers, William, had died in action while serving aboard a B-24 bomber over the Caroline Islands the previous April. Sam had been the one to break the news to Gast during one of their training maneuvers back in England. Gast bowed his head, swallowed hard, and managed to whisper, "Roger, sir, thank you for letting me know." Sam asked him if he needed time to himself, to which Gast replied by shaking his head and saying, "No, sir, my job is here with you, and that's the best way I can avenge my brother."

Now, they split some canned crackers and cheese spread as they drove the country trails from one field to another. Sam wanted to spot-check the progress of maintenance on the Shermans, half-tracks, and peeps spread out in an eight-kilometer radius among the verdant fields and thick hedgerows. Mechanical reliability was one thing the Sherman had going for it. Still, for every hour rolling, the American vehicles needed two hours of maintenance.

Soldiers who were not on security were stirring, climbing out of the shallow foxholes they'd dug beside their tanks and covered with pup tents. Vehicle drivers were checking oil levels, not just the performative "kicking tires"—looking busy when the colonel approached in his peep.

They knew lives depended on their machines running flawlessly. Some were waist deep in engine compartments while others shimmied faceup on the dirt as they checked gearboxes and hydraulic lines.

The peep crested and dove through rolling hills, sunken roads, and thickly overgrown hedgerows twisted with roots and packed earth as Sam traversed the battalion perimeter over to see C Company. This was Sam's chance to congratulate a few of the crews for their first successful combat performance. Morale seemed good after a reviving bath and warm food. Lieutenant Jake Sitzes had an ear-to-ear grin. His platoon's casualties were light—only a few slightly wounded—and he'd taken a couple of Luger pistols off German prisoners to send home as war trophies.

As Sam chatted up the crew of another C Company "Mae West" tank, a messenger roared up on a Harley motorcycle with a note calling Sam to the regimental command post. So much for getting around to each company for a welfare check. Sam finished his Camel cigarette, then left to finish checking on maintenance. Gast radioed for Major Travis M. Brown, the Third Battalion's operations officer, to meet the CO at the command post (CP) of the Thirty-sixth Infantry Regiment.

It was about 7:45 A.M. when Sam and Travis walked into the tented area set up by the M3 half-track that served as Colonel Roysdon's CP. A hard-charging infantry officer, Roysdon looked even more rugged wearing a couple of days of scruffy beard underneath the camouflage netting of his helmet.

Within the tent, all was abuzz with activity: soldiers moved about the cramped interior updating maps and preparing orders while two others sat monitoring radios mounted in the half-track bed. I bet we're getting orders for the next big attack, thought Sam as they walked inside. He greeted his fellow commanders, Rosie King and Bill Lovelady, both of whom were in their forties. At twenty-eight, Sam was one of the youngest battalion commanders in the army.

They opened the meeting by confronting the fact that the tough fight on Hill 91 had exposed quite a few weaknesses that needed to be remedied. The Sherman's 75-mm rounds (the diameter of the projectile in millimeters) were totally inadequate against the frontal armor of the Panther tank. The forty-five-ton Mark V Panther was better armored than the thirty-three-ton Sherman. The German cannons on both the Mark IV and the Mark V could knock out a Sherman at greater range, 1,000 meters, than the Sherman was capable of with its own short-barreled cannon. Shermans needed to get within 300 meters to guarantee a Panther kill through its frontal armor.

The officers added that the few Shermans they received that were "upgunned" to the 76-mm round did only marginally better—in volume it was comparable to the German tank rounds, but it held a smaller powder charge—so even with a slightly elongated barrel it still lacked the punch of the enemy's cannon. And neither American cannon could penetrate the hedgerows to get at the entrenched enemy defenders.

In contrast, the enemy's 75-mm gun tube was almost twice as long, resulting in a stunning three-thousand-feet-per-second muzzle velocity that could penetrate the American tanks from one side through to the other. The battalion commanders provided their recommendations on how to counter the enemy's advantages, such as Captain Cramer's discovery that using high-explosive instead of armor-piercing rounds could damage the German tank's optics and concuss the crew within.

The commanders also realized that being a heavy division had its drawbacks. They didn't have enough infantry support, particularly in the face of the portable and powerful German antitank weapons that leveled the playing field between a foot soldier and a tank. In addition to the lack of infantry, coordination was difficult, as the infantry's SC 536 AM "handy-talkie" radio could not communicate with the tankers' onboard FM radio. All these shortcomings needed to be addressed before the next attack, or more people would get killed and the Allies could be stuck on this Normandy perimeter for months.

Colonel Roysdon acknowledged their concerns. Better equipment was on the way, but for now the plan was for the Americans to bridge the gap through tank-infantry teamwork combined with aggressive use of airpower and artillery.

"Now to the business at hand," the mustached colonel crowed in a fast, raucous Chicago accent. "Gents, we have word from our division headquarters that the Twenty-ninth Infantry Division has pushed out as far as they can into a salient pointing to the little Norman village of Villiers-Fossard." A lit cigarette stuck out of the corner of his mouth as he pointed to a spot on the large map tacked to plywood in the middle of the tent. "We have a job to do, and we're going to do it, whatever the cost. We must throw caution to the winds and be completely reckless. When you have casualties and lose vehicles, keep right on going. If a company commander becomes a casualty, the second-in-command takes over immediately. As soon as you stop, in addition to wasting time, you're going to have more people killed and hurt. So whatever happens, absorb your losses and keep moving!"[1]

He went on to explain that a top-secret offensive, dubbed Operation Cobra, was Bradley's audacious plan to break out of the Normandy perimeter and race for Paris. But two corps of hardened SS troops lay ahead, surely digging in using their hands-on experience of preparing defenses in depth against giant Soviet tank armies.

The SS (short for Schutzstaffel, or "bodyguard") were the elite unit of the German armed forces. Similar to Special Operations forces, they were a relatively small unit that received the best training and most advanced equipment. The SS originated as Hitler's personal bodyguard—they were recruited for their loyalty and fanaticism. Ruthless and brutal, they generally took no prisoners.

As Roysdon's warning order went on, Sam's mind raced ahead—thinking not about tactics but about life and death. The specter of fear brought up acid in his belly. That first battle had been so costly, and he feared that what awaited his boys was surely worse. Get your people ready, stack the odds in our favor to make it out alive and back home, he thought. The preparation and necessary buildup of combat power meant two things—Sam's boys could get a short rest, but they also had to use that time to organize and prepare and digest some lessons learned from their first major attack. For this operation, the battalions would beef up into task forces.

What, you may ask, is a task force? Also known as a battle group, it is a "pure" tank or infantry battalion—like Sam's Third Battalion of the Thirty-third Armored Regiment—that is reinforced and organized according to its mission or task. This helped solve the problem of the tanks' vulnerability to infantry armed with antitank rockets: team up the armor with infantry to protect each other. Your mission is to attack a defensive line in a wooded area? You will need those foot soldiers to protect the tanks from enemy tank-killer teams hiding among the trees. Are you expecting obstacles, mines, or a river crossing? You will need engineers to find and deactivate the mines or throw up a bridge that can hold your tanks to get them across a river. Enemy aircraft nearby? The higher headquarters had better loan you a couple of M3 half-tracks, with quad .50-caliber machine guns mounted in the back, manned by farm boys with steady nerves ready to put down a wall of lead against enemy fighter-bombers screaming in at 350 miles per hour.

Task Force 3 became their new moniker for this crucial step in breaking out from the Normandy bocage and onto the fine tank country of northern France. Their reinforcement was a company of infantry. The infantry—the foot soldiers or GIs (for "government issue")—sometimes called themselves "doughs" in tribute to the World War I infantry doughboys.

In the tank division, they rode into combat aboard lightly armored, open-top half-tracks. The front wheels made them light enough to be fast while the rear track, like a tank's treads, gave it better cross-country mobility than a standard cargo truck. Two hundred riflemen mounted on half-tracks from the Thirty-sixth Armored Infantry Regiment joined the fold. The Thirty-sixth was the Third Armored Division's infantry regiment, one-third of its combat power. The remainder were the two tank regiments: the Thirty-second and Sam's Thirty-third.

A company of scouts from the Eighty-third Reconnaissance Battalion and a company of engineers also reinforced Task Force 3. The combat engineers dealt with any German *Schrapnell Minen*—S-mines—or "Bouncing Bettys." These nasty little inventions of Teutonic ingenuity, when detonated, set off a small charge propelling a larger charge in the air, exploding about a meter off the ground and slinging steel balls out-ward at waist level, right where a soldier's major organs are found. GIs dreaded them. In the best-case scenario, you survived but stood to lose your "family jewels"—the mildest of the soldiers' euphemisms.[2]

Sam and Travis drove from Roysdon's command post back to the battalion camp. En route, they choked down more canned rations—mystery meat and gelatinous beans in a can, washed down with canteen water—then called a meeting of the company leaders. The brains of the unit, the task force CP was always a hive of activity, with radios crack-ling, runners coming in and out with messages, and soldiers tracking all aspects of a battalion on the move.

The backs of the parked battalion commander's and operations offi-cer's half-tracks opened up into a medium-sized tent erected by the effi-cient operations staff, assisted by Gast and Sergeant Phil D'Orio, Sam's orderly. Orderlies ran orders from the commander and helped him to administratively run the unit, sometimes also acting as a bodyguard. For Sam, however, Phil was a valued adviser on the affairs and morale of his enlisted soldiers, akin to what a command sergeant major does to-day. There were folding chairs, the much-needed coffeepot, and a type-writer for cranking out orders and reports.

Sets of radios mounted in the half-tracks enabled the commander to radio his superior unit, the combat command, as well as his subordi-nate units, each with their own frequency, or "net." This included the tank company net. The mortars, and any attached artillery, were on the "Fires" net. Maps mounted on boards showed the locations of friendly units and their boundaries. Known enemy locations, marked in red, and the forward line of troops rounded out the information.

The small CP was abuzz with soldiers moving about and Sam's sub-ordinate commanders arriving. There were greetings and handshakes as they climbed out of their peeps accompanied by their executive officers (XOs) and first sergeants (tops). These were the most experienced and highest-ranking noncommissioned officers (NCOs) in a company. The first sergeant title came from the Roman legions—where a career "pri-mus pilus" (first spear) led each "century" of one hundred men.

Sam was at the center, a large map tacked to a five-by-eight wood board with acetate overlays passed down from the combat command showing routes and enemy positions behind him. His sky-blue eyes radiated warmth, but with a touch of hard-earned wisdom—the heavy responsibilities and loneliness of command. High cheekbones hinted of pioneer stock mingling with Native American blood. He had an easygoing confidence about him, backed by years of training and tactical competency, that was contagious to the men in his command.

As one officer described his commander: "He has a slim build—about 1.80 meters tall—and is slender. He has a deep voice, is slow of speech, almost nonchalant, but he weighs his words carefully. He has an optimistic disposition, smiles easily, and has an air of mockery. He is daring and combative. When he smokes a Camel, it is often a sign that great decisions are impending."[3]

Sam was smoking a Camel.

He gazed warmly at these young men he had grown to know so well over almost three years of training stateside and then in England. It was time to issue the order for the next battle.

For the group, the operations order, or OPORD, was just like a hundred others they had received in training—yet this time it was different. They were playing for keeps now. A dozen kilometers ahead was an experienced enemy, dug in and ready to kill or be killed.

Sam didn't hesitate. "All right, team, this is it, what we've trained for all these months. Operation Cobra is the plan to get us out of this perimeter and onto the flat, good tank country that will take us through the liberation of France. We have the next seven days to prepare twenty-six officers and 470 men for this action. Now, you know the drill. Major Brown will describe what is facing us and what we're going to do next."

Major Travis M. Brown stood to address the men. Called "Brownie" by his peers, he opened up with his slow southern twang. "Thanks, sir. Gentlemen, here we are." He pointed to the map. "For this mission we're supported by infantry with the scouts in the lead. In front of our corps is the German Seventh Army, composed of the Fifth Parachute, Second Panzer, and Panzer Lehr Divisions. Intel says that the 116th

Panzer Division, the Windhund [Greyhound], is out there somewhere." An ominous murmur rose from the gathered soldiers at the mention of the Windhund Division, for they had received that nickname for their speed and punching power.

Brownie quieted the men and moved on to translate Sam and the higher brass's guidance into tactical plans on the map. Company commanders and their platoon leaders scribbled notes, beginning to plan where they fit into the big picture. After this brief, they'd run back to disseminate the information to their own smaller units and begin reconnaissance.

"Our mission from higher: Task Force 3 will spearhead Combat Command B's attack toward Coutances, which will set us up for the breakthrough out of this Normandy perimeter we're sitting in," Brown said. This was the big battle that would launch the Allies through France toward Germany, but for the sake of the men he tried to sound as calm as possible.

Company commanders—Captains Ben Creamer and Carl Cramer and Lieutenant Ed Wray—exchanged excited glances. Ben Creamer was from Owensboro, Kentucky; a brave and competent leader, he was one of the founding officers of the Third Armored Division, and reported as a young lieutenant to Camp Polk, Louisiana, in 1941. Hard years of training had transformed Ben from a shy, lanky country boy to a robust and confident battle captain.

Ben pointed to the map and whispered to Jake Sitzes, his senior platoon leader, "This is where our light tanks can really make a difference in screening the task force flanks."

Jacob Marion Sitzes Jr. nodded, a mischievous gleam in his eyes. Slight of build, Jake was "full of the devil"—a small package of energy. He was combative and just what you want in a tank commander. When reminded how tough German tanks were, he encouraged his tankers by telling them, "I'm going to shoot them 'til they burn." Given the tiny 37-mm "pea-shooter" cannon on his M3 "Mae West" tanks, this was a bold statement.

Back in England, Jake was always getting into trouble with the Old

Man (Third Armored Division commander Major General Leroy Watson), probably in an attempt to be transferred out of headquarters and into a tank platoon. He wanted to be leading troops, not shuffling paper in the rear areas. He got his wish shortly before the embarkation for Normandy.

Jake belonged with troops. He was a natural leader, and his soldiers, after only a short time of knowing him, were ready to follow him anywhere. They knew he would be the one leading the way and that he would never ask them to do anything that he would not do himself.

Brown went on. "My staff and I are passing out the map overlays showing our sectors. Remember, anything in front of the forward line of troops"—he swept across the line marked "FLOT" in red on the map—"is the enemy."

Sam chimed in: "We must stay behind the FLOT until H-hour. Massive saturation bombing will soften up the enemy, but expect that they will fight hard and use the terrain to try and slow us down."

Brown concluded his part of the brief. He and his operations staff would stay busy as they tracked the battle and kept the reports that fed the hungry beast at regimental and division headquarters with hourly updates on location, disposition, casualties, status of supply, and readiness of the men and machines.

Sam strode up to the map confidently and with a sparkle of anticipation in his eye. He would personally show his commanders and staff his concept of maneuver. He began in a calm but commanding voice. "Scouts: you are our eyes and ears." He looked over at his lieutenants, Clark Worrell and Robert Resterer, and their senior sergeant, Shorty Wright.

The battalion's scout platoon sped forward into the unknown (or the vague and often inaccurately known, painted by G2 intelligence) in their M8 Greyhound six-wheeled armored cars, backed up by the occasional Stuart light tank, to find the enemy. Their 37-mm guns—known also as the "door knocker," for their inability to penetrate enemy tank armor—were no match for even the lightest German panzer, so they had to rely on stealth and speed. Their mission: find out where the enemy is, then hide, keep eyes on them, and report. The lieutenants and their sergeant jotted down notes as Sam continued: "Don't scrap with the enemy—find them and report back."

He continued, "Keep your air identification panels on at all times so you don't get strafed or rocketed by friendly air." Sam glanced at his air liaison officer. "Air support is going to be key, especially against entrenched hidden enemy. I need you to stay in constant contact with the IX TAC [Tactical Air Command] to keep those P-47s employed whenever they are on station. You'll ride next to me in your tank."

Helaman P. "Ted" Cardon stood up. "Roger that, sir. I'll keep those birds gainfully employed." Ted had been commissioned out of the University of Arizona's ROTC program. He joined the regiment just in time for its desert training in 1942 and was good at everything he did, from maintenance commander to air liaison.

Sam used a long stick as a pointer. "George Company will lead as we move out in columns." He pointed to the map. "At Phase Line A, we shift into company wedge formation in preparation for contact. Don't present a single line for the enemy gunners to shoot at us like ducks at a county fair. Stay dispersed."

Captain Carl H. Cramer of G Company scribbled notes furiously while thinking ahead on how to get his tankers ready. Often mistaken for a West Pointer due to his ramrod-straight posture, Carl was actually a "sixty-day wonder" graduate of Officer Candidate School—OCS, the army's solution to its tenfold expansion since Pearl Harbor. OCS turned experienced enlisted soldiers into officers in just two months, compared to four years in ROTC or at West Point.

The former regular army staff sergeant from Patoka, Indiana, led his soldiers with the tough-love, no-nonsense approach of a senior sergeant. He looked up from his notes briefly to whisper to Ben, "I really can't wait until we win this war and I can return to being someone important again."

"Yeah? What's that?" retorted Ben.

"A regular army noncommissioned officer."

Ben smiled at his buddy. They both knew well, as good officers do, that NCOs are the backbone of the US Army, its first-line supervisors. They take care of the day-to-day needs of troops, see to their discipline, and manage the myriad details required to keep them trained, fed, and equipped so that the officers can focus on the planning and execution of battle.[4]

Sam went on: "H Company, you follow George until Phase Line A, where your tanks will form the right wing."

Ed dipped his chin in acknowledgment, then said, "Sir, I plan to lead with my dozer tank and I go second."

"That's right, Ed," Sam continued. "Terrain and the enemy dictates your formation. I won't tell you how to crack that egg—you know the mission. How you get your tanks there is up to you and Top Filyaw [H company's first sergeant, Ernest C. Filyaw]." He managed to crack a grin. "You have my full confidence, especially after your exemplary actions on Vents."

Ed had been working as a clerk in the Hotel Charlotte in North Carolina when Japan attacked Pearl Harbor. He shelved his goal of becoming a hotelier and volunteered for the Armored Corps. Sam's confidence in Ed was well founded—he had already put him in for a Silver Star, the third-highest award for valor, for his actions under fire at Hill 91.[5]

"Ben, your Charlie Company tanks are the reserve, but you will actively screen our flanks, keeping in contact with the neighboring Thirtieth Infantry Division screens."

Ben gave a thumbs-up. "We're ready, sir. I was also talking with Lieutenant Sitzes about how our small tanks can navigate the tight roads better." Sam nodded.

"Now let's talk fires." He looked to Lieutenant Tom Magness and Sergeants Arnold Schlaich and John Grimes, who would coordinate indirect fire. "We're all counting on you to suppress and kill any German dismounts and their antitank weapons. You'll need to carry with you plenty of high-explosive, smoke, and illumination rounds." Sam then motioned to the map, where "free fire areas" and friendly unit boundaries guided where indirect fire could drop or not, in order to prevent wounding or killing friendly forces or civilians.

Tom Magness jotted down and exchanged notes with his sergeant as he listened on. He was in charge of the M8 assault guns, a light tank chassis with a snub-nosed, low-velocity 75-mm gun used to take out small fortifications and machine gun nests. An assault gun fired like a tank, in direct-fire mode, or indirectly, like a mortar. It was not designed to square off against tanks, having less armor and slower muzzle velocity than the already outgunned, outarmored Sherman, but it could take out unarmored vehicles, antitank guns, and small bunkers. Sergeant Arnold "Slack" Schlaich was Tom's senior NCO. The native of Herscher, Illinois, was anything but a "slack," but his men never could pronounce his last name in the kaiser's German.[6]

Also scribbling furiously, calculating ammo, fuel, and food requirements for the march, was Sergeant John Grimes. An old hand going back to the Fort Polk birth of the regiment two years earlier, he led one of three mortar crews and its "track."

Each M3 half-track mounted an 81-mm mortar—a tube five feet high and about the thickness of a soldier's thigh—in the open bay of the vehicle that resembled a pickup truck with dual tracks instead of rear wheels holding up its armored bed. Soldiers dropped an explosive projectile inside the mouth of the tube, then got out of the way as a small propellant charge ignited and sent the round spinning in a high arc toward unseen enemies kilometers away.

Surrounded by one hundred rounds of ammunition, a trained crew of eight could fire off projectiles weighing six pounds at a rate of eighteen per minute out to a range of four kilometers. The mortars could also fire smoke rounds to foil the enemy's ability to aim at friendly tank formations trying to outflank them. Armed with a .50-caliber machine gun in front and a .30-caliber in back, the mortar tracks were expected to not only take care of their own security but also assist in clearing objectives taken by the tanks as the latter licked their wounds and prepared for a counterattack, or to pursue a defeated enemy.

Grimes was a short, lean farm boy from a town in Missouri that remains difficult to find on a map to this day. His soft face held narrow, piercing eyes that showed the kind of determination in a person that only adversity can bring. The other sergeants called him "Little King"—at five foot five, he was short in stature but big in boldness and action.

Little King was a pro: "I have no questions, sir. I just need to get back to brief my men and get them ready."

The assault gun platoon and the 81-mm mortar tubes mounted on M3 half-tracks were the only artillery Sam and his company commanders directly controlled. The cannon artillery or howitzers were a division or corps asset shared among units. Sometimes another combat battalion had higher priority—which, in the heat of battle, can be heartburn-inducing for the commander under fire.

Unlike artillery battalion support or air support, like the P-47 Thunderbolt fighter-bombers, the mortars belonged to the battalion. Also, unlike the aircraft, they could support by fire in any weather, day or night—critical assets in the months ahead.

"Now let's talk beans, bullets, and fuel." Sam needn't remind the tankers. They knew well that, although not as sexy as riding steel horses into battle, the jobs of the rear echelon of the battalion—the fuelers, ammunition bearers, and medics—were just as important as that of the "trigger pullers."

Major Stewart Walker, Sam's second-in-command, took the pointer. Walker, bookish with glasses, was one of the original cadre assembled in 1941 on the dreary bayou of Camp Beauregard—closer than most to his hometown of Winfield, Louisiana.

"All right, men," he began in his Cajun-accented twang, "expect pushes of fuel at the assembly area here, then daily resupply along the march. Same with ammunition. Plan on rations for three days, as the supply train won't be able to keep up with the tanks in the muddy terrain—enjoy your hot chow while you can."

Walker had commanded a tank company as a captain. Now a major, he was responsible for keeping the supplies of ammunition, fuel, water, food, and medical necessities flowing, but also to stand ready to assume command if the CO was killed or incapacitated. His young face, shy smile, and glasses looked to be a better fit for a math teacher or librarian, but underneath these was a reliable and spirited officer.

As Walker wound down, in walked a lean, mustached officer with a red cross on white background painted on his steel helmet and brassard.

The younger officers smiled warmly at their battalion surgeon, Captain Louis Spigelman—a nice Jewish doctor from New York. Though not a combatant, he was an important member of the battalion staff.

Doc supervised the battalion aid station and its medics, who moved forward under fire to retrieve wounded in their two armored half-track ambulances. His men treated everything from trench foot to dysentery to shrapnel wounds. They provided the critical care needed immediately on the battlefield, stabilizing wounded soldiers enough to move them, sometimes under fire, to hospitals in the rear and their only chance at survival.

"Thanks, Major Walker," he began in his Brooklyn accent. "As per standard operating procedure, the battalion aid station will be with the rear echelon, a few kilometers back from your forward line and out of enemy artillery range." Medics were interspersed with the accompanying infantry or in their armored ambulance half-tracks, ready to respond to the dreaded cry of "MEDIC!"

Doc continued: "My medics will run a casualty collection point next to the battalion command post, and from there we'll move the wounded by armored ambulance to the aid station." He closed with "I sincerely hope I don't see any of you or your men at the aid station—but if I do, know that they're in good hands."

With that, Sam stepped back up to the front of the map to conclude the battalion OPORD brief. "Good luck, everyone. Stay aggressive. I will be right out there with you."

Each company commander departed to his respective sector. The basics of the battalion plan had been briefed early on, giving the captains maximum time to, in turn, prepare and brief their subordinate platoon leaders and sergeants.

So began preparation to unleash hell on the German line facing them and break out of the Normandy perimeter. The next seven days were a whirlwind of activity as the Allies waited for the rainy weather to clear so the bombers could do their job. Incoming artillery and the evening bombing raids by trios of German Ju 88 night bombers reminded the American soldiers that only more danger lay ahead.

Over the next few days, Sam and Brownie perfected their plan as new information came in. Sam also visited each platoon—he wanted to spend a few hours a day walking the lines, sitting down with each captain and lieutenant, pulling out his dog-eared copy of *The Armored Force Field Manual* from his musette bag to review theories of armored warfare. Sam did not lecture but discussed specific events from the last attack to hammer home points on tactics. *Where could we have outflanked this German antitank section? How could we have integrated artillery better on this attack?* Sam continued to worry about how green and inexperienced they all were compared to the Germans facing them.

He felt an older-brother affection for his young soldiers. His thoughts often flashed back to the small farm in south Texas where his mother and father struggled hard to provide for him and his sister. Many of his soldiers were the sole providers for their families, just as he was, and Sam hoped he could get as many of them back safely as possible.

The soldiers, sergeants, and officers looked to him for leadership. At twenty-eight, he had only three years' more experience in the army than his soldiers, many of whom were still in their teens. Still, Sam knew he had to project confidence and a calm, steely resolve.

There was only one place where an officer could prove himself, and that was in combat. In the back of his mind, there were doubts. How far could he push his mind and body? Could he conquer his fears, or would his fears conquer him? Was his troops' training enough for them to hold their own against the battle-hardened German army? These thoughts ran through his mind, but he had to pack them away.

For two and a half years, they had trained for war. A cadre of officers and NCOs had assembled from across the tiny prewar army in the swamps of Louisiana at Camp Beauregard in 1941. Camp Polk hadn't even been built, and the Third Armored Division was a newly created unit standing at four thousand troops—one-quarter of what its war-time strength would grow to be.

The first trainloads of "selectees" arrived to a greeting by Major General Walton Walker and a brass band. Young men, some in sharp double-breasted suits and fedoras and some in denim coveralls and rough farmer's shoes, stepped off the train after the weeklong ride from cities like Chicago, Indianapolis, and Cleveland. They received a hot meal and lined up through supply to get their uniforms, boots, and linens. From there, it was basic proficiency on how to march and fire their individual weapons, and an introduction on how to be tank crew members: drivers, gunners, loaders, or mechanics.

Sergeant John "Little King" Grimes, NCO in charge of one of the mortar sections, was typical of the boys making up the battalion. He was nineteen years old, from tiny Forbes, Missouri. His father had died when he was four, so John dropped out of school at age fourteen to earn a little money to support his family, dredging a river for the Civilian Conservation Corps. He then drove a truck from Texas to Missouri, hauling fruits and vegetables. He could barely look over the wheel. This Depression-era program was run with the help of the US military, so this gave John a little bit more experience than most selectees.[7]

He arrived at Camp Polk initially to be a mechanic, given his experience as a truck driver, but before the end of training he had learned all about firing mortars. Indirect fire, artillery, and mortars are critical in modern warfare. Grimes and his fellow mortarmen became experts at the difficult task of accurately firing high-explosive shells in a steep arc where the gunners never see the target. The mortar rounds must be guided onto the target—"called in"—by other soldiers spotting the target, usually through binoculars. The size of the powder charge, type of round (high explosive, smoke, illumination), wind, air density, and rotation of the earth all must be calculated to hit the target with accuracy.

The senior officers and most of the sergeants at the OPORD briefing had been present at the birth of the Third Armored Division at swampy Camp Beauregard. War had not touched the United States yet, and many selectees were counting down the days to complete their required eighteen-month selective service obligation. That all ended on a Sunday morning in December. Soldiers were sleeping in from a night out dancing with local dates at an event put on by the Service League—a predecessor to today's USO. The radio announcement, "Unidentified aircraft are attacking Pearl Harbor," changed it all.

After the shock wore off, the members of the nascent Third Armored Division cinched down their steel helmets as the war declarations on Japan and then Germany came in. Leaves and furloughs were reduced. Soldiers soberly packed their civilian clothes with mothballs, unsure when or if they would get to wear them again.

Training took on a new urgency. The entire division, personnel and vehicles, loaded onto trains headed west. After a week on the rails they arrived at a desolate tract of the broiling Mojave Desert, a flat bowl surrounded by forbidding brown ridges in the distance. Spirits were immediately deflated but, shaking off that sinking feeling, the soldiers began clearing the sagebrush and rocks.[8] They set up an enormous tent city that would be their home from July to October 1942. Slit trenches for bathrooms and a light coating of dust on everything were included among the luxuries.

But typical of the ingenuity of the tank crews—anything to get a little more comfort and civility—a lieutenant carried, strapped to the side of his tank, a folding metal chair with an oval hole cut in the middle of the seat. It worked wonderfully when positioned over a slit trench, and it was the envy of the other tank crews.

One day, the lieutenant, after a hard day of riding around on maneuvers in the desert and eating heavy canned rations barely fit for human consumption, was sitting down to a relaxing "shite" while reading a copy of the *Stars and Stripes*.

He thought he could count on some privacy: he had hiked a bit to the far side of a knob away from his platoon laager. There was the rumble of tank engines, but he thought nothing of it. The sun was going down and the desert had begun to cool off. He almost felt like a human being again.

Suddenly the lieutenant looked up from his periodical to see another tank company's convoy turning the corner to "his" side of the knob. There the officer sat on his "throne" as five tanks rolled by not one hundred feet from him, the tanks' crews riding with hatches open. All turned heads as one, looking at him quizzically from their turrets. All the lieutenant could do was smile and wave as the convoy rolled by. Everyone cracked up later at the incident.

With the US officially at war, more trainloads of draftees (no longer one-year-term, lottery-picked selectees; the draft was in effect so citizens were now drafted for the duration of the war) arrived to swell the division's ranks. It was ironic, but fairly typical of big army planning, that the armored division conducting desert training was destined not to go anywhere near a desert but to fight instead in fields of thick, green, overgrown hedgerows and hilly, forested terrain in near zero-degree temperatures.

Nevertheless, the maneuvers in the California desert pushed men and equipment to their limits, as lessons learned from fighting the German Afrika Korps filtered in and the temperatures reached 115 degrees. Rattlesnakes abounded, and soldiers checked their boots each morning for scorpions and spiders. In the rough conditions, the troops jelled, whether they liked one another or not, learning how to work as members of a tank crew, a team working in concert to move a thirty-three-ton machine at speed while spotting and firing upon enemy tanks. They learned the critical importance of radio communications, maintenance, and resupply of water, fuel, and ammunition.

In October 1942, the division moved back east—another weeklong-plus train trip, this time to Camp Pickett, Virginia, where the battalions continued to grow to full strength with new officers and men arriving from their induction stations.

From there, it was on to Fort Indiantown Gap, Pennsylvania, which—with its permanent barracks, good infrastructure, and rail network—was a huge improvement over the bayou, the desert, or Camp Pickett's mildewy particleboard huts. Training continued with individual skills such as reading and navigating from maps, this time in heavily wooded areas, and collective tasks of moving and maneuvering as a platoon or company in formations of three, six, and up to fifteen tanks.

They learned how to use the terrain to protect themselves and the formation, firing on the move while flanking the enemy. Each officer and enlisted man was required to complete an infiltration course in which they crawled through barbed wire, with explosive charges firing off and a machine gun bursting overhead.[9]

Troop scuttlebutt came back to Sam through trusty Sergeant D'Orio.

"Sir, the soldiers are asking, 'Why practice being miserable?'" With this feedback, Sam encouraged his officers and enlisted men by reminding them that they each had to recognize how far they could push themselves and each other during periods of fatigue, lack of food and sleep, and constant stress.

Sam learned that he could make it on little sleep provided he took a thirty-minute catnap here and there when time permitted. There was a careful balance between the tasks that had to be performed and how little sleep a human body could take before decision-making became compromised.

All these travails served to teach the men about each other and themselves. Officers who showed promise moved up. Old-timers identified sharp soldiers to wear sergeant's stripes. Sergeants who excelled in technical and tactical proficiency as well as leadership skills were selected for commissioning programs so they could become officers. Fraternal bonds were forged. The vast majority of these boys were good, but, as in any society, mixed in were a few bad apples.

These soldiers were identified early by experienced sergeants and were either motivated to become team players or were eventually discharged or moved to training units or staffs that would not be deploying overseas. Kitchen patrol—KP, as unglamorous as it sounds—was one "corrective action" that worked wonders. In the days before armies of civilian contractors pushed hot meals out to troops from fortified field operating bases (FOBs), units had to prepare their own hot meals, or chow. Cooking meals for five hundred men involved labor-intensive potato peeling, pot scrubbing, and sweating in the hot field kitchens. Soldiers assigned to help the mess sergeant were known as KPs.

Under the direction of the mess sergeant, the KPs followed recipes calling for hundreds of potatoes, pounds of butter, or dozens of cans of powdered eggs. "You're on KP all week" was a sure way to prevent the recurrence of sleeping while on guard duty. Honest mistakes could be made in training, but backstabbing or a lack of integrity were not tolerated, as they would produce casualties and endanger the success of combat missions.

Finally, in early 1944, fully manned and equipped, the division loaded up three troopships and sailed to England. Ten days and nights with eighteen hundred of your best friends on a ship built for nine hundred. There were long hours of cramped boredom, games of poker, nausea, cleaning weapons, and the occasional but welcome interruption of an "abandon ship" drill. There was still the real threat of a German U-boat sending the packed troopship to the bottom of the Atlantic with a couple of well-aimed torpedoes. Only a couple of "real" alarms occurred, though, and the escorting ships dropped depth charges with no result.

After setting up a pup-tent city in the frigid, foggy plains of Salisbury, the division conducted more maneuvers and combat exercises, intermingled with the occasional visit and pep talk from Allied brass, such as Sam's old tactics instructor, Lieutenant General Omar Bradley, and Field Marshal Bernard Montgomery. The vast majority of soldiers would have traded the pep talks for a few more forays to Sutton or Warminster to dance with English girls.

For most soldiers, though, there was a feeling of "let's get on with it," especially those that had been training since the bayou days in Louisiana.

Get on with it they did, rolling onto Omaha Beach seventeen days after D-Day aboard LSTs (landing ship, tank) as the huge cargo ships beached onshore. Now, camped on the fields of Normandy after their baptism by fire on Hill 91, Sam and his officers knew that the battalion and their leaders at division were still green. Training can instruct you in the theory of warfare, but only war can create a veteran. While Sam and Travis coached, mentored, and planned, Walker made sure that replacement tanks arrived for the three that were lost in combat and that spare parts flowed in and heavy oil was available for the daily maintenance of the tanks, half-tracks, trucks, and peeps.

Sam also had Walker ensure that at least one tank per platoon was fitted with the newly improvised hedgerow cutters, large prongs cut out from German steel antitank obstacles that resembled a giant jack from a kids' game, about the height of a man. These cutters would enable the tanks to avoid German kill zones by cutting through the thick wooded hedgerows that divided every plot of Norman farmland in the bocage.

After the day's tasks were complete, there was time for a little poker among the company commanders and their lieutenants. Sitting next to the cover of a half-track or tank with their foxholes nearby, the young officers sat smoking and joking over cards, blowing off steam and the precombat jitters. Sam would occasionally join in, aware that his presence probably made the younger officers a little less relaxed than if he wasn't there.

The summer nights were cool even as the sun went down late in the evenings—around 9:30 P.M. The mood was good. It was late July and the soldiers felt ready to fight their way out of the Normandy bocage in a few days.

"All right, boys, who among you will give up all your hard-earned pennies tonight?" began the trash talk. Sam sat down to look on at some of the good-natured ribbing. "Ben, if only your luck was as bad as your tanks, I'd stand a chance tonight," chided Carl Cramer.

The cards were drawn and the game began. Ben Creamer's luck was phenomenal. He drew three cards to fill, made inside straights, and drew two cards to flushes.

"Woohoo, I'm on a roll, boys!" drawled the Kentuckian. He was unbeatable. "I may have to take all these earnings on a three-day pass to Paris next month."

The others chimed in, "Nah, fella, you and your light tanks will be guarding the division command post the entire French campaign." Sam grinned; it was good to see morale was back after the losses they took at Hill 91.

The game wound down after an hour or so. Officers began drifting off to check on their perimeter guards or to their respective holes for some shut-eye in the warm confines of their "fart sack" (sleeping bag or bedroll). Ben, a wide grin on his face, was among the last to retire, winnings in hand, to his bedroll, spread out and comfortable in a narrow foxhole under the starry Normandy sky.

All was quiet save for the occasional thunder of artillery harassment fire far to the south. Sporadically, there was also the staccato of US antiaircraft fire shot into the night sky to deter Luftwaffe night bombers—named "Bed Check Charlie" by the GIs, for their proclivity to bomb US assembly areas in the dark of night.

It was the night of July 28, 1944, and the eerie calm was brusquely interrupted by a high-pitched whistle, like that of a mortar round but smaller in size, followed by a zip, a thud, and a gasp.

What made that noise? Perimeter guards looked around but found nothing amiss. It was not until Jake arrived at dawn to rouse his commander that the tragedy became evident. One of the US antiaircraft rounds, a .50-caliber bullet, about the size of a large Magic Marker, had come down and gone straight through Ben's heart as he lay sleeping in his foxhole.

For many, including Sam, Ben's death confirmed a fatalistic acceptance of destiny: when a bullet or artillery shard has your name on it, there's no stopping what's coming. In a sick way, it was almost comforting. The cards always fell however they pleased.

Sam had had no illusions about being able to bring all of his men back in one piece, but to lose another commander so early on and to such a freak incident put Sam in a somber mood that he had to shake himself out of. There was no time to mourn or ponder the twists of fate—C Company needed a new leader, and Ted Cardon stepped up.[10] Jake and Ted somberly inventoried Ben's few possessions for eventual shipment to his widow, Dorothy: uniforms, rank insignia, socks, field gear, a fountain pen, and a small album of family photographs.

A Graves Registration team from the First Army came, took an imprint of his dog tags, and interred him next to some of the Hauts Vents casualties adjacent to a little orchard near the village of La Cambe. Ben was twenty-five years old.

As the start date for Operation Cobra drew closer, Sam tried to scratch out a few minutes to himself in his pup tent, pitched alongside the command half-track. There was little time for reflection. He was always on the go: meetings, coaching his officers, planning, and giving guidance. Here was time to collect his thoughts and maybe catch up on mail. He wrote letters to his parents, Dodge and Mary, in faraway Pharr, Texas, always closing with "you all write often."

Sam tried to reassure his parents and his wife, Belle, and told them how pleased he was with this outfit, how they had the best equipment, plenty of it, and were well trained. He hoped for more letters from his father—some encouragement from someone he looked up to who wasn't a general officer barking orders. Unfortunately, Dodge's health was not good, but Mary promised him canned jalapenos to dress up the bland tinned "mystery" meats. She planned to surprise him with a Texas fruitcake, soaked in bourbon to preserve it, if the Americans weren't home by Christmas.

The precious few minutes to himself were also a time for introspection. Loneliness is a commander's constant companion. There really was nobody around to whom he could vent. He knew that being a leader implied knowing his people, having rapport but not friendship. In the coming battles, he would have to order these five hundred soldiers—men he cared about, boys with mothers, siblings, and young kids—into battle, from which many would not return alive.

If Sam became too close to anyone, close enough to complain or ask for advice, he risked hesitating at the moment of giving an order. The unit could break down. He wished he could write to his father about some of the frustrations and worries saturating his mind—the pressure from the brass to "get the troops bloodied." But he could not—the mail censors would never let it pass. Still, Sam was never one to complain. He would affect what he could. *I'll be damned if I waste any of my boys' lives needlessly,* he told himself.

Sam knew that, as a battalion commander, he would often be shot at, but rarely would he be able to fire back. He had to decide for himself, based on the situation and as quickly as possible, whether to move forward in the face of enemy fire or to back away and press for a flank. Sometimes, he knew, the Germans would decide for him. Would he be up to the task?

On the humid midmorning of the day before the attack, Sam gazed up from one of his interminable battalion commander tasks to the echoing moan of wave after wave of B-17 bombers blanketing the evening sky overhead, their long contrails visible against the canopy of summer sky blue. Sam thought for a moment about the brave crews traveling in subzero temperatures in a metal cylinder packed with bombs heading for the enemy's heartland. After staring in awe for a few moments, he got back to work.

3

★ ★ ★ ★ ★

OPERATION COBRA: BREAKOUT FROM NORMANDY

AUGUST 7–12, 1944

The day after those bombers flew overhead, Task Force 3 received orders to take a ridge to secure the Allies a point of departure for further advance. Near the village of Chérencé-le-Roussel, the three companies of tanks occupied the ridge without incident, then waited for the foot soldiers of the Thirty-ninth Infantry Regiment, Ninth Infantry Division to pass through their lines and occupy the line of departure.

The tankers looked on from their open hatch positions with interest at the GIs marching by. The infantry soldiers and their sergeants plodded forward in worn uniforms and thoroughly broken-in boots. Many carried captured German pistols in leather holsters as their backup weapons. They looked ahead with the steely-eyed resolve of hardened veterans who had been there and came out the other side.

A tanker shouted out to them: "Hey, Joe! What's that stenciled on your helmet, Alcoholics Anonymous?"

"Nope!" answered a salty infantry sergeant. "It's our motto: AAAO. Anything, Anywhere, Anytime—Bar None." The tanker nodded in respect.

The Thirty-ninth had stormed ashore at Algiers in 1942 and fought under Patton in Sicily before splashing onto Utah Beach a couple of weeks prior. On their perches, the tank sergeants glanced knowingly among themselves; they could tell who the replacement soldiers were. They wore less faded olive drab and looked nervously about, marveling at the size and mean silhouette of the Sherman tank. The veteran foot soldiers were unimpressed; they'd already seen German Tiger and Panther tanks as well as their effects on a Sherman in a one-on-one matchup.

Once the show passed them by, the tankers returned to checking their oil levels and track tightness, and added camouflage to their mounts. Some crews even added sandbags to bolster their frontal armor and were busy tightening the chicken wire that held the bags in place.

Out of nowhere, a low hum grew louder, turning into an earsplitting shriek of aircraft piston engines. The racket interrupted the crews, who looked toward the noise and spotted enemy fighter-bombers streaking in low from the valley below them. Captain Ted Cardon, perched in his own tank turret, roared at anyone who could hear him, "Those are not friendlies!"

Shouts of "ENEMY AIR!" rang out as tankers scrambled into their turrets. Several crewmen ratcheted back the heavy bolts on their hatch-mounted .50-caliber machine guns and turned them toward the threat.

The three Focke-Wulfe 190 fighter-bombers, Iron Crosses painted on their fuselages, zoomed in and unleashed a barrage of rockets and cannon fire. US machine guns swung violently toward the fast-moving planes, trying to intercept one with a stream of lead. The German fighters were too fast and too low, but thankfully they caused no damage, and they disappeared before any US fighters came on station.

Some of the more experienced soldiers got an uneasy feeling in their guts. This was no random strafing. The Germans were up to something.

The battalion did not know it yet, but they were in the path of Hitler's answer to Cobra: Operation Luttich, a four-division counterattack to recapture coastal Avranches, a mere eighteen miles from Sam's positions. In one move, the Germans could split the US First and Third Armies in two. Cut off from supply, Patton's Third Army, without its daily 25,000 gallons of fuel needed to move, would languish and die at the hands of mobile German *Kampfgruppe*, the enemy equivalent of an armored task force.

The night prior, August 6, division orders to the regiment had been to prepare for a couple of days of rest and refit after the hard fighting at Hauts Vents overlooking the Vire River. Not anymore. Sam put the task force on alert as they straddled the strong position on the ridge protecting the Chérencé-le-Roussel road. The tank commanders and the attached infantry—engineer and tank destroyer leadership—gathered for a huddle.

"I think the Germans are coming and will hit us hard." Sam turned a serious look to Carl Cramer. "Captain, I want your platoons spread out here on the reverse slope." He pointed to his folder map with a slender left index finger.

"Lieutenant," he said, turning to the tank destroyer platoon leader, "I want you to intersperse your TDs to where they can ambush enemy tanks coming along these draws here." He then pointed on the map at the terrain below.

The open-topped M10 tank destroyers (TDs) were part of the flawed doctrine that had been championed by General Lesley McNair, according to which the Sherman would not fight other tanks as much as break through enemy lines in support of infantry. TDs would protect the Shermans from enemy tanks. TDs were lightly armored and fast, but with a bigger gun that could destroy the enemy's armor.

It was only in the lessons learned from battles in North Africa and Italy that the brass began to realize that the best weapon against a tank is another tank. Tank destroyers were useful, but were vulnerable to artillery because of their open tops. They were also limited—one battalion of fifty TDs to be shared across the entire sixteen-thousand-soldier division.

Sam's hasty battle plan moved on. "Ed, you are our reserve, but I want your tanks and infantry tied in here on the right with the neighboring unit."

Wray nodded, adding, "Sir, it's sure going to be a nice change with the enemy attacking our prepared defensive positions rather than the other way around."

By early afternoon, commanders placed their units in covered and concealed positions, and the attached engineer company aided in digging in tanks to a "hull down" position, where the turret was the only thing visible among the copses of trees. Now they waited.

Jake Sitzes and Ted Cardon, dug in along the mile-wide defensive line, looked on through their binoculars from their pit under the hull of Jake's command tank.

"Sir, do you think they're really coming at us?" asked Jake.

Ted thought a minute and answered, "The colonel seems to think so, and the Nazis have to do something right now: their chances of pushing us back into the sea are shrinking by the day."

"Roger that, sounds about right." Jake took his eyes out of his binoculars for a few seconds. "What do you want to do after the war?"

"Well, Jake, I have a wife and a farm in Arizona to go back to." The tank speaker suddenly hissed alive as one of the scout observation posts reported in. "Blue Six, this is OP 1. We can hear tank engines and smell diesel smoke on the other side of the hedgerow."

A murmur of a half dozen Maybach diesel engines reached the ears of Jake and Ted, amplified as they sat crammed into the hole under their tank.

"Shit, sir, I hear them coming." Ted nodded, then wrote down coordinates off his map, in preparation for a radio call for tactical air support.

Out of the southwest, six German tanks turned out of the field they were in and gathered in a wedge formation to cross the hay fields between them and the task force positions. Eight hundred yards separated the combatants.

Jake excitedly grabbed Ted's elbow. "Those are Mark IVs, we can take them!" The Mark IV was Germany's workhorse main battle tank. It was smaller and less well armored than the Panther or Tiger tanks, but still packed Sherman-killing power in its high-velocity, long-barrel, 75-mm cannon.

The radio crackled again. This time it was the colonel's slow Texas twang, calm and smooth. "All units, this is Six, we have eyes on six enemy tanks in the open, hold your fire until the TDs open up."

The German Mark IVs rolled closer, cutting swathes of dark earth beneath their treads. Their turrets scanned the folds of the earth to their front and sides, turning slowly, like a cop on beat in a dangerous neighborhood. Now they were at seven hundred yards.

Sam, located next to the tank destroyer platoon leader, looked on intently through his own binoculars. The lieutenant fumbled for his "pork chop" microphone. Sam, still sighting the enemy tanks through his binos, gave him a pat on the shoulder and a second later, the command *"Fire!"* burst over the radio airwaves.

Three M10 tank destroyers and six Shermans opened fire. Jake gave out a war whoop as he saw the lightning bolts of nine antitank rounds blaze away toward the valley below. *CRUNCH, CRUNCH—BOOM BOOM BOOM* as the cannon rounds found their target. The six enemy tanks stopped in their tracks or sputtered a few dozen feet from sheer momentum, then exploded in sparks and smoke. A cheer erupted on the ridgeline from the jubilant tank crews, infantrymen, and engineers.

Sam got on the radio to his immediate superior officer, Combat Command B (CCB)'s Colonel Truman Boudinot.

"Ontario Six, we've stopped a strong attack by six German Mark IVs, all enemy tanks destroyed." Sam reported to higher headquarters that this was likely a strong probe ahead of a major counterattack.

"Roger, this is Ontario Six, report to my POS [location] for additional orders-out." With that, Sam was hastily summoned due south of his task force position in the neighboring unit's area of operations for new marching orders.

Back ten kilometers at CCB headquarters, the CP was buzzing like a nest of wasps. Battles were breaking out all along the Allied front.

Boudinot was all business. "Sam, good job stopping that enemy probe. CCB is now attached to Thirtieth ID. All available armor in the area will move to the sound of the guns to help break the attack. Report to General Hobbs for your orders." Sam saluted and moved out, intent on getting the real scoop from Boudinot's operations chief.

The order was to reinforce their friends in Old Hickory, the Thirtieth Infantry Division, as Operation Luttich began to hit them head-on. Initial reports were that the Second SS Panzer and Seventeenth SS Panzer Grenadier Divisions had already encircled a battalion of the Thirtieth in the valley town of Mortain. An attack by the Fourth Infantry Division to seize a strategic crossroads had been stopped cold by the SS armor backed by strong artillery.

Sam shook hands with the ops chief, took some maps and overlays, then briskly walked out of the jumble of half-tracks and tents toward his waiting peep. The driver, Private Charles Gast, Sergeant Phil D'Orio, and Sam sped away, the sounds of artillery booming to their south at Le Mesnil-Adelée. An uneventful six-kilometer ride put them outside a massive dug-in divisional command post.

Sam and Sergeant D'Orio exchanged glances. "Who's in here, sir—Churchill?" joked D'Orio.

"I'm about to find out," said Sam flatly. "Why don't you and Gast find the mess tent and get yourselves some warm chow? I might be a while."

Sam strolled in past eight-foot-high earthen berms put up by engineer dozers. The site was large and not very mobile. Inside Major General Leland Hobbs's impressive divisional command post, things were hectic. Sam wrinkled his nose unconsciously for a second, thinking, *This CP should be mobile and closer to the action.*

His thoughts were brusquely interrupted by Major General Hobbs. "Colonel Hogan, right over here, we need your tanks immediately." He waved Sam toward him through the maze of desks, radios, runners, and battle trackers.

Hobbs gave Sam a quick overview in his thick Massachusetts accent. He was known as an impatient, vociferous commander who fired anyone at the slightest indication of inefficiency or hesitation. In contrast, Sam was not one to scream or berate. His voice was commanding, firm, but fair. These qualities and his sincere care for his soldiers' well-being meant that they did all they could to never let him down.

In addition to the opposite leadership styles, there existed still some discord between the Third Armored and Thirtieth Infantry leadership over General Bohn's firing and the traffic jams coming off the beach toward Hauts Vents. Sam never took things personally, as long as his higher leadership let him work. He knew the on-the-ground commanders would move past any bad blood—their men's lives were at stake.

Hobbs continued, "Your tanks will take the crossroads near the town of L'Abbaye Blanche [White Abbey] to block the German advance. My operations staff will give you further details." A firm handshake and that was that. The situation was still evolving so the division staff had little else to add.

Leaving the safety and security of this rearward fortress, Sam raced back to his task force perimeter to get them prepared for what was next. This was obviously a major German counteroffensive. What lay ahead? How much could the Thirtieth absorb? And would the Americans be able to hold the ground they had taken at such heavy cost over the past weeks?

Sam had a bad feeling about this one, and as his peep sped away he thought ahead to all that needed to be done. He had no idea at the time how correct his gut instinct was. Near L'Abbaye Blanche, the Germans were massed for their main attack of Operation Luttich. Worse still, Sam's objective happened also to be the unit boundary of the two German SS Divisions—the Second Panzer and the Seventeenth Panzer Grenadier.

It was dusk by the time they returned, and Sam caught a short nap after checking that his three understrength companies and the attached infantrymen of E and F Companies, 119th Infantry Regiment, of the Thirtieth Infantry Division were at their jump-off positions loaded up with ammunition and fuel. He spot-checked that vehicles had air recognition panels laid out on their back decks, their only defense against Allied airpower striking them by mistake. The tragic friendly fire on July 12 at Hauts Vents had made him extra cautious.

An even more catastrophic friendly fire incident had killed Lieutenant General Lesley McNair two weeks after the battle on the same hilltop. The stateside chief of ground forces, McNair was visiting the

Thirtieth Infantry to observe the Operation Cobra preparatory bombing. On July 25, B-17 bombs dropped short of the German lines, killing the general and several hundred Old Hickory soldiers.[1] They would need strong coordination with the air corps to preclude any more friendly fire tragedies.

At midnight, Sam radioed for the unit to start moving toward the line of departure for the morning kickoff. Night movements involved less risk of getting shot by snipers or an antitank ambush. They allowed you to sneak up on the enemy and keep him reeling. However, moving more than five hundred men and fifty-five tanks plus assorted other vehicles, in the darkness, into an unknown country with no headlights or taillights came with its own complications.

Of course they had trained for this, too, but once again, it's all different when your life depends on it and there's a heavily armed enemy waiting for you to make a mistake. Drivers and commanders learned to run convoys at night relying on blackout lights, tiny slits of light let out by encasing the taillight in a metal sheath. It did not project a beam, which could be seen from the sides or front alerting the enemy. Instead, it was a small enough glow that the friendly vehicle behind, close enough and knowing what to look for, could see and follow the tiny red taillight. Often, in the dark of night, this was all the driver and assistant driver could see. This made for stressful, slow going.

Despite all these challenges, things were going relatively smoothly. A calm before another storm. Sam's tanks and infantry moved on schedule in the direction of the main objective: Mortain. Sam rode in his command tank with the hatch opened so he could monitor progress and double-check his map with known features as they passed them. At the first dark-blue glow of the coming dawn, Sam mentally checked off passing terrain features. A pretty stone farmhouse here, a hilltop to the southeast there.

Task Force 3 stopped to refuel well after daybreak at a hamlet called Le Neufbourg. Fuel trucks set up in an adjacent field, and it took the better part of two hours for the tanks, half-tracks, and jeeps to pass through for their gas. Soldiers took any free minutes to wolf down some crackers or lay back in their vehicles or the shade of a tree for a quick nap. Seeing the mass of vehicles awaiting fuel made Sam thankful for Allied air superiority. He tried not to gag on a can of veal and pork C rations, hunger helping him make the best of it. Sam then shut his eyes for a fifteen-minute catnap. He knew he would need it.

A little after 2:00 P.M., as planned, Sam was gently roused by Sergeant Phil D'Orio.

"Sir, the recon platoon is moving out in ten minutes." It was time to shake the sleep out of his head and accompany the reconnaissance platoon, the eyes and ears of the battalion, to see what maps alone could not tell them.

"Right, let's go." Escorted by four Sherman tanks, the small formation left the task force behind and headed toward the objective crossroads. At an old Norman cemetery—adorned with wrought-iron fencing, stone crosses, and pretty poplars—the convoy made a slight left turn following the old country roads visible on the map.

Sam saw a small country manor by a hand-painted wooden sign pointing down the road with the words "L'Abbaye Blanche"—it conjured up images of cobblestone streets and a hamlet made up of lovely wood-framed houses dressed in white stucco, crowned with maroon clay tiles. But past the little house, this fantasy gave way to the reality of dark brown fields with increasingly thick hedgerows on all sides and undulating terrain. Artillery duels thundered to the south. A life-and-death struggle lay ahead.

Moving swiftly, they reached the forward line of US troops, where a Lieutenant Springfield of the 823rd Tank Destroyer Battalion stood with sunken eyes, looking haggard after several dustups with the advancing Germans. He pointed a soiled, sinewy finger to a gently rising slope bordered by hedgerows, stating flatly, "There are plenty of enemy up that hill."

Sam nodded. He was glad to see firsthand what the terrain looked like—this confirmed the need for dozer tanks in the lead and plenty of infantry to protect the tanks from the Panzerfaust-armed dismounts. The little reconnaissance party retraced its steps, linking up with the main body of Task Force 3.[2]

On the move again, Sam could hear over the radio the lead tanks passing checkpoints that meant they were arriving in their last assembly area. From it, they would launch their attack on the crossroads: Road Junction (RJ) 278, so named for its map reference number. The tension continued to ratchet up. After crossing a railroad, the vehicles spread out according to plan, straddling either side of the dirt trail that turned into a single-lane country road. Carl Cramer's G Company on the left and H Company, led by Lieutenant Ed Wray, on the right.

Ahead, more of those damned thick hedgerows, crisscrossing randomly across the entire front.

The Allies had been beating their heads to a pulp against the ubiquitous hedgerows of the bocage. The earthen walls stopped formations cold, sheltered enemy tank-killer teams, channeled tanks into kill zones, and enfeebled any US numerical advantage.

Handy GIs in Sam's sister regiment, the Thirty-second, had found a technical, ingenious solution in late June: two spearhead-shaped prongs soldered low in front of each track. However, technical solutions are just a gimmick if tactics to use them are not developed in parallel.

Back during the buildup, Jake had already demonstrated how even one of his light tanks, fitted with a set of prongs, could crush through the bocage and open up a hole for the tanks. Jake insisted on testing them himself. From the hatch of his little tank, twenty yards from a section of bocage, Jake lowered his goggles, then ordered his driver to *GO GO GO!*

At his command, the small tank jerked forward, gained a little speed, leaving a cloud of dust in its wake, then, with a *CRUNCH* and a rev of the engine, the prongs dug up the twisted mass of roots that anchored the wall of packed mud and vines. Smoke poured out of the Stuart's back-end muffler. Then, miraculously, the tank's momentum carried with it the entire section of wall, leaving a hole for tanks to follow. The little tank did a victory lap through the clouds of dust and debris back to the start point, where the other crews looked on.

Jake flashed an ear-to-ear grin and hopped off his tank in two bounds.

"So that's what Superman feels like!" he quipped. The gathered tankers clapped, whooped, and hollered. They could now come at the entrenched Germans at a place of the Americans' choosing to flank and destroy their strongpoints.

Now, with more experience, but facing a juggernaut of German tanks and infantry surrounding Mortain, the tactic was to use a dozer tank fitted with the improvised prongs to lead each company, the platoon or company commander guiding it from the second tank. The dozer tank would open up a way through the hedgerows, avoiding main roads and intersections surely well covered by German antitank guns and artillery.

Through the opening, the tanks and infantry would rush through and attack the enclosed corners of the adjacent field. Speed and surprise were of the essence to catch the German cannon crews before they could reposition themselves, aim, and fire.

The infantrymen of E/119th were with G Company and those of F/119th on the right with H Company, the GIs providing the tanks protection from any German foot soldiers armed with antitank rockets. The light tanks of C Company spread out short of the railroad crossing, with Sam and his headquarters in the middle. Past the eastern edge of Mortain they advanced until within sight of the railroad station at L'Abbaye Blanche. The task force spread out as they entered fields astride a country road that led straight to RJ 278, their objective.

It was late afternoon. Artillery rounds boomed ahead with a *POP POP POP* as they left their tubes. Although he couldn't see them, Sam guessed they were probably coming from positions on the other side of Mortain. Sam felt that cold moisture on the back of his neck again, but this time his pulse remained steady.

Artillery fire crept in on the advancing formation. Shouts of *Incoming!* surged over the radio as the tankers buttoned up and the infantrymen grabbed their helmets and curled up into a ball, making their bodies as small as possible. They looked around to ditches abutting the road, selecting where they would jump off to if the need arose. This was no harassment fire—this was heavy, organized incoming artillery.

The first handful of rounds came in with a whine that grew louder, like a freight train. From Wray and Cramer's tanks, infantry spilled off Shermans as they jumped, rolled, and sought cover in the nearest ditch or hedge. From there, everything went to hell in just a few quick seconds. Instead of occasional *POP POP*s separated by minutes, a wave of blasts and dirt hit the advancing tanks. *BOOM BOOM BOOM* as clouds of dust mixed with fiery blasts, sending hot metallic shards zipping through the dirty air. Thankfully, the shards pinged harmlessly off the Shermans' armor.

Infantry hugged the ground close—the action had just gotten heavy. More rounds came in with eardrum-shattering explosions, some ahead of the tanks and some in between. Panicked shouts of *"I'm hit!"* and *"Medic!"* began to ring out.

Platoon and company leaders knew to keep moving in the face of artillery barrages. The last thing you want to do is sit still unless you have prepared positions to shelter in and are on the defensive. Over the internal radios and out to the infantry walkie-talkies crackled the commands: "All elements! Keep pressing forward, twelve o'clock, 150 meters!"

In between the volleys of enemy artillery, the foot soldiers crouched up, shuffling quickly forward from cover to cover until the next shouts of *"Incoming!"* drove them back down as low as possible on the sodden ground.

The lead tanks of both companies arrived at the first line of hedgerows and punched through them with a loud roar of the engine and a ripping crunch of sunbaked mud mixed with dry, twisted vines and tree branches. The dozer tank backed up, and the formation funneled in, led by Shermans. Infantry poured through the newly created gap after them, through a haze of smoke and dust.

One, two, three—the tanks moved through, machine guns blazing at the corners of the field they had just entered. The tanks, hatches buttoned up, kept moving, with their turrets and bow-mounted machine guns scanning for targets in the far-off hedgerows.

Inside his command tank, Ed Wray spotted a camouflaged PAK-40 (Panzer Abwehr Kanone, an antitank cannon) and crew, wide-eyed and panicking as they struggled to turn their unwieldy piece around to fire at the Americans who had just unexpectedly surged up on their back.

"Gunner! Antitank gun ten o'clock, in the corner of the hedgerow!" The Sherman's hydraulic turret whizzed around to the left as the gunner began spraying .30-caliber machine gun fire from the coaxial gun fitted next to his cannon barrel. *"On the way!"* was the call as the gunner let fly. Clouds of dust, torn camouflage fabric, and crimson blood splatters filled their periscopes' field of vision as the German crew and cannon were ripped to shreds. The tank turret scanned around looking for the next target. There was none. "This field is cleared," reported Ed as the follow-on US infantry surged through the gap behind him.

On the left wing, G Company pushed through another hedgerow with its own tank dozer and deployed on the far side of the field to cover the road intersection five hundred yards ahead. Inside tank G-16 *Ground Gainer* sat tank gunner Wilson Whitehead. His tank commander, Staff Sergeant James V. Curry, called out to him, "Wilson, keep your gunsights on the crossroads ahead. We have to wait until H Company comes on line."

"Roger, Sarge," came the reply.

Whitehead leaned in to look through the gunsight reticle, then turned the turret with a push of a button to align it on target. Even inside the closed-up tank, he could hear heavy artillery and mortars exploding to their back and to their left. At least it's not landing on us, he thought.

There was still nothing but empty road through his gunsight. Hedgerows sprang out to both sides of the intersection, so his field of vision through the gunsights was only about the diameter of a Coke-bottle bottom.

Whitehead blinked. There was movement. A long, camouflaged barrel rolled into his sights from the right. It came slowly into focus until the large angular hull also appeared.

The G Company net came alive: *"Panther tank, eleven o'clock, four hundred meters!"* The word "Panther" or "Tiger" struck terror in an American tanker's heart. It meant that a vastly superior tank to your own had spotted you before you had spotted it. This meant that one of your fellow Shermans, or maybe your own, was about to be impaled by a high velocity 75- or 88-mm shell that could pass through both ends of your Sherman's armor, vaporizing everything in its path.

Whitehead hardly noticed that he had just sent out the alert over the radio. He now waited for Staff Sergeant Curry's command. A 75-mm armor-piercing shell was already in the breech. Wilson breathed heavily as he waited for the Panther to come up broadside into the center of his gunsight. It felt like an eternity until he heard Curry's accented order, "Faarrr when ready." With a grunt and a hard tap on the floor-mounted trigger, the round shot out. "On the way!"

The breech flew back, rocking the tank and sending cordite fumes into the crew compartment. Whitehead kept his eye on the target. In just a few seconds, the Sherman's cannon round struck home . . . then shot up to the sky as it deflected off the enemy tank's thick armor. An anticipated hit turned into curses of disappointment as the round failed to make a dent in the dreaded Panther, which ignored the Sherman's attack like a horse dismissing a gnat and crossed the road to disappear behind a row of hedges.[3]

Suddenly, seconds after Wilson Whitehead opened fire, the front exploded with two large muzzle flashes and machine gun fire. The two green tracers found their mark upon two Shermans, producing a shower of sparks and rising smoke that immediately stopped the tanks dead in their tracks. The crews jumped and rolled, finding any available cover from the lines of machine gun tracers sweeping the field. The German MG42 machine guns, with their incredibly fast rate of fire of twelve hundred rounds per minute, sounded like a giant zipper ripped violently apart.

Meanwhile, large artillery fragments began peppering *Ground Gainer* as it scanned for more targets while suppressing the hedgerows with machine gun fire. The rattle of shrapnel bouncing off the slope armor swelled into head-jarring explosions as several heavy-caliber artillery rounds detonated within feet of the tank.

The Germans were bringing in divisional and corps artillery to bear: 150-mm behemoths and even 100-mm cannon captured from the French army in 1940.[4] Staff Sergeant Curry moved quickly to close his turret hatch as a shell detonated in a violent and accurate airburst right above it, knocking him back in a violent shock wave of superheated air and pieces of glowing-hot metal.

Wilson Whitehead—sitting below and in front of Curry's seat—was slammed against the turret wall, knocking the wind out of him and severely bruising his clavicle and arm. The Sherman filled up with dust and smoke.

Whitehead shook away the ear-ringing and head fog to find Curry slumped partly over him and partly over his small back support. He was bleeding heavily onto Whitehead's right shoulder.

The sight of his tank commander made him grimace: Curry was almost decapitated, his tanker's helmet half covering his face and grievous wounds on his jaw and neck. There was no doubt he was dead. Whitehead, loader Private First Class John Gunther, and driver Tech 4 Pedro Vasques stayed put inside the tank as they tried to wait out the artillery barrage that had killed their commander.

Taking advantage of a short lull, the three survivors bailed out of the stricken tank. They crawled sixty yards to a parallel hedgerow, occupied by a gaggle of GIs. Wilson saw a young infantry lieutenant pacing nervously, ranting to himself incoherently, the wild look of shell shock in his eyes.

Their medic rushed over to Whitehead and began pulling off his coveralls.

"What are you doing, mac? I'm not wounded." Whitehead grunted.

"You're covered in blood," replied the medic.

"It's not my blood, dammit!"[5]

Back on the line, Shermans lobbed desperate return fire with main gun rounds as they struggled to make out any enemy muzzle flashes to target, and bow gunners opened up with .30-caliber machine gun rounds. Shouts of "Where are they at?!" and "Take out those AT guns!" saturated the company radio nets. The German guns were camouflaged to the point of near invisibility. They were using flashless gunpowder that was almost impossible to sight in on.

On the other side of the next field, more volleys hit two more

H Company Shermans. One was put immediately out of action, while the front wheel sprocket of the other was destroyed, sending fifty-pound pieces of the heavy metal track flying through the air in a lazy spinning arc. The stricken tank ground what was left of its track into the loose soil as it began sharply turning toward its still-functioning right track, exposing the tank's thinner side armor.

From behind high-grade optics, the German cannoneers turned a crank, shifting their long-barreled cannon steadily toward the crippled Sherman. They didn't want their prey to escape. *"Feuer!"* was the shrieked command that sent a second volley blazing toward the Americans. In an instant, the Sherman burst into a giant torch. Two of its crew, Privates John H. Flavell and Earl Wyatt, didn't make it out.

H Company pulled back. Cramer's Sherman, driven by Tech 4 Luis Alamea and gunner Corporal Frank Plezia, backed up behind some covering terrain and dismounted to check on the Sherman commanded by their platoon sergeant, Wayne Axel Kron. Alamea crawled as close as he could to the disabled Sherman, where Kron lay writhing in pain on the oily ground.

Both of his feet were gone from an armor-piercing round that had penetrated his tank. Still twenty yards away from him, Alamea stopped as bullets tore up the ground between him and Kron.

"Don't let me die!" pleaded Kron. Alamea yelled over the gunfire to hold on and they would get him back to the aid station. Alamea's tank, still serviceable, was about to be overrun. He crawled back and got in through the bottom escape hatch. The fire was too heavy to get to Kron—he would have to hold on until nightfall.[6]

Though G Company shielded itself somewhat using the folds in the terrain, Carl Cramer's command lost a tank to another well-camouflaged antitank gun. Lost was tank G-3; its platoon leader, First Lieutenant Thomas Cooper, was wounded. Cooper had commented on his way up to the line that maybe he could get the "million-dollar wound" and head home.

Looking at the flesh wound, Doc Spigelman retorted, "LT, I think it's more like a two-hundred dollar wound," with no return home ticket tied to it. "You were lucky, Tom—you still need to come off the line." Cooper did not like the idea of being away from his platoon.[7]

Captain Cramer continued rallying his tankers and infantry. His command tank was a flurry of signal flags, radio calls, and occasionally visuals as the tall, spindly captain supplemented his radio commands with karate chops of the hand into the air indicating where he wanted forward movement.

"Let's go! Up and at 'em!" Cramer added drawling exhortations to the grunts within earshot, as he pressed his platoons forward from his tank turret. The high-strung OCS graduate pressed on in the center of the action, ignoring the pings and whizzes of bullets and shrapnel striking the turret below him.

Despite their élan, the infantry on both wings of that attack were unable to advance in the face of the accurate incoming artillery and heavy volume of machine gun fire. One platoon of E/119th Infantry was caught entirely in the open, and most of its members were wounded or killed. The attack stalled out. It was a little after 5:00 P.M. when Sam called a halt as the tanks and infantry barely occupied the first line of hedgerows they had reached.

The Germans followed their standard defense-in-depth tactic. They inflicted casualties on the first wave of attackers, then pulled back to a secondary line if the attackers persisted. Then, from that second line, they could counterattack as the attackers consolidated on their first line attained.

The two Panther tanks that fired earlier had pulled back. Sam radioed his tank commanders Carl Cramer and Ed Wray as well as his attached infantry companies, so understrength that they amounted to one company (about one hundred soldiers), under Lieutenants Warren Fox and Ed Arn, telling them to hold positions, dig in, and prepare for a German counterattack.

During the battle, Travis Brown's operations staff had set up the task force command post in the field just short of the railroad underpass and ahead of Sam's reserve, C Company. Sam and his command tank moved one hundred meters toward the rustic CP.

There had been no time or thought of setting up a nice tent, folding chairs, and map boards in between the two tracks—the artillery barrage had made that impossible. Instead, soldiers dug large holes underneath so that their vehicles provided overhead cover. Under the battalion commander's half-track, driver Charlie Gast was busily digging the trench deeper under the chassis. With nothing but a canvas top over the cab, under the half-track was the safest place to be. From this CP they would plan the next attack while coordinating a defensive perimeter for the night. A sunken road nearby served as the casualty collection point, where medics could give initial treatment to casualties before they moved them back to field hospitals in the rear.

Doc Spigelman and his intrepid medics were doing God's work. After digging themselves in under their own half-tracks, they prepared the aid station. The dreaded call *"Medic!"* came far too often.

Doc sweat bullets in the makeshift aid station, applying bandages, tourniquets, and intravenous drips to the first casualties among the infantry. Medics rushed toward one of the smoking H Company tanks.

Doc's medical aides, Sergeant Raymond Kuderka and Corporals Derrick Filkins and John Skuly, plus one of the infantry medics, crept forward, crouched low with their olive-drab stretcher and medic bags slung on their chests. Panting, they crossed the busted-up hedgerow toward the line of battle.

"Come on. We're almost there," Kuderka exhorted.

There, in the shade of the hedge, was a tanker, face burned crimson, his body showing burns under the ashy shreds of his coveralls. Machine gun fire cracked overhead. Two infantry soldiers crouched over the tanker, giving him sips of water from a metal canteen.

The tanker's eyes were fading.

"Come on guys, help us load him up," Kuderka said. "Easy now." The burned soldier gasped in pain as the infantry and medics gently rolled him onto the stretcher.

Kuderka administered a shot of morphine from a little glass syrette in his medic bag. "Okay, let's go! Prepare to lift." Each soldier grabbed his corner pole of the stretcher. "Lift!" The four moved out at a low crouch, bouncing up and down over the uneven ground and back through the hole in the hedgerow. They were still in enemy artillery range, so they hugged the next hedgerow, then stopped at the remains of another low hedge.

There they took a knee as two medics climbed over, then passed the moaning soldier over the low wall to the others. The two front stretcher bearers then waited for the remaining two to climb over to help with their share of the 170-pound soldier's weight.

One final clearing to cross and they would be home free under Doc's care. If only the tanker could hang on—shock was setting in. "Hey, soldier! Stay with me."

Two enemy mortar rounds burst behind them. They got down again and began crawling with the soldier, stretcher poles on the ends tucked over their elbows. One heave of the arms—"All together now . . . heave!"—then a push forward with their legs on the loose dirt. The final fifty yards they stood up and ran.

Doc was on his feet, holding an IV bag, as another soldier was loaded on an M3 armored half-track ambulance for the trip back to the regimental aid station. Finishing that, he went over to the burned tanker. He made a quick assessment and began to cover the worst of the burns with clean bandages soaked in distilled water.

"You're going to make it, trooper." Doc stood up and directed the team loading up the ambulance. "This one needs to go to the field hospital." He gently covered him to prevent hypothermia, then patted his litter bearers on the back to move out.

This process continued as the task force licked its wounds. Whoever Doc couldn't treat was stabilized, then transported on a half-track to the regimental aid station. After that, they would move to a First Army field hospital, then back home—if they made it. If doctors expected a complete recovery, the wounded soldier stayed on the continent to rejoin his unit somewhere down the line.

For Doc's unarmed medics, it was dangerous and stressful work, especially since enemy units oftentimes used the red cross painted on the sides of half-tracks as convenient targets for their guns.

Sam got on the radio to his immediate commander, Colonel Truman Boudinot—one of the original Third Armored Division senior officers—to inform him of the halt and send the initial casualty report.

Boudinot's response over the radio was angry: "Take your casualties and keep driving on to the crossroads."[8] Sam clenched his jaw but held his tongue, irritated that someone kilometers to the rear in the safety of a regimental CP was so cavalier about the lives of his men.

Instead of getting into a back-and-forth, Sam informed him that the casualty report was being prepared and that his unit needed fuel, water, and ammunition moved up immediately before any new attack. He signed off "Blue Six, out," then ordered Lieutenant Tom Magness to bring up his assault gun platoon and set up an observation post (OP) at the most forward position he could find ahead of the task force.

Tom saluted and moved out. As he and Staff Sergeant George Gregan loaded up for the OP, Tom remarked, "I'm so glad you made me bring our trailers full of extra ammunition." Little did either of them know how much they were going to need all that ammunition.

Well camouflaged, the OP would give the unit eyes on the crossroads as well as any route for a German counterattack upon the small armored force sitting three farm fields away from the front line.[9]

Sure enough, as dusk began drawing heavy shadows from the hedgerows, there was the unmistakable whistle of incoming artillery and shouts of *"Incoming!"* as everyone dove for cover. Sam, his small operations staff, Travis Brown, and Sergeant Phil D'Orio all dove under the half-track.

Two rounds kicked up dirt one hundred meters away and sent whitehot shards of metal exploding in a starburst, followed by large clods of brown earth. A third round landed just to the side of the battalion command half-track and CP. The blinding flash and ringing in the ears were immediate. Sam felt sharp pain in his right ear as his eardrum ruptured. The right front wheel of the half-track was shredded to bits.

This is bad—this kind of barrage means a big attack is coming, thought Sam through the pain. The Germans were accurately landing mortar and cannon fire of all calibers—"everything but Hitler's mustache." With an air of levity belying his injury and current deadly predicament, Sam yelled out to his peep driver, Charlie Gast, who was frantically digging the hole under the half-track even deeper: "Gast, I'm going to charge you with AWOL if you don't stop digging and pick up a weapon!"[10]

Meanwhile, two hundred yards in front of the task force, on a wooded knoll overlooking the German positions, was Tom Magness. He was covered in sweat and dirt after several close hits of artillery. Staff Sergeant George Gregan was severely wounded by shrapnel as they moved up to set up the artillery observation post. Without eyes on the enemy positions from the OP, it would be impossible to accurately land indirect fire on the advancing enemy from the mortars and assault guns behind them in the hedgerows. Tom carried the wounded sergeant back fifty yards where Sergeant John Grimes, section leader of the mortar platoon, helped Gregan into an armored ambulance for his trip to the regimental aid station.

Magness was back alone at the OP, but with a working radio. Now's time for some payback, he thought as he observed German helmets bobbing up and down among the trees below. A platoon of enemy infantry was preparing to attack. It would be a close one, calling in artillery on an enemy only two hundred yards away. He had a plan: use the assault gun's flat trajectory to flush the Germans out with special "Willy Pete" rounds that exploded in blooms of white-hot phosphorus. Then he would hit the exposed troops with a barrage of 81-mm high explosive from the three half-track mounted battalion mortars.

Magness, pushing away images of a sniper round striking him in the forehead as he observed the Germans milling about, radioed excitedly back to the assault guns and 81-mm mortars. They were positioned and ready to fire from a sunken road two hedgerows away from the task force CP.

"Hawk, Hawk, this is OP 1: Fire Mission, German infantry and vehicles in the open, Grid RJ 45312 28191, Willy Pete, fire for effect, over."

Fifty yards behind him, the battalion mortars, assault guns, and two platoons of 81-mm tubes from the 119th Infantry Regiment were ready to fire. Two NCOs led the ad hoc force. Sergeant Arnold W. Schlaich, the assault gun platoon sergeant, also took over leadership of the infantry mortarmen after the German artillery barrage killed their lieutenant. With a dull *thud, thud, thud,* the three assault guns fired off the Willy Petes. From his perch, Magness observed the rounds arcing away toward the enemy with a *POP, POP, POP,* followed by their trademark white-hot blooms and smoke as the rounds struck home among the hedgerows.

Grimes, now acting platoon sergeant of the half-track-mounted mortars, prepared his crews to send rounds downrange. The three mortar platoons received the radio transmission, adjusted their tubes, checked leveling bubbles, and dropped 81-mm HE rounds, each weighing thirty pounds, into the barrel—quickly ducking and covering their ears.

Magness grinned and fired off a few rounds from his M1 carbine as his call for fire was answered with a series of dull pops less than sixty seconds after his handheld radio's last squelch. He could see the gray shadows on blue sky as the rounds arced to the right and above his position, then descended into the hedgerow down the hill and opposite the US lines.

The rounds from eighteen mortar tubes and three assault guns blew up in a line of explosions that lit up the tree line in the fading light of the day. A chorus of screams rang out before desperate-looking figures sprinted out of the brush to scrape off the embers of white phosphorus burning through clothes, leather, and flesh. Then the mortars whistled in and detonated among the German infantry, sending clumps of dirt, flesh, and gear flying.

"Splash, out," exhaled Tom into his radio, indicating to the mortarmen that he had observed their rounds hit on target with deadly effects.

Dusk was coming, and observation was getting difficult in the fading light, but the mortar fire had successfully halted the German counterattack, which petered out amid the screams of wounded and dying infantrymen two hundred yards below the US positions.

Sergeant Grimes and his men quickly repositioned their half-tracks and emptied out into predug trenches. Sergeant Schlaich dismounted his mortarmen into foxholes. Unlike the operations staff, nobody wanted to be in or near the mortar half-tracks' open bays when the German artillery returned fire, since each contained one hundred rounds of stowed ammunition.

"Bring it on, you Kraut sons of bitches!" yelled some of the younger, full-of-piss-and-vinegar GIs. Slack and Grimes just cinched down their helmets and grimly awaited the enemy response.

Before the final blanket of darkness covered both German and US positions, facing off across a small valley of fields now littered with German bodies and several smoldering hulks of wheeled vehicles, the German artillery opened fire again.

This time, a barrage of mortar rounds landed on E Company, 119th Infantry positions. Captain Warren Fox, the company commander, was killed in the attack.[11]

As the enemy held the high ground surrounding Mortain and the encircled battalion of the Thirtieth Infantry Division, it was time to dig in for the night. Hogan's task force lost six tanks, with both infantry companies (E and F of the 119th Infantry) severely mauled.

Tank crews slept at their positions or under their Shermans. It would be an uneasy night, with half the force on guard at any one time and leaders scrambling to plan the next day's attack, replenish fuel and ammunition, and maybe catch a couple of hours of desperately needed sleep.

But little sleep was coming, despite the exhaustion. The sun had set late, at 10:00 P.M., and things were relatively quiet as soldiers on guard struggled to stay awake while the ones whose turn it was to sleep struggled to rest. Every crunch of boot under earth, every pop in the distance, jolted them awake.

Out of the shadow of a hedgerow in front, a German patrol crept up, swishing through the knee-high wheat of a farmer's field below and toward the center of the American position. They moved in a wedge formation, their sergeant silently guiding them by hand signals, creeping up like ghosts.

Their mission was to get in close and throw grenades under the American commanders' vehicles, thus decapitating the enemy defense.

They crossed the field past a burning tank, leaving a swathe of upturned soil in their wake. The Germans fumbled for "potato masher" grenades tucked in their leather belts.

Clicks and clangs alerted one of the US sentries. The discipline of Hogan and Fox's troops paid dividends.

"HALT! Identify yourself!"

The Germans froze. The sentry, knowing that no group of half a dozen should be walking around at that hour, let fly with rifle rounds. Several Germans threw their grenades. Tired American tankers and infantrymen responded to the commotion. They joined in, opening fire on the creeping shadows of the German infantry squad, and drove them off with fire from their short M1 carbines and .45-caliber pistols.[12]

At eleven o'clock came the radio call from General Hobbs, call sign Chaos Six: "TF3 will remain in defensive positions and actively defend gains made during the day until relieved."

No shit, thought Sam, and acknowledged: "Roger wilco, Chaos Six, Orchard Blue Six out."

AUGUST 10

Zero-dark-hundred, a chilly morning, and the surrounded Americans were under the cover of tanks or in foxholes with a foot of earth covering the top. The leadership of TF3 spent the night in their unceremonious command post—the hole dug underneath the immobile half-track in the middle of the battalion perimeter. Sam, Travis Brown, and Stewart Walker gathered the company commanders for a quick huddle before the artillery started raining down again.

"Here's the situation," Sam started off. Things looked dismal, and Sam never sugarcoated. TF3 had taken 30 percent casualties among the infantry, and G and H Companies had lost close to half of their fifteen Shermans. Neighboring units also had not had a good day: TF2, made up mostly of Thirty-sixth Armored Infantry soldiers, lost its leadership to a German artillery shell that landed smack in the middle of the command group. To TF3's front, SS Panzer divisions, the First and Second, had tightened the noose around the Thirtieth Infantry's surrounded units inside Mortain. Frenzied radio transmissions decoded and jotted down during the night by Brown's radio operators painted a still dimmer picture.

"Colonel," said Brown, "the Germans even overran the battalion aid station of the Thirtieth's Second Battalion, 120th Infantry, taking the battalion surgeon and all wounded troops prisoner."

"That's pretty bad, Brownie, and we're the only armor in the area."

"Right, sir, and get this—the 120th's radio call sign is 'Custer.'"

"Well, this isn't the Little Big Horn—Custer or no Custer, we have to get to them," Sam replied somberly.

The 120th Infantry was in dire straits. The enemy, however, was wedged in between Task Force 3, the 120th, and the next unit to the right and down the hill—the Twelfth Infantry. Intelligence reported that the enemy had emplaced antitank guns and dug-in tanks along all paths TF3 could take to the crossroads. Proving that this was not the imaginative report of an intel weenie: to their right, three dug-in enemy tanks brutally halted the Twelfth Infantry's attack toward Sam's task force.[13]

"At least resupply is coming," added Sam optimistically, "arranged by Major Walker and Captain Marcus Schumacher." Just in time.

Fuel and ammunition were running low. The supply of drinking water was getting down to critical level, too. Cramer was already threatening to court-martial any of his G tankers caught shaving or taking helmet baths. Not that anyone had the time or inclination.

Captains, lieutenants, and senior sergeants returned to their respective units to make their final preparations, foremost of which was resupply.

Now, in the glow of the coming dawn, ammunition and fuel arrived. Even the kitchen trucks were pressed into service to haul crates of tank rounds or five-gallon cans of fuel.

Resupply was laborious even in peacetime. Everyone helped. Soldiers who had been on guard or fighting most of the night put out their cigarettes with a resigned grunt, then lined up to offload the heavy cans of fuel. Supply soldiers handed the cans, one at a time, down from the truck bed to the waiting bucket brigade. They lined up without complaint, handing off the cans down the line to the thirsty tanks. Fifteen cans were needed to fill each Sherman. Their crews waited at the end, hefting each can up and leaning it into the thirsty gas port.

"Quickly, let's get it done," yelled a sergeant, "before Jerry starts shelling again!"

The same process continued for the ammunition. Heavy wood cases full of shells were handed off the truck to a waiting line of grimy tankers and soldiers. At the end of the line, the box was cracked open and the three-foot-long shells were raised one at a time to the gunner and loader waiting in the turret to fill their ammunition racks. Once finished, crews made final checks of track tension and oil level, and prayed—some silently to themselves, some as a tank crew or infantry squad.

Captain Marcus Schumacher's fuel and ammunition trucks completed their crucial mission, knowing that they were prime targets. German observers were watching from the cover of the hedgerows, binoculars in hand. Schumacher climbed into the cab of the last truck and patted his driver on the back.

"Get us out of here," he muttered, just as a series of sickening thuds reverberated in the distance. There were shouts of *"Incoming!"* as the enemy mortar rounds arced, then descended with a high-pitched whine. The artillery barrage came in like rolling thunder, creeping up on the line of trucks as they roared out of the perimeter one at a time. Schumacher's truck waited its turn to leave when another low whistle came in accompanied by shouts of *"Take cover!"* Schumacher and his driver dove out of the cab and onto the ground just in time—the truck was destroyed. Schumacher felt a burning sensation on his flank. Bloody nosed, with shrapnel wounds on back and shoulders darkening his olive-drab shirt, Schumacher helped his driver to his feet as the truck began to burn. The two soldiers helped each other one hundred meters back to see Doc Spigelman and his medics. The well-aimed barrage destroyed one truck but did not stop the resupply.[14]

By midmorning, Task Force 3 rolled toward the crossroads again in two large armored inverted Vs made up of just twelve G and H Company Shermans—the only remaining tanks out of the twenty they had started with. Riding on the tanks and trudging along on foot were what was left of the infantry from E and F companies of the 119th Infantry Regiment. Squads that started off as twelve riflemen were down to six or seven.

The infantry looked downtrodden, with their chins down and their rifles held low, muzzles pointed to the ground. Exhausted looks emanated from their eyes. Encouragement to *Stay alert, boys,* from their few remaining sergeants were met with worried and apathetic looks. Nevertheless, they kept trudging forward—"One foot in front of the other."

As planned, Carl Cramer's tanks on the left pressed the enemy front to fix their attention on that side. To his right, Ed Wray's H Company tanks were tasked to hit the Germans on the flank. Ed didn't like the look of it. He was down to six tanks and a dozen infantrymen. He remembered the tactical classes taught out of thick manuals at Fort Knox almost two years earlier: an attacker against an entrenched enemy on defense needs a three-to-one advantage in numbers. But that was theory—this was reality.

H Company rolled out, a dozer-blade-equipped tank leading the way. Sergeant Emmett Tripp's tank dozer crunched through the dried-out mass of dirt, roots, and vines of the hedgerow, then backed up to let Ed Wray's command tank through. Ed was leading from the front, one of the many reasons his men respected him. Tripp drove back into the breach to provide covering fire, followed by the remaining tanks and infantry. The armored wedge moved forward methodically across the farmer's field and onto the next set of hedgerows, where the second German line stood to meet them.

The tree line opened up with a volley of rockets swooshing out from Panzerfausts fired by German infantry hiding in the hedgerow. Ed's Sherman was struck and immediately rocked to a halt. The warhead of the Panzerfaust had found its mark and impacted the armor with a sickening metallic chomp. Smoke began pouring out as H tanks and infantry fired back into the tree line. The American flanking attack faltered.

Now the senior officer on that field, Lieutenant Arn of F/119th Infantry, saw Ed Wray making it out of his stricken tank and onto his knees on the loose, dark dirt of the farmer's field. One soldier remained alive inside the tank.

Instead of running to the safety of the nearest tank or back to the hedgerow from where they started, Ed climbed back on the smoking tank to get the survivor out. Arn and his radio operator looked on from the tree line as bullets zipped over their heads.

From cover, Arn shouted encouragement: "Get back here to cover! First squad: get ready to help them when they get closer." He looked through his binoculars. The top half of Ed's body was hidden inside the hatch. His lower half swayed as he obviously pulled at something within. After a few seconds of struggle, Ed's torso began reappearing as he pulled on the shoulders of his crewman.

"Keep firing into the woods around them!" Arn called out to his squads so that they would cover Wray's movement back to safety and away from the middle of the clearing. Ed Wray and his limping gunner, their coveralls stained with soot, turned toward friendly lines and began hobbling back.

Arn called out, "A few more yards and you're in the clear!"

Suddenly, a sickening burst of machine gun fire from the German-occupied hedgerow flashed out. Both the tankers jerked and stumbled as bullets cut through them like a scythe, leaving them both crumpled up and motionless on the muddy ground. Arn lowered his binoculars and waved his soldiers back into the bushes to regroup.[15]

It was just before 11:00 A.M., and the chaotic first twenty minutes on the right wing of Task Force 3's attack toward RJ 235 settled into an uneasy din. SS troopers and a thin line of F/119th Infantry faced each other from opposite hedgerows. Toward the far end of the field, closer to the SS lines, Captain Ed Wray's Sherman tank poured smoke, the dark columns drifting lazily in the summer breeze.

Lieutenant Arn scouted with his binoculars, looking for a counterattack. None came. Instead, a handful of SS troopers in mottled camouflage, loaded down with belts of machine gun ammunition, grenades, and entrenching tools, nonchalantly walked up to Wray's derelict tank looking for souvenirs or some of the prized American canned rations, maybe some cigarettes.

Arn couldn't believe his eyes. His grunts looked at him wide-eyed as he held up his hand and continued to look through his binos.

"Let them get closer," he said.

Two or three minutes felt like an eternity as the SS troopers milled about, the American bodies lying behind the wrecked Sherman. Arn's troops were all looking down the sights of their M1 Garands and carbines. Everyone aimed at an SS trooper. Finger on the trigger, ready to squeeze it.

Arn raised his hand high and brought it down. Before he could align the sight of his own carbine, his men opened up in a loud volley that dropped the half dozen SS troopers into a writhing mass of camouflage and gray steel. Satisfied smiles crept onto the faces of the infantry grunts—dirty, tired, their numbers decimated over the past twenty-four hours, they realized there was no counterattack forthcoming in their sector and they had avenged that brave tank lieutenant and his crew.[16]

Sam felt a sharp jab in his chest, a pang of guilt and loss, when the battalion net crackled that H's "Six" (commander) and his crew were missing and presumed dead. He bowed his head for a moment, whispered a short prayer. The task force commander had ordered the attack, and Ed Wray had saluted and moved out despite any misgivings.

Sam needed to shake off the feeling for the moment, shove it deep down inside. This was his chosen path in life. A combat commander must make life-and-death decisions. The same commander must live with the consequences and lead his soldiers on. Switching back to a sharp focus on eliminating the enemy in front of his task force was the only way to keep from taking even more casualties.

On the left of TF3's attack, Captain Cramer's G Company Shermans were still attempting to find the German line's other flank but halted their attack in the face of a wall of machine gun fire and accurately placed mortar barrages. The other tankers in his company could see Cramer hopping down from his tank, M1 carbine slung over his shoulder, with total disregard for the flying bullets, striding purposefully up to the nearest tank, banging on the commander's hatch, and then pointing toward where he wanted his force to fire upon the German position. "Two o'clock! I said fire to your two o'clock!"

He did this several times, a hands-on leader. Striding to a tank to coach a platoon leader or tank sergeant, then hopping down and calmly walking back to his command tank. Climbing back into the turret he called out energetically, "Okay, let's get going!"[17] Despite Cramer's slow and steely demeanor, there was even more urgency than usual. Staff Sergeant Kron continued to lie wounded in the field. Nothing could save him but the advance of the American line.

Just then, the German counterattack they'd been fearing kicked off. It started with a short but brutal artillery barrage. Rounds zipped in and denotated in blasts of fire and earth. There was a short pause, then they heard the distinct clapping of tank treads and saw plumes of diesel exhaust shimmering from the sunken roads before them.

Three Second SS Panzer Division tanks turned off the sunken road, quickly formed a battle line, and charged forward relentlessly. Coaxial machine gun fire began immediately, spraying the American-held hedgerow. Tank rounds burst among the trees and over foxholes of the left flank held by the depleted and tired infantrymen of E/119th. The German Mark IVs advanced in a roar of engines—churning mud behind and belching fire in front.

US bazooka rockets fired from the hedgerow with a hiss and a pop, only to ricochet off the panzers' frontal armor. The helpless infantrymen began to fall back.

From his observation post, Tom Magness saw the American line bend under the pressure from the enemy tanks. He again pleaded for fire over the radio. White-knuckling his field glasses to his face, he observed the rounds that rained down on the attacking German tanks. The explosions crimped treads and sent wheel sprockets flying off.

The impacts of high-explosive shells from the 75-mm Sherman assault guns and the 81-mm mortars again somehow managed to drive the Germans back. The attacking tanks pulled back reluctantly, not wanting to engage the American-held hedgerow under a rain of artillery. They retreated, but not before they had managed to push back the American line several hundred yards.

The US soldiers reloaded clips into M1 rifles and new magazines into carbines, took swigs from their near-empty canteens, and looked on as the retreating Germans pulled back to their side of the hedgerows to regroup and lick their wounds. The GIs grunted, unsheathed their entrenching tools, and began digging in with blistered, dirt-caked hands.

Three hundred yards back, Sam was busier than a one-armed paper hanger. He coordinated the movements of the two tank companies and the accompanying infantry while Walker handled resupply and the movement of wounded back to the battalion aid station. Back at higher headquarters they were thirsting for information: Where was the forward line of troops? Where was the latest casualty and missing report? What was the status of fuel, water, and ammunition? The operations staff sent what information they had and requested immediate resupply.

On the battle line, the two tank companies needed to stay linked together while also avoiding crossfire between friendly forces. Even worse, two RAF Typhoon fighters had mistakenly strafed the US positions with rockets earlier in the day—as if the German heavy artillery weren't enough.

Now was the time for another counterpunch, but none of the US tank or infantry commanders were able to identify the location of the German antitank guns that had stopped Captain Cramer's G Company tanks. At 4:00 P.M., the task force made a final attempt to push on the German line and get Staff Sergeant Kron back. Despite their best efforts to save their buddy, the attack stalled again in the face of heavy artillery and small-arms fire.

By 5:00 P.M., daylight was waning, with G and H Companies both stalled—the latter with Ed Wray, her commander, presumed dead. Sam ordered a halt to operations for the day. Carl Cramer was snorting mad. The lanky former NCO pounded on the side of his tank in frustration over having to leave someone behind—if only for the rest of that bloody day. He knew Kron's chances were not good. Carl was devoted to his wife, Juanita, back home in Indiana, and thoughts of her helped calm the beast within. Yes, they would attack again at first light—this time with air support.

The evening situation report went back to the regiment and division encrypted over the radio. Sam's report: "We've pushed on several fields but encountered antitank fire from three different directions. Our infantry is hit bad."[18] The Americans counted two enemy tanks and one PAK antitank gun destroyed against the loss of four tanks, a dozen wounded, and three killed.

So TF3, now just one hundred weary infantry and eight tanks, settled in for another night facing approximately two hundred dug-in German infantrymen protected by antitank cannons and handheld Panzerfausts. Nearby enemy tanks awaited their chance to break through any gaps in the US line. The darkness of another sleepless night for the officers and men of TF3 was inching its way over them. Pulling security. Checking and rechecking equipment for the soldiers. Redistributing ammunition, fuel, and water. Planning the next day's assault for the officers and noncoms. Then came word from Colonel Boudinot that TF3 was surrounded and to be prepared for a major German counterattack.

"Colonel, I'm sure glad we handled resupply this morning," Walker remarked.

"No kidding," spat Sam.

AUGUST 11

Combat Command Headquarters insisted on reports about "enemy movement to the north," and Sam instructed the radio operator to respond, "We are unable to tell anything about movement to the north of enemy forces. Enemy tanks moved in last night and we are in contact with the enemy on all sides. Road behind us is cut by the enemy and reported mined. Request friendly forces clear the road for evacuation of the wounded and for resupply."

At least there was some potential good news. Soldiers on guard through the night reported that the Germans had taken Staff Sergeant

Kron with them as they retreated. If they did not intend to render him aid as a prisoner of war, they would've just killed him in place or left him there.

It was time to try another approach, thought Sam. The fast and nimble light tanks of C Company could find a way around the unguarded German right flank. Once they found the gap, he could direct the heavier Shermans of G and H, supported by infantry, to exploit the breach and roll up the German line. For this task, Lieutenant Robert Resterer, with Jake Sitzes's platoon, moved out while G and H Shermans distracted the Germans to their front.

The five M5 Stuarts, led by Sergeant Emmett Tripp's trusty Sherman tank dozer, moved out with some difficulty clearing paths through the hedgerows. They moved steadily but cautiously, across fields of wheat and clusters of apple trees. The fast, agile Stuarts zigzagged easily. Jake kept a sharp eye out from his commander's position, a hatch-mounted .50-caliber machine gun ready to rake the next hedgerow in their path.

After close to thirty minutes, the small group slogged to within eight hundred yards (according to their maps, at least) of RJ 278. Jake raised his fist as his tank shuddered to a halt. The tanks in his wake stopped as the crew inside wondered if their LT had just spotted a hidden German antitank gun. Sergeant Tripp, in the second, dozer tank, saw the lieutenant run up to the side of his tank.

"Emmett, we're going to have to turn right around." They had encountered something the maps didn't show, a steep cliff that dropped thirty feet down—impassable by tanks.

Meanwhile, Sam directed the two-pronged diversion from his command tank and received artillery fire as SS dismounts moved up the slope toward them, using the terrain for protection. Moving in disciplined rushes, the SS troopers would roll to the side, then pop up just long enough to run—not giving enough time for the US riflemen to get a bead on them. They rushed forward in mottled camouflage tunics, carrying the high-tech Sturmgewehr (StG) 44—the world's first assault rifle, outwardly indistinguishable from a modern AK-47.

The steep terrain up which the SS charged made it impossible for

Sam's tanks to lower their turret guns enough to fire. The Shermans' hulls got in the way. It was time to rely again on the hard-pressed 81-mm mortars and M8 assault guns under Tom Magness.

The call crackled over the Fires net: "Hawk, Hawk, enemy infantry in the open, HE, timed-fuse, fire for effect." Timed fuses made the round explode in midair above the target, showering it with shrapnel. It was ideal for neutralizing troops caught out in the open.

The mortars were ready, and Grimes's troops plotted targets on their map board along the possible approaches the enemy could use in a counterattack. Within thirty seconds, the rounds traveled the five hundred yards from the tubes to the enemy, whistling in, exploding just above the steel-helmeted heads of the SS troopers in puffs of black smoke as the attackers scrambled for cover.

In response, the German guns shot up and over the American lines toward the little puffs of smoke of the US mortars. The crews dove for cover as mortar shells boomed around them. Sergeant Robert Cordell, Sam's fellow Texan, cried out, "I'm hit!"

"Hang on, Rob!" Grimes yelled back, visibly dismayed that one of his guys was hurt. Cordell squirmed in pain. Blood stained his shirt bright red. Seconds seemed like minutes as Grimes rose up from his shallow hole, then sprinted toward Cordell.

"I'm here, Rob, you're gonna be okay." Grimes pulled out an aluminum case from Cordell's pistol belt, snapped it open, and unwound the white-and-beige bandage within, stanching several jagged wounds on Cordell's shoulder.

"Damn, King, this hurts," moaned Cordell. "I hope I make it."

A short lull in the German fire allowed Grimes to drag his friend to a waiting peep, which took him to the aid station trailed by a cloud of dust. Once Cordell was secure, Grimes returned to the guns with splotches of his friend's blood still on his soiled coveralls. He immediately yelled out commands to his three half-tracks.

"Ready fire mission!" The mortars and assault guns kept firing, each half-track shooting ten to twelve rounds per minute over the next thirty minutes.

Through all the noise of the battle they heard a dreaded hum. Infantrymen in their shallow holes looked up at the drone of incoming aircraft. *What now? Another strafing run?* Some GIs started digging deeper; others grabbed on to their helmets and hugged the bottom of their shallow holes in anticipation of an ear-shattering bombing run.

But in the center of the task force perimeter, Ted Cardon let out a whoop as he popped his head out of the hatch of his tank: "We have TACAIR [Tactical Aircraft] on station!" Finally, some good news. US Thunderbolt fighter-bombers were moving in, poised to strike.

Cardon leaned over his turret, map board in hand, and twisted his neck to try and catch sight of the friendly aircraft. He raised the pilots and oriented them to their attack run: "Rattler Five Zero, this is Charlie Six, proceed along attack run, target is enemy tanks and infantry at grid RJ 582127. Friendlies are eight hundred meters north—over."

Half a minute later, two US P-47 fighter-bombers appeared behind their backs, zipped in, and unleashed a stream of swooshing rockets from pods on their wings. On the ground, the soldiers whooped and shouted approval as they watched the rockets, smoke trailing in a downward sloping path, crash on the German line with bursts of fire, smoke, and dirt. Finally, the German attack broke up in a hail of shrapnel from aerial rockets, 81-mm mortars, and the assault guns.

But the enemy still had an air force, and Hitler directed Luftwaffe chief Hermann Göring to spare no fighters and crews to support Operation Luttich. Thirty minutes after the US TACAIR departed station, another drone of piston-engine aircraft was heard in the distance. This time there was no mistaking it. From his hilltop position, Tom Magness spotted Iron Crosses and swastikas on the aircraft.

"TF3 elements, this is OP 1, enemy air incoming." The few soldiers milling about scampered for cover, and the tankers descended into their open hatches, pushed the bolts forward on their turret-mounted machine guns, and hunkered down.

The droning got closer. Then came the unmistakable *SWOOSH* of rockets and the staccato clap of aircraft cannon on a strafing run.

But this time, it was the Germans' turn to learn that "friendly fire" was anything but. It was the golden hour of sunset, the Focke-Wulf 190 fighter-bombers zoomed in from the east, the dying sun to their back, and unleashed their rockets and machine guns at the German line.

The Americans looked on in awe as the German aircraft let loose with a stream of hot metal. The Germans sent up green flares in an attempt to signal to their air support that they were friendly. The sight of the Germans' desperation resulted in hooting and hollering from the exhausted US soldiers looking on. Sam felt a surge of joy and actually let out a chuckle for this small bit of payback.

That night, fifty-four US cannons trained their fire on the German line. The order from the Thirtieth Infantry Division chief of staff to the chief of division artillery read, "I want you to rain steel down on the Germans in Mortain. I don't want a single thing left alive."

At 2:00 A.M., Task Force 3 sent up a coded radio report to higher command: "Large amount of enemy vehicles heard moving north and northeast of our positions."

"Roger," came back the bored reply. *Were the Germans attempting a night assault?* The Americans hunkered down and waited for dawn and the possibility of more air support.

Unknown to the division, overnight, Hitler reluctantly authorized his Operation Luttich units to withdraw. Faced with a stalemate at Mortain, the prospect of cutoff by the British to the north, and Patton's surging Third Army to the south, Field Marshal Günter von Kluge, the German commander, began pulling back his forces.

At 8:00 A.M. the next morning, Task Force 3 elements pushed out for one last try with the fuel they had left. G and H Companies crossed the open hedgerow where Ed Wray's tank lay covered in soot, hatches open. The infantry rode on the tanks, which stopped only to clear hedgerows. The troops maintained nervous caution—their advance seemed deceptively easy.

Another field to cross. Sam halted the advance when radio contact was established with the 120th Infantry Regiment. He ordered the task force to secure the area. Sam and Sergeant Emmett Tripp walked down to RJ 278, passing the burned-out hulks of US tanks and the mangled bodies of Germans killed by US artillery. *Where did they go?*

Suddenly, the sound of machine gun fire began popping to their front. Sam's command tank pulled up, ready for him to mount and fight.

"Sir, Custer reports a Panther tank guarding the road ahead."

In two bounds, Sam shot up into his command hatch. He plugged in his tanker's helmet and began scanning for targets. On the other side of the road junction there was more fire and US infantrymen shouting commands. *"Flank him!" "Bring up the bazooka!"* Before Sam's tank could see past some stone farm buildings, there was a swoosh and a crunch. Smoke began spewing from the other side of the buildings. More machine gun fire rang out.

The German force had indeed pulled back, leaving a lone Panther to delay the Americans—GIs of the 120th Infantry handily dispatched the enemy tank with several bazooka rounds. And just like that, after five days of costly combat, Task Force 3 had finally linked up with the 120th Infantry.

Sam slumped back in his turret and let out a sigh of relief.

His radio crackled. *What now?*

It was Colonel Boudinot, at combat command headquarters ten kilometers back. He had heard the radio reports that the Germans had pulled back under cover of darkness. Boudinot radioed Sam's command post to suggest that he drop in for a look. Sam frowned when he heard the radio chatter, quickly took to the microphone, and said, "Ontario Six, this is Blue Six, we are still dealing with sporadic sniper fire and haven't cleared for mines—over." That ended Boudinot's tentative boondoggle to the front line.[19]

Tripp and Sam returned to Task Force 3 as the troops consolidated on the objective. Infantry fanned out searching for any straggling German troops and for their American comrades missing in action.

American infantry flooded the fields and hedgerows northwest of L'Abbaye Blanche as the 120th, the Twelfth, and Task Force 3 finally linked up. Back in front of the H Company sector, Lieutenant Arn's foot soldiers wearily returned to the field where a charred Sherman rested, its suspension collapsed from the heat.

Two bodies in US olive drab lay sprawled a dozen yards away. Arn walked toward them, carbine at the ready, as his soldiers spread out to clear the opposing hedgerows. It was Ed Wray and his gunner—both dead. Pushing down his anger and tears, he radioed Sam with the bad news.

Back at the crossroads, Sam winced at the confirmation of what he already suspected. He lowered his head slightly, thoughts of his last meeting with Ed in his mind. He shook his head and radioed back, "Roger, Task Force 3, this is Six, consolidate on the objective and prepare for possible pursuit, acknowledge, over."

But there was no pursuit—the battle of Mortain was over. Ed was posthumously awarded a second Silver Star for his bravery in returning to his burning tank to help recover his crew.

Both G and H Companies were hit hard. Killed on the first day of battle were Privates John H. Flavell and Earl "Tex" Wyatt, who never made it out of their tank. Tex Wyatt's cowboy boots, arranged carefully in his duffel bag for an anticipated night on the town in Paris, survived the conflagration. They were packed up later with his other effects to be returned home to his parents.[20]

As for Staff Sergeant Kron, Sam and Carl learned a few days later from the Red Cross that Kron had bled out in German hands. Retreating Germans picked him up, but he passed away early on the tenth inside their aid station.

The mission of taking pressure off the Thirtieth Infantry Division units surrounded at Mortain was accomplished, but the toll was a steep one—twenty killed, 142 wounded, and sixty-four missing. The battalion also lost fourteen Sherman tanks, two M5 Stuarts, one M10 tank destroyer, one M8 assault gun, three half-tracks, and six peeps.[21]

With the battle over, the brave doughs of the 119th Infantry Regiment were released back to the Thirtieth Infantry Division to await replacements and bring themselves back to fighting strength. The Third Battalion, Thirty-third Armored Regiment also stood down for a few days of rest and recuperation.

Back at Third Armored Division headquarters, the mild-mannered Major General Leroy Watson was relieved of duty for lack of aggressive spirit. The soldiers on the line hardly noticed. They were too exhausted to care. But they would soon know their new division commander, for he was tough but fair—demanding, but never of anything he himself wouldn't do. He eschewed rear-echelon command posts, always seeing the front line with his own eyes. He was a tough, ramrod-straight cavalryman, a veteran of World War I and the campaign in North Africa: Major General Maurice Rose.

For the task force soldiers, officers, and NCOs, there was little actual rest. Damaged vehicles needed repairs and new equipment needed to be requisitioned. Personnel replacements had to be integrated and trained. There was no end in sight: as Sam's former West Point tactics instructor, General Omar Bradley, rightly stated, "After weeks or months on the line, only a wound can offer [the combat soldier] the comfort of safety, shelter, and a bed. Those who are left to fight, fight on, evading death but knowing that with each day of evasion they have exhausted one more chance for survival. Sooner or later, unless victory comes, this chase must end on the litter or in the grave."[22]

Bradley himself led the planning for a wide-arc offensive to trap the German forces defending the coast in the Falaise pocket, and it was in high gear.

There was much to do. But first, it was obvious that something had to be done about H Company. Ed Wray was its last experienced leader. Sam figured the division would not have any officers to spare but mentioned it anyway to Boudinot at the nightly update briefing back at combat command headquarters.

"Sam, I can't spare any lieutenants, much less captains. What's your plan?"

"Well, I have a Lieutenant in mind. His men would walk barefoot through a prickly pear patch if he told them it needed to be done."

That was all Boudinot needed to hear—Jake Sitzes took over H Company.

4

★ ★ ★ ★ ★

THROUGH FRANCE
LIKE BUTTER

To dispel any myths about the glamour of riding into battle inside a tank, imagine five men who haven't showered in a few days, crammed inside an unforgiving steel capsule whose interior adds up in volume to about the size of a modern minivan and is painted an unfriendly shade of dull pistachio green. The hull is crammed with the beer-keg-sized breech of the main gun sticking out into the middle of the turret space, a crew member seated on either side and the commander above and behind it—legs in the hull and upper body in the turret. The driver and the bow gunner/assistant driver are packed in the front of the hull with the tank's gearbox and ventilator wedged between them. Cannon rounds, three feet long, surround the crew in every possible nook and cranny. A dozen shells are lined up around the inside of the turret, with ten more in the ready rack within reach of the loader. The remainder of the combat load of seventy-one rounds was stacked along the sides of the hull or under the floor. Fuel tanks holding 170 gallons of highly flammable gasoline sat behind the crew compartment, saddling each side of the engine.

All around was hard steel. There were periscopes, sights, fixed metal seats, elevation levers, handles for ammunition rack doors, stacks of wires, and all manner of knobs, metal boxes, and levers that stuck out, waiting to ensnare the folds of a uniform or connect with skull or face at every bump and jolt of the thirty-three-ton tank. Even the forty-pound hatch over the driver, bow gunner, or commander's position could knock a tanker out cold or shear fingers off if not secured when open and the tank's movement caused it to slam shut.

Once the tank was moving with hatches closed, or "buttoned up," it became a nauseating trap rocking and lurching forward with nothing but small slits or periscopes for the crew to look out into the outside air. The environment within the crew compartment ranged from sweaty and hot in the summer to bitterly cold in the wintertime.

The smells of body odor, burning fuel and oil, and gunpowder were a persistent heavy air for the crew members to breathe. Firing the main gun sent the breech recoiling backward violently. Standing in front of it at the wrong time could result in a broken hip or femur. If all went well, the loader then removed the hot, spent shell—smoke still rising from its opening—grabbed a live shell, pushed it in with a closed fist (to prevent stripping off a fingernail between the shell and the chamber), then slammed the breech shut. The heavy breech block was also another dangerous moving metal part. The slamming breech resulted in many noncombat injuries such as shattered fingers or broken wrists.

Should the tank take a direct hit, the crew inside was exposed to a wide array of painful and potentially deadly effects. Best-case scenarios, where an antitank round failed to fully penetrate, could still result in a concussion or ruptured eardrums.

If an antitank round defeated the Sherman's armor and you survived the round cutting through hull, body, or limbs, the scuttlebutt among the veteran troops was that you only had six seconds to exit before the tank burned up.

With gallows humor, soldiers nicknamed their Shermans Purple Heart boxes or Ronson lighters (Ronson's well-known catchphrase was "It Lights Every Time"). This was due to the high probability of the tank catching fire, since it drew power from a gasoline engine and its onboard ammunition was stowed along the side walls of the turret and hull.

The combination of fuel, high explosives, and the crewmen's grease-covered overalls made for an incendiary blend that resulted in horrible deaths for tankers on both sides. Lessons learned from the First Armored Division in North Africa led to most of the ammunition being stowed under the floorboards of the Sherman as well as extra patches of armor being welded on to better protect the ammunition and crew.

There were tradeoffs. The infantry GI fights on foot, exposed to the merciless scythes of bullets and artillery fragments. Nothing but a thin steel helmet protects his skull—he moves from cover to cover or hugs the dirt. If in one place for long, he must dig a foxhole to survive.

The tanker, like the mounted knight of old, sits protected by armor. Inside the protective cocoon, the crew are safe from flying bullets and artillery—anything but a direct hit. The trade-off is that the tank is also a magnet for the enemy's biggest guns. You're the biggest threat, the biggest target, and you're trapped in there.

Still, the Sherman and the Stuart were the tankers' home, despite their shortcomings. Tankers got used to the smell of the stale air, sometimes welcoming it because they had grown to rely on and love their machines and fellow crew members. For many, it was a love-hate relationship.

Smoke was still rising from the Mortain battlefield when the orders for the next battle came down by runner. With the German counterattack, Operation Luttich, having been parried at great cost, the way was now open out of the bocage into much smoother tank country. The tanks were to liberate the rest of France as they rolled toward Germany. Up roared a motorcycle messenger from Colonel Boudinot's headquarters with an alert to get moving.

Sam was finishing with a helmet bath—stripped down to the waist, the steel shell of his helmet filled with water, dabbing a washcloth to remove dust from face, neck, armpits, and perhaps wiping down his "junk." He dried off and closed a letter to his parents and sister, signing off with the customary "you all write" (he requested some canned tamales and a Texas flag in their next care package). The Harley rider would take the letter back with him.

Back at Brownie's operations half-track, the company commanders and their top sergeants assembled, ready to get the basics of the plan before sitting down to refine it. Company leaders briefed their platoon leaders, and then the plan was passed down to each individual tank crew, infantry squad, and mortar section.

Sam strode in with the orders and some map overlays on acetate. First, Task Force 3 was now called Task Force Hogan, as the division began naming the battle groups for their commanders who had managed to survive the first battles unscathed and unfired. Second, the Third Armored Division was directed to turn east and north in a race to cut off the enemy's Army Group B before it could consolidate into a defensive line.

With the British heading south from Caen, the Americans and the Second French Armored Division would converge in two wide arcs centered near Falaise. Sam's division became the main armored force of the US VII Corps, First Army, and they in turn formed the southern arm of the envelopment to trap the entire German army group, including the Seventh Army and the Fifth Panzer Army.

Commanders and staff got down to business. Walker made sure the ammunition, fuel, and chow was either on hand or at points along the route. He also made sure spare parts were ready and that the maintenance program was keeping the hard-pressed tanks, half-tracks, trucks, and peeps ready to roll and not break down along the route. Everyone pulled their weight: drivers knew their vehicles were their lifeblood.

Travis "Brownie" Brown not only translated Sam's intent into the tactical maneuvers required, he also kept the command post moving along with the troops. His sharp sergeants and soldiers methodically found a suitable position, even if only a deep hole underneath a half-track, then put up map boards, strung telephonic wire, and made sure the wired-in field telephones and HF radios were up and running and could reach the spread-out tanks, infantry, and mortars. A section of dispatch riders mounted on Harley-Davidson motorcycles provided a third alternative, especially helpful if radio silence was necessary to disguise preparations for an attack.

Redundancy was the name of the game. If mortar shell fragments cut the field phone wires to the artillery, they could rely on the wireless radio to communicate—in code, because enemy intelligence was always listening. Sergeants kept this war machine running smoothly. You could guarantee there was a quick-thinking NCO making sure that even the drainage was appropriate for the battalion camps so they did not all wake up ankle deep in rainwater after an evening storm.

NCOs such as First Sergeant Hoyt D. Rogers—deep lines etched on his face from his experiences in World War I and dozens of "field problems," as the old timers called training exercises—managed the day-to-day workings, ensuring the line soldiers got their chow, that they kept their bodies and equipment in working order, and that the morale was as good as could be. They also looked after their officers. Sergeants like Phil D'Orio always checked on the colonel or others at the company level on "my lieutenant" to make sure they were getting a bare minimum of sleep or took some expectorant for that persistent cough.

Sam was continually amazed that the battalion worked so well. His boys were no longer fresh-faced selectees. He had been there to receive many of them at Camp Polk in 1942, still in their civilian clothes. Their tanned faces reflected youth, but the eyes projected a determined, quiet confidence. Moreover, there was trust between him and his subordinate commanders and sergeants. They trusted in Sam's tactical and technical competence. They knew he was not one of those glory seekers willing to risk soldiers' lives. In turn, Sam trusted his subordinates to accomplish the mission with little supervision. This allowed him to focus on the big picture of the day, as well as the next mission.

On August 12, the division rolled out of Mayenne in two enormous, armored pincers along an axis of advance centered on the towns of Carrouges, Rânes, and Fromentel. Division intelligence reports filtered down to the combat command and battalion commanders: remnants of thirty-two German divisions were attempting to withdraw. If they could capture the high ground near Rânes, the allies could block the German withdrawal, putting these enemy divisions permanently out of commission.[1]

From Mayenne, Sam's task force moved on as the right prong through rolling lush farmland interspersed with pine forests and little farming communes. The small towns were untouched, a welcome sight after the devastated pile of rubble that remained of Mortain. Through the little villages of Le Ribay, Javron-les-Chapelles, and Pré-en-Pail, G, H, and C tanks and piggybacking infantry rolled, stopping only to clear pockets of resistance. The battalion supply units kept up a few miles behind with their vital ammunition, fuel, and water relays. There was danger for the supply trucks, too, as it was a battle of "meeting engagements"—units bumping into each other, where whoever spotted and fired on the enemy first normally came out on top. Firefights at less than one hundred yards were not uncommon.

Upon reaching Pré-en-Pail, the task force swung north toward Rânes for the final thirty-kilometer march. Casualties were light. German units were isolated and bypassed, as they failed in their attempt to delay the Americans.[2]

Somewhere along this mechanized Tour de France, the Third Armored Division began to be known by an honorary nickname. Corps and army headquarters battle orders consistently opened, "This operation will be spearheaded by the Third Armored Division." First noticed by war correspondents filing their stories, the word "spearhead" filtered down to the line, and—soldiers being soldiers—they proudly adopted it. And so, the Third Armored Division became known as "Spearhead."[3] The troops began stenciling a stone spearhead on the side of their helmets. General Rose, recognizing the impact and morale-boosting effect of this moniker, made it standard across the division.

On the topic of morale, during a pause where mail caught up with the task force, Sam received a care package with treats from home.

Sergeant D'Orio walked up with a big smile: "Colonel, sir, you've got a parcel." Those words brought a grin to Sam's face as he hopped off his perch by the radio and maps.

"Thanks, Sergeant, just what I needed!" As he took the carefully wrapped box addressed "Overseas Military Mail and European Theater of Operations," Sam didn't wait. Over the hood of his peep, he brought out a small buck knife and carefully cut the tape holding the top flaps together.

He gently peeled back the cardboard folds. A letter from his mother and another from his wife were at the top. Underneath, there were canned jalapeños, vitamins, magazines, and a book titled *Texas: A World in Itself.* At the very bottom was a folded Lone Star flag.

Unfolding the nineteen-by-eleven-inch flag, Sam looked up at D'Orio. "I think this will look great flying from our radio antenna."

The flag was from his uncle Vaughan Miller. Sam planned to fly it from his tank or peep antenna, then send it back as a souvenir and a thank-you for the care packages and letters.

Miller's boy Vaughan Jr. was like a brother to Sam. They had grown up fishing on the shores of the Gulf of Mexico, as well as getting into the occasional mischief. One day, the two rascals got ahold of some dynamite and blew up an abandoned brick kiln out in the desert. The blast blew out windows in town and, years later, the local newspaper still remembered the incident, marveling at how the boy-turned-tank-commander was still blowing things up—only now it was German tanks.[4]

From then on, Sam flew the Lone Star flag from the radio antenna of whatever vehicle he was riding. German intelligence already knew that the US stenciled identification numbers on their tanks, and so they recognized and targeted the command tanks. Sam shrugged off the risk of making himself a target. If anything, the flag showed his troops that he was right there with them, where the action was.

In one village, the column stopped and a French lad pointed curiously at the Lone Star flag on the command peep's antenna. In his south Texas "French," Sam tried to explain.

"It is the flag of the free Americans" was interpreted by the boy's grandfather, who matter-of-factly informed the onlooking villagers, "*Mais oui!* That is the flag of the American resistance movement!" A war correspondent nearby jotted the encounter down in his notes. The story made *Stars and Stripes* as well as several Texan periodicals, where amused and proud chuckles ensued.[5]

Soon after Sam flew the Lone Star, Jake Sitzes flew a flag made from a liberated bedsheet—stenciled on it was a Missouri mule in full kick. His men always knew where to find Jake, leading from the front. Now they could see his Missouri flag fluttering in the cool Norman breeze.

The flags were the talk of the unit. During a short pause when Sam and Jake's tanks were near each other, their respective sergeants remarked about the banners. Sergeant D'Orio remarked to First Sergeant Filyaw of H Company, "Hey, Top, between the colonel's Lone Star and Lieutenant Sitzes's mule, they're really confusing the hell out of the enemy about who their opponents are."

"Yep, I reckon so," Filyaw chuckled back, as he puffed another cigarette.

Small morale-building tokens like the flags cemented Task Force Hogan's esprit and combated the stress-monotony-stress cycle. That exhausting, bone-jarring rhythm of plan, prepare, move, attack, repeat—with no end in sight.[6]

The advance continued on August 13 and 14. Sam's casualties were a few slightly wounded and no major vehicle losses. The French Resistance—French Forces of the Interior (FFI), or *maquis*—appeared often, helping the lead US units identify possible ambushes, minefields, and concentrations of troops and armor.

In one instance, a brave FFI member stopped the column short of a bridge. Jake's tanks were in the lead. Scouts reported the far bank unoccupied by enemy forces. It was a narrow gap to cross, but ten feet below ran a small creek. Jake looked on, wondering what was going on. The slender Frenchman looked back, held up a hand in a *wait a minute* signal, then gingerly hopped under the bridge.

"What the . . . ?" said Jake, as he dismounted to see.

The young FFI member pulled wire cutters from his coat pocket, then began expertly snipping demolition wires hidden along the insides of the booby-trapped bridge supports.

"I'll be damned," Jake muttered. The Frenchman crawled out the other side. With a smile and wave, he beckoned the column across, and they rolled on.

In some of the villages where the Germans had no time to set up a strongpoint, the task force rolled in unopposed to the warm reception of the local population. French country families in wooden shoes filed out of cellars onto the streets. Often led by their priest, they gathered at town squares to celebrate their liberation. One mademoiselle presented Sam with a small, embroidered flag made from US parachute fabric, with the coat of arms of two gold lions on a red background and the word "Normandie" embroidered on it.

Shouts of *"Vive La France! Vive l'Amérique!"* and *"Okay, okay, hello, boys!"* emanated from exultant villagers. Soldiers riding on tanks and half-tracks were kissed on the cheek. They posed for photographs and accepted gifts of eggs, butter, and jars of milk, or the occasional bottle of champagne or calvados (Norman apple brandy). The villagers selflessly shared these tokens of their country, which had been painstakingly hidden, sometimes buried in their front yards, for the four years of German occupation.

A liberated bottle of calvados made its way into the hands of Captain Carl Cramer's tank commander, Sergeant Lloyd Small. During one of their long stops to await resupply, the bottle came out. Taking a swig, Small's face broadened into a smile. He elbowed Corporal Frank Plezia, the tank's gunner: "Plezia, this stuff tastes like ground-up grenades." He passed it for a sip.

Resupply took too long to arrive, and Small had a few too many sips. They were all standing around waiting for Captain Cramer to come back with the next objective. Plezia and Ellis Butler, the radio operator, nudged Small up as their commander power-walked back to his tank.

The liquid courage got the best of Small as he proceeded to tell Cramer that he could give him a lesson on leadership. "Sir, leeemmeee tell you how IIIII woulda done things at Mortain . . ." As soon as he opened his mouth, Small knew he was in trouble. Plezia and Butler firmed up to attention while still holding Small up.

Cramer, the tough former NCO and disciplinarian, stood with his hands on his hips, neck slowly getting bright red, blood vessels bulging, until those around him thought he would blow his top. Small swayed and began tipping over before the captain could chew him a new one.

Landing on his side with a thud, all Small could do was crack up. The entire group, Cramer included, burst into hoots of laughter.[7]

The roads began to heat up, however, as the division approached the main bodies of the retreating German units. By August 15, the fighting stiffened sharply when Spearhead approached the hinge of the door closing the Falaise gap. Closing the gap looked simple on General Bradley's paper, but the enemy had a say and would not make it easy. A narrowing corridor between Falaise and Argentan was their escape route, and they intended to keep it open at all costs. The Germans were revitalized under a new commander—Field Marshal Walther Model. The monocled Model was a tough and energetic commander. He came with years of experience on both offense, such as Operation Typhoon, the attack on Moscow, and on defense; several times he had restored order to the German line in the face of superior numbers of Red Army tanks, infantry, and artillery. An Allied aircraft strafing attack had wounded Rommel in July, and now Model, Hitler's favorite defensive tactician, was coming in to save the day again.

To protect the division's right flank, Sam was ordered to take his task force past Rânes to seize the village of Écouché. The town's capture would cut off any German retreat along Highway 24 toward Paris.[8]

Écouché was at a critical crossroads but also at the unit boundary of the First and Third Armies. Unit boundaries existed on paper—on the map. There were no fences or walls, but there might as well have been, for units were restricted from crossing into each other's zones. This helped prevent friendly fire incidents. Furthermore, in a top-down hierarchy, information flowed up and down the chain of command of large units like a field army. It did not flow as well horizontally. These two facts made attacking the administrative seam of two units very desirable from your opponent's perspective.

On the flank of the Third Army were the Free French troops of General Philippe Leclerc. The French Second Armored Division was ready to avenge the defeats of 1940 and was a little too overeager, eschewing Third Army–directed fire coordination and road control measures designed to prevent friendly fire casualties. It was up to Sam to not only secure the division's right flank by taking Écouché, but also to keep their French allies from killing anyone other than Germans.

From his tank flying the Texas flag, Sam radioed for his attached scouts from A Company, Eighty-third Reconnaissance Battalion to establish a screen. Then he reached out to his French counterparts. Sam sure could have used Clem Elissondo's elementary French, but Clem was recovering from shrapnel wounds. His childhood reading and West Point basic French would have to do. "Mon Colonel" reached out, a meeting was set, and the two commanders understood each other. There were no friendly fire issues. The French armor surged forward with gusto on TF Hogan's right to help close the Falaise pocket.

Operation Cobra and the Normandy campaign were reaching their climax. At stake was whether General Bradley's grand plan could fulfill what every generalissimo in history had dreamed of since Hannibal at Cannae—namely, to envelop an entire enemy army, cut it off, then capture or destroy it.

"This is an opportunity that comes to a commander not more than once in a century," said General Bradley to a visiting dignitary.[9] The accomplishment of such a feat would leave the way clear all the way to the German border. There was even talk of "home by Christmas" as the Allied columns rolled forward to close the Falaise-Argentan pocket.

From the heights on the far side of the little stone town, Spearhead tanks and artillery observers saw the jaw-dropping sight of twelve hundred enemy vehicles of all types passing in the valley below. On a hilltop, officers and sergeants trained in calling in artillery and close air support began their deadly work. Ted Cardon, Tom Magness, Arnold Schlaich, and others white-knuckled binoculars to their eyes, jotted down coordinates, then raised divisional artillery on the radio.

"Oshkosh Three-Five, this is Hawk. Fire mission!" rang the call. The radio calls were followed by satisfying blasts from somewhere to their rear as the seventy-pound high-explosive rounds left their tubes and, seconds later, thundered in the valley below accompanied by white blasts, a smoky puff, and then the resounding explosion as the racket reached the observers' ears.

While the observers had a field day calling in artillery and air strikes on the columns retreating nine kilometers due north, at the halfway point between Falaise and Argentan, the tankers and infantry held a tight perimeter, fighting off probes as the enemy sought to expand or hold its perimeter by counterattacks.

To Task Force Hogan's left, Colonel Roysdon's command captured Fromentel on the seventeenth, after sharp duels with antitank guns and tanks from the Second Panzer, First SS Panzer, and 708th Infantry Divisions.[10] It truly was mayhem, with tanks dueling at only seventy-five to one hundred yards away from each other.

One tank destroyer, commanded by Corporal Joseph Juno, turned a sharp corner around a Norman farmhouse to find two Panther tanks less than thirty yards away. From the confines of his turret Juno calmly ordered his gunner, "Panther tank, hit the left one. FIRE!" The enemy tank's turret stopped turning, smoke and fire lashing out of the hole in its hull.

"Quick! Load AP!" The loader pounded the long round home, slammed the breech, and yelled, "AP up!" The gunner turned the turret and, without waiting for the command, sent the second round toward the second Panther, hitting it on its flank. The enemy tank crews began streaming out of escape hatches.

Juno, hearing their screams, vaulted over his open turret, jumped off the hull, and ran to the stricken Panther to get the stuck enemy driver out before his tank burned. He struggled to climb the tall tank. Once on top, Juno reached a hand toward the tank driver as he struggled to free himself. A massive blast stopped their efforts as the Panther's onboard ammunition cooked off. Juno and the stuck Panther driver were killed instantly.[11]

All along the Third Armored Division line the fight raged on. In addition to heavy use of artillery, the US IX Tactical Air Force fighter-bombers helped overcome the odds. However, the fighting was at such close quarters that the exploding ordnance proved dangerous to both friendly and enemy forces. Colonel Roysdon himself was slightly wounded from one such "danger close" air support mission.

Finally, by noon on the eighteenth, the entire division occupied its assigned objectives on a line from Fromentel and Rânes to Écouché. Between them, the two commands destroyed fifteen German tanks and took four hundred prisoners in a vise centered on the three towns. Nevertheless, the battle was not over. The Falaise-Argentan corridor remained as German columns streamed toward crossings on the Seine, day and night.

Controlled chaos was the order of the day as seventeen Allied divisions—US, British, Polish, and French—converged on the remnants of fifteen German divisions from four directions. It is no surprise that in Clausewitz's "realm of chance and uncertainty" the Germans were able to keep the corridor open. From somewhere up the US chain, the order to stop came down. Politics and the fog of war played into the situation, as Montgomery's troops stopped short, too. Finger pointing would follow, but the Germans fought like lions trying to squeeze out as many troops and tanks as they could.

On August 21, the last German units crossed on ferries to the relative safety of the far bank of the Seine. The enemy succeeded in getting out some of their armor and most of their field army and division commanders. Many enemy formations and their experienced soldiers would fight again. Task Force Hogan was destined to clash again with several units they had faced in Normandy, chief among them the 116th Panzer "Greyhound" Division.

The knockout blow was not delivered—but despite this fact, the Reich's loss of somewhere between two hundred thousand and four hundred thousand killed or captured in the Falaise pocket, plus associated tanks, artillery, and wheeled vehicles, opened the way to Paris for the Allies.

The City of Light lay 130 miles to the east. General Leclerc's Second Armored had already sent advance units, unbeknownst to their US allies, even as their scouts shook hands with Sam outside Écouché.

The Reich tightened up its lines and immediately began rearming its battered divisions. Hitler still had millions of soldiers under arms. Furthermore, despite Allied strategic bombing, Albert Speer's factories were cranking out tanks, airplanes, and *Wunderwaffen* ("wonder-weapons") like never before.

His scientists continued to devise and rush into production weapons straight out of American science fiction: guided bombs, jet aircraft, and ballistic missiles. V-2 rockets began raining death and destruction on London by early September. The Germans produced armaments to revolutionize modern warfare, like the "Vampyr" infrared night vision sights for their assault rifles and tank cannon.

A game of cat and mouse between Model's Army Group B and the US First Army began. Nobody knew how long it would last, but first, the massive armored columns of Spearhead needed to execute river crossings at the much-fought-over Marne and Seine Rivers.

Since the time of Julius Caesar, river crossings have presented a tough challenge for the attacker and an advantage to any outnumbered defender. The task is compounded when the enemy holds the opposite bank and brings artillery and direct fire to bear on your armored columns—channeled, clustered, and immobile as they stop and prepare to cross. Whether a squad crossing a creek using a rope bridge or a division crossing multiple bridges under cover of air and artillery support, a lot of planning is necessary to secure the far side, arrive at the bridgehead, cross under fire, then hold long enough to expand the bridgehead and move out again.

Spearhead halted until August 24 to prepare to move out again and cross those rivers. Tanks, half-tracks, and other vehicles were in dire need of maintenance. Fuel and ammunition supplies needed to catch up to the front.

Profiting from the few hours of downtime, Major General Rose presented some awards, including Silver Stars for Travis Brown and Dorrance Roysdon. A small consolation for Roysdon, who was soon after relieved due to personality conflicts between him and Rose. Some Spearheaders, who had watched Roysdon's XO, Major Winston Gilkey, die in his arms from shrapnel wounds during the move to Mortain, whispered that the incident affected the colonel so much that he was fired for being overcautious in protecting his troops.[12]

Sam was to receive the Silver Star as well, his only notice to the family delivered in one of his longing letters home—humble, perhaps with a touch of survivor's guilt, he simply wrote: "I have been awarded the Silver Star." Period.

On the night of August 24, Task Force Hogan approached the Seine along the center route with the other Spearhead commands on each side. The German Forty-eighth Infantry and Ninth Panzer Divisions persisted in their attempts to hold ground until the situation was untenable, then they melted away, allowing themselves to be bypassed, then attacking supply convoys and depots. Spearhead's Twenty-third Engineer Battalion underwent its combat bridge-building baptism by fire, throwing up pontoon bridges over the Seine to augment an existing bridge south of Corbeil.[13]

It was 11:45 P.M. on August 25. The two-hundred-meter-wide Seine flowed slowly, dark and forbidding across the entire fifteen-hundred-meter front occupied by Task Force Hogan. This was not the Seine that gaily reflected light off magnificent Parisian buildings and elegant quays thirty-five miles upriver. This was a wide, black antitank barrier. Here the banks were swampy and the opposite side cloaked in mystery and darkness. The nearby village of Melun slept peacefully unawares.

With a prearranged flashlight signal and a wave forward, Sam's scouts proceeded across the old stone bridge and two sets of pontoons put up by the engineers. Ted, Carl, and Sam squinted through the darkness, trying to follow the M8 Greyhound scout car's tiny red tactical lights. Behind the officers, tanks and mortars—spread out to avoid massive casualties from one lucky direct artillery hit—waited nervously. They were locked and loaded, waiting for an order to light up the opposite bank if the scouts met any resistance.

Sam took a few deep breaths as he stood on the dark bank. Reflected on the turbulent surface of the Seine were a few stars. He looked up to the heavens for a minute, thinking back to the "big sky" country of his boyhood.

This was the point of danger. His task force, though spread out as much as possible, was still funneled in at the approaches to three bridgeheads. One Luftwaffe night bomber could cause havoc. Just in case, a section of antiaircraft half-tracks, four .50-caliber machine guns mounted behind each, stood guard at each bridge entrance.

Fifteen or twenty minutes passed that seemed like an eternity. The signal flashes of light cut through the darkness from the far bank. Lieutenants Worrell, Resterer, and Sitzes and Sergeant Shorty Wright, each responsible for scouting a sector, flashed the all-clear sign.

More than sixty engines cranked up, instantly drowning the peaceful night in mechanical growls and screeches. Across the three bridges moved the long stream of tanks and half-tracks. They set up positions on the opposite bank and waited for their brothers of the rear echelon—unarmored kitchen and ammunition trucks, peeps and ambulances—to cross over.

Finally, an hour later, in the last hours of the night, the last vehicle crossed the Seine and Sam sat back in his canvas-and-metal peep seat. This crossing had gone surprisingly well, but an untold number of similar crossings loomed in their future.

There was little time to fuel up and reconnoiter the road, and then it was on to the next river: the Marne. General Rose, always at the front, made it clear the pace was to be unrelenting—keep the Germans reeling and off balance. Jake Sitzes and C Company, Missouri mule pennant flying from his little M3 Stuart tank, were outstanding in mopping up pockets of resistance and screening Task Force Hogan's advance.

The Third Armored Division swung wide northwest around Paris in an enormous wedge befitting the name Spearhead, with the First Infantry Division—the "Big Red One," so nicknamed for their shoulder patch, a big red number 1 on a green shield—and the Ninth Infantry Division following behind and on each side. They cut off German-occupied Paris and passed the honor of liberating the City of Light to French armored units.

By the last day of August, Spearhead had rolled on to the Aisne River, liberating objectives with names like Soissons and Sedan. These names brought memories of the Great War—with its hard, stalemate fighting—for some of the senior officers like General Rose. Beyond was the West Wall, also known as the Siegfried line. German units were fighting a disciplined withdrawal to those fortifications, built prior to the war and upgraded since that time with the German expectation of fighting a two-front war again.

On their advance through the French countryside, the German Luftwaffe made a rare appearance over Sam's armored column. The only alert for the Americans was an unfamiliar low, mechanical wail that started to the northwest. In very little time, a sleek black aircraft zoomed in high on a path to bisect the long olive-drab column of US vehicles. The alert hissed out of radios: "Orchard elements: unknown aircraft, possibly enemy, at three o'clock to the line of march." Some of the troops pointed out, with startled murmurs, that the aircraft had no propellers.

The antiaircraft sections from the division's 486th AAA Battalion were left behind to guard other river crossings, so tank commanders—including Sam, Carl, and Jake—readied their hatch-mounted machine guns. They followed the dark object's path with the gunsights, unsure of whether they'd have any effect whatsoever on the high-flying fast mover.

"That's gotta be one of the Nazi wonder-weapons," called a voice over the internal net. The sleek form dropped down on a path toward the US formation. Sam exhaled, a determined but worried look drawn on his forehead, jaw clenched—images of rockets or some newfangled robot bomb raining down on his men rushed through his head.

"All elements, this is Six, hold your fire. It's far out of range." His body eased forward as his driver let off the gas. He got back on the net. "This is Six, keep up the speed of march, don't speed up or slow!"

The black bird yawed up and right in a graceful arc that revealed black Iron Crosses under its wings. No more mystery as to its origins. But was it preparing to fire rockets? The tanks were sitting ducks, nothing but flat fields of grain on either side. "Still out of effective range! Hold your fire."

Two propless engines under each wing pushed it along at an amazing speed. This was one of the new jet bombers, the first in the world, though no visible ordnance hung under its swept wings. The bird stayed on its high-altitude arc—the troops didn't know it at the time, but it was silently taking photographs. This was a reconnaissance bird, though the American ground-pounders had no idea.

Ted Cardon, in a tank trailing Sam's, finally got Air Corps liaison on the radio. "Stand by, ground element, we have friendly air coming on station—over." Five endless minutes later and a pair of P-51 Mustangs approached fast from the south.

The ground soldiers looked on; the enemy plane was too fast and out of machine gun range, but they expected the show of a dogfight. It was not to be—suddenly the dark, sleek enemy jet turned in a tight curve and screamed off back toward Germany, leaving the Mustangs in the dust of fluffy white contrails. Sam exhaled a sharp breath of relief.

It was the end of August 1944 and there was no end in sight to the fog of exhaustion mixed with shots of the exhilaration of combat as Sam's task force approached north-central France. Things were going too smoothly—something had to give. Near the town of Herbigny, radio orders directed all Spearhead units to halt and "coil" in place. Commanders were to report to "Omaha Forward"—General Rose's advance command post—forthwith.

The coil formation was standard for units way out front ahead of friendly lines in enemy territory. When the unit had to stop to await supplies, or to camp overnight before an attack, the scouts would find a good bit of dry and preferably high ground off the main route of march. The column coiled with the tanks facing out 360 degrees and infantrymen dug in on the approaches. The headquarters, mortars, supply trucks, and battalion aid station sat within the relative safety of the "circle of wagons," or, in the parlance of previous wars, the laager. Slit trenches were the only "comforts"—that is, if they stayed there long enough. Otherwise, it was dig a hole next to your tank with your entrenching tool, do your business, then cover it up with a few spadefuls as a courtesy to others. One's fellow crewmen would not be happy to step on a "stinky mine."

The task force's coil was in view of road signs that said "Sedan—95 KM." Tracing their way back two kilometers to the Spearhead's advanced command post at Seraincourt, Sam, Travis Brown, and Phil D'Orio crammed into a peep. One of Jake's light tanks led the way for security. This was standard operating procedure, since cut-off Germans were known to string up wire to decapitate American soldiers driving by in open-top cars. Also, squads of German infantry had been captured attempting to ambush supply convoys from the woods north of what they called on their maps "Route Blue," so a little firepower in the lead was a prudent precaution for the command group. A commander can't account for everything, but at least the risks can be minimized.

Thirty minutes later, the peep and light tank escort arrived at General Rose's command post. Since they were on the move as fast as their vehicles could carry them toward Germany, the divisional CP consisted of nothing more than two half-tracks and a peep pulled to the side of the road. Sam saw Colonel Robert "Bobby" Howze—his new regimental commander—standing tall, Combat Infantryman's Badge pinned conspicuously above his left breast pocket. Colonel Howze was the new link between Sam and Spearhead's commander for this operation.

The commander of the echelon above Sam seemed to change about every couple of weeks, depending on which combat command was the main effort for the Third Armored Division. The combat command was one of three regimental-sized battle groups, with a strength encompassing two to three task forces like Sam's, plus add-ons depending on their mission. Which combat command led with tanks also depended on the rotation of units, where one was the main effort and the other held in reserve—the reserve usually being the one that had just participated in heavy action. This was done so that the unit could rest, bring in personnel replacements, and maintain their much-abused tanks and wheeled vehicles in preparation to assume the lead again in the next battle. Still, as one of the few tools a commander has to influence a battle at its climax, his reserve had to be just a call away from action.

Sam considered Colonel Howze a lucky draw to be his new commander. Working under the fellow cavalryman Howze reminded him of his early West Point days, when he was the first in his class to choose cavalry as his branch. He loved the idea that he would get to ride horses fast for a living. Well, it wasn't that easy.

Apart from basic horsemanship, which every cadet had to take, those who picked the cavalry arm went through intense daily training conducted by none other than the famous African American regiment—known in old Western days as the buffalo soldiers—of the Ninth Cavalry Regiment. On the first day, the cadets lined up on one end of the colossal indoor riding hall with a line of horses on the other end. At the command of *"Charge!"* the cadets had to sprint sixty yards on sawdust toward whichever looked, to them, like the best horse. Invariably, some cadet got the short straw. A buffalo soldier drawled out, *"Aright, sirs, who's going to ride old Diablo?"* Sam, however, lucked out and got a beautiful chestnut gelding, whom he renamed Tex.

So Sam was glad when it was the tough but fair Howze he pulled to be his new commander. Being a former cavalryman turned infantry commander, Howze knew how to employ the tanks. This was something his infantry admired, because they knew he would use the tanks to punch through, sparing the infantry from taking unnecessary casualties. They in turn protected the tanks from German tank-killer teams. A quick nod and handshake and the two slim officers were leaning over a map board along with several of the other combat command and task force commanders.

"Group! TENCH. . . . HUN!" Colonels, lieutenants, enlisted drivers, and orderlies all snapped to attention. In walked an immaculately tailored and tall general officer, with the purposeful stride of someone who knew what he wanted and how to get there. General Rose walked confidently toward Sam and the other commanders.

"AT EASE, gentlemen." His voice immediately commanded obedience. His stern visage was rarely—if ever—cracked by a smile, and wordlessly intimated *I'm all about business and am not someone to be trifled with.* General Rose epitomized confidence and professionalism. All who were assembled instantly understood that this was a serious man who pushed his men and machines relentlessly. The general welcomed his commanders one by one with a nod and a firm handshake.

Like Sam, Rose possessed the impeccable posture of a polo player on the saddle. He too carried himself with a calm, dignified confidence that inspired respect and confidence. It was not a posture of arrogance but the inspirational sureness of a good leader, well versed in his trade, tactically and technically competent.

Rose met his task force commander eye-to-eye at six feet tall—Sam noticed Rose's lean, straight frame clothed in pressed field pants, shined combat boots, and a tanker jacket, the two shiny stars of a major general visible on his pressed shirt collar points and steel helmet.

"Gentlemen, we have a change of mission. The entire division is going to turn ninety degrees and head north to seize Mons, Belgium, as our objective." The assembled commanders exchanged surprised glances. Sam's mind flashed back to military history classes at West Point, where they had studied the Battle of Mons during the Great War as a major turning point for the Allies.

The division intelligence officer, Captain Bill Castille, interrupted Sam's thoughtful scrutiny of the map as he dragged on a Camel and said, "Army Air Corps has identified a major German movement involving units of the German Seventh and Fifteenth Armies. These units must not be allowed to retreat and take their positions on the fortified German border." Castille pointed to arrows on the acetate map overlays— big, red, and headed east. "You'll be facing elements of the elite Sixth Parachute Division, as well as four motorized infantry divisions."

General Rose chimed in: "The pace is to continue, unrelenting. We have a unique opportunity to hit these five German divisions in their flank as they stream eastward immediately north of us. They'll be pinned against the British forces north of them in the Low Countries." He paused for effect. "From me on down to the Tech 4 Sherman driver, everyone in their hearts must understand that maintaining the initiative—keeping the enemy reeling—is the quickest and least bloody path to victory and the ship ride back home."[14]

Rose gave broad instructions: they would disengage from the enemy facing them to the east—*break contact,* in tactical terms—and head north. A VII Corps Infantry unit, the Ninth Infantry Division, would come in to take over the line while the Spearhead combat commands wheeled north along French routes 9 and 11. A ninety-degree turn from the most forward position facing the enemy was no easy feat. Months later, Patton would brag about a similar operation taking only twenty-four hours for his Third Army units—however, Spearhead was about to attempt it in a fraction of that time.

General Rose informed the gathered commanders that the division order and additional details, including map overlays, were forthcoming in the next two hours. The battle rhythm was already practically muscle memory. With this initial bit of information, Sam and Travis Brown could return to the task force and begin preparations for the turn north. A thorough map reconnaissance, detailed route, logistics, and contingency planning would follow. All the while, the logistics and signal personnel topped off vehicles and ammunition, picked up communications wire, and cleaned weapons, while their leaders planned how they would move and sustain the force on their new routes of advance.

Sam crammed his lanky frame back into the little peep, banging his kneecap into the metal dash. Left-handed, he'd always had two left feet as well.

With a grunt and *let's go,* the task force leadership roared down the little forested country road back to the coiled tanks and half-tracks, itching to get the word out to the troops that they were to close in on their old nemesis, Army Group B, yet again.

The pain in his knee reminded him that he'd already had two tanks shot out from under him—statistically speaking, the odds were already against him if it happened a third time. That pesky law of averages. He accepted the probability and a wave of calm resignation surged over him. Still, the questions remained unanswerable: *How many battles were left? How many more enemy could they kill or capture before the Reich sued for peace?*

5

★ ★ ★ ★ ★

INTO BELGIUM

The command group raced back to the coiled Task Force Hogan in a swirl of dust and into the perimeter of circled wagons where captains, lieutenants, and sergeants eagerly awaited news of what their next objective would be.

Sam leapt out of the narrow confines of his peep, then walked briskly toward the gaggle of officers gathered around the operations half-track. There were a lot of smiles and pats on the back. Doc Spigelman was there, too, next to a tall, slender tanker in brand-new OD coveralls.

The officer turned toward his incoming commander. Sam and Sergeant D'Orio both smiled widely as they recognized a familiar face. The young man looked fit—but under his coveralls, jagged pink scars testified to a close brush with death. His gray-blue eyes gleamed still but with a barely perceptible tinge from the strains of past combat. It was Captain John Barclay, recovered from the wounds incurred at Hauts Vents.

The young captain straightened up and saluted: "Sir! Captain Barclay reporting! I got back as soon as I could." Sam returned the salute and they warmly shook hands.

"John, we're damned glad to have you back." Sam turned and motioned at a smiling Jake Sitzes. "This Lieutenant here has been doing a bang-up job." John put an arm around the shorter officer. Jake was glad to have his commander healthy and back. He happily relinquished command to become Barclay's executive officer.

Sam cut the celebration a bit short. "Welcome back, Captain Barclay." He paused briefly and his tone changed back to business. "Now, men, we have a change of mission—prepare to copy." Small notebooks and pencils were pulled from coat pockets.

Sam looked at the half dozen young men in front of him. Some, like their commander, wore steel helmet shells over their football-style tanker headgear—a hard lesson learned from watching men killed and wounded from shrapnel in the battles after Normandy. The tanker's helmet was only designed to cushion the soldier's head when bumping against the hard insides of the tank during movement—not to stop flying hot metal. So, as soldiers so often did in the field of battle, they'd improvised.

Some stood with cigarettes in their mouths or a canteen cup of black coffee at hand. They were clothed in grimy overalls, some with the light tanker's blazer on their upper bodies. They all looked older than their years. Sam lit a Camel and walked over to the upright map board.

"We're headed due north into Belgium to seize Mons and prevent a large body of Germans from escaping east to man the Siegfried line fortifications. The entire division will move along routes between Hirson"—Sam pointed and swept up—"and Vervin."[1]

The plan was thus set. One company of the Third Battalion, Forty-seventh Infantry Regiment of the Ninth Infantry Division—the "Old Reliables"—with attached heavy machine gun section, would fall in with each of the tank companies, G and H, riding on top of their Shermans. A rifle company would follow behind in their own two-and-half-ton ("deuce-and-a-half") trucks. Carl Cramer's G Company would lead with Shermans, the very first one without the clinging infantry, and, upon contact, would return fire—allowing the trailing tanks to unload their dismounts and maneuver through the woods to flank any antitank ambushes from cannon, Panzerfaust-armed infantry, or any combination thereof.[2]

Like skirmishers during seventeenth-century warfare, C Company light tanks would patrol off the road into firebreaks and secondary trails, to foil any ambushes or units hanging behind to cut off the advancing Americans. Headquarters traveled in the center, accompanied by engineers. Service Company—the mechanics, supply clerks, and medics—brought up the rear with some of the M8 assault guns interspersed among them for protection.

It would be a thundering, sweeping river of American steel.

Surprised but eager looks greeted the change of mission. The men had assumed they were going "balls out"—maximum speed, in railway terminology—straight east to Germany. But now the entire division, eighteen thousand troops and hundreds of vehicles, was turning ninety degrees to the north to ram a huge formation of Germans right in the flank as they retrograded east to man the Siegfried line.

Already, Travis Brown was alerting the reconnaissance platoon to prepare to set off ahead of the main body. Carl Cramer, John Barclay, and Marcus Schumacher broke off in different directions—hasty farewell handshakes and last-minute cigarette bumming taking place. This was a well-oiled machine, but the division was changing directions in the middle of a dense forest with little knowledge of what lay ahead to the north.

The Third Battalion, Forty-seventh Infantry joined the fold. They arrived in canvas-topped, unarmored deuce-and-a-half trucks. Their commander was a soft-spoken but tough-as-nails, six-foot-tall New Yorker named Donald C. Clayman. Don had been a star football player at Syracuse University before the war. He was dark-haired, with fierce and determined brown eyes. His handlebar mustache went handily with his bravado in battle. He introduced himself to Sam, saluted, and after a hearty handshake, prepared his troops to fall in with the column.

Within two hours, the entire Combat Command, with Task Force Hogan on the right, wheeled around—Sherman tanks uncoiling their armor to face east, and turning around to head northwest toward Mons. The command group fell in behind the advance guard, Sherman tanks in the middle and the mortar half-tracks interspersed, with the little M3 Stuarts securing their now-vulnerable tail and right flank. It was late afternoon on August 31. The task force—over six hundred men loaded into fifty tanks, a dozen half-tracks, and thirty-five trucks—belched exhaust fumes and roared forward; the metallic *frap, frap, frap* of tank treads and almost a hundred gearboxes shifting at once boomed through the forest.

Sam sat back in his command tank with an exhausted sigh. All seemed to be progressing according to plan. He knew he had twenty minutes of quiet as the task force retraced its route, but they were on unknown ground and needed to be alert for enemy ambushes. The slim twenty-eight-year-old from the sparse caliche plains of Texas had somehow found himself responsible for a regimental-sized (three battalions) column aimed directly at the German army as it attempted to escape back to man the Siegfried line. This was the rhythm of war: periods of tension and anxiety with very few moments for self-reflection. He fired off a short letter to his wife, Belle, and to his parents, Dodge and Mary. His normally buoyant personality was a bit deflated. Still, he felt a need to reassure his family, and he himself looked forward to every little letter he got from home.

After thirty minutes of slow movement, radio chatter indicated that the recon element four hundred yards ahead had forded a river, the Thon, near the town of Bucilly and were now receiving fire from German infantry advancing on their position.

It was time to fight again. Radio checks came in from the companies as they hit predesignated checkpoints. Sam eased back into his commander's hatch and made some quick calculations as he reviewed his map. He then stood back up on the metal seat to just about shoulder level out of the hatch to check that the terrain matched what was on his map and that his large formation was progressing on schedule. When the tank was buttoned up, the tank commander—who was also sometimes the platoon, company, or battalion commander—could only see through the rotating cupola periscope, which afforded a limited line of sight. Sam had learned at Hill 91 that, for the tank commander, it was good practice to not always stay buttoned up when advancing to contact. Through the periscope or tiny vision slits, it was almost impossible to see the muzzle flash of an enemy tank or antitank gun. On the receiving end of an antitank gunshot, the speed of sound made sure that no one heard the round leaving the enemy gun. The rounds traveled so fast that the only telltale sign that one was on the way was a small burst of dust and a muzzle flash coming from an otherwise invisible, deftly camouflaged, low-to-the-ground German antitank cannon. Here again, chance encounters and the law of averages could play against a commander's longevity on earth.

Additionally, a man's head poking out of the tank commander's position made a tempting target for any sharp-eyed German sniper. If enemy artillery happened to land nearby, a sliver to the head as small as a needle could kill you if the round exploded within fifty meters. Then again, a half-open hatch could help diffuse overpressure that occurred when taking a direct hit—hopefully sparing everyone a concussion. So here again, Sam and his commanders had to decide what they were comfortable with, balancing the needs of the mission and good leadership with not getting your brains blown out. For Sam, the solution was to put the steel shell of an M1 helmet over his tanker's helmet and ride with the commander's hatch open, but showing very little above the neck. So far, it had worked.

So far.

THE TIP OF THE COLUMN slowed as the Thon River crossing loomed ahead. It was not a wide span, but stout stone houses and a church, fortified during medieval times, guarded the approaches. Sam, Don Clayman of the Forty-seventh Infantry, and two of his officers forded a shallow canal running parallel to the river, then advanced to the high ground overlooking a possible crossing point.

BRRRRT! Fire burst out abruptly. Two hundred yards ahead, out of the shadows of the low buildings, figures in gray and mottled camouflage darted in and out of cover. They moved in the Americans' direction. Sam's little group took cover from the bursts of German MP 40 submachine gun fire. The squad of six German infantrymen rose up, one or two at a time, sprinting then taking cover in turns, firing up the hill at the small group of US GIs.

Clayman calmly took a knee, then signaled his infantrymen behind him as he drew up his M1 rifle. Before the enemy could race up the hundred-yard incline, US infantry atop the lead tanks dismounted and sprinted up the knoll toward the party of Americans. They arrived just in time to roll grenades down onto the advancing German patrol to break their attack.

With eyes now on the far side of the river and no enemy to contest the crossing, Sam directed accompanying troops of the Twenty-third Engineers to throw up a span over the river, and the expert engineers did it quickly. Scouts forded then secured the far side as the engineers drove forward in trucks with bridge sections, backed into the riverbed, then dropped the sections. After securing the bridge, the lead vehicles streamed forward. The column narrowed into the funnel formed by the narrow bridge. This was the dangerous part, but the tanks with piggyback-mounted infantry, trucks, and half-tracks moved quickly. The river crossing was so fast and efficient that it left the enemy stunned. Speed and surprise kept the Germans off balance and US casualties minimal.

Darkness approached and the combat command halted three-quarters of a mile southeast of Hirson, within view of the little town, with its cobblestoned square, tall church belfry, and low stone buildings. Reconnaissance elements pushed into the town with G Company tanks in their wake. The River Oise bisected the town, creating another danger area to cross. Captain Cramer roared up to the bank in his Sherman to get a view of the far side.

Cramer's narrow silhouette protruded from his commander's hatch as he squinted into the night trying to see signs of enemy life. A fireball erupted, lighting up his surprised face. He radioed: "Small, Plezia, get ready to back up."

Cramer's probe was rewarded with a fireworks show as the Germans blew up a train of ammunition that they thought might be captured by the hard-pressing Americans. There were no injuries, though the sky remained aglow for several hours, burning to the north as G Company and its accompanying infantry cleared the town.

By 10 P.M., the enemy pulled back and left several dazed rearguard troops who were taken prisoner. Task Force Hogan secured their bivouac, some resting, some pulling guard and preparing their weapons and tanks. Sam tried to unwind with a cup of coffee, a Camel, and a map reconnaissance of the route to Mons. He would try to get a thirty-minute catnap before rousing himself to check on the men and the preparation for the next movement.

It was still dark and cool when tank and half-track engines revved up again to continue the advance. Drivers rubbed their eyes and swallowed canteen cups of cold coffee and canned biscuits. Some, those lucky enough to not be driving, wolfed down a dreaded can of ham and lima beans while waiting for the vehicle in front to roll out. In his half-track, Sergeant John Grimes kept a keen eye on his driver, squinting through the dark and trying to identify the small tactical taillight of the vehicle in front. Grimes would tap the driver's right shoulder with his boot when they needed to turn right, left shoulder for a left turn.

The yellow glow of the ammunition fire cooled off, leaving a burnt-orange line silhouetting the little town's buildings, their fronts still cloaked in purple darkness. The column of vehicles dipped down toward the bridge over the Oise like one loud, gargantuan serpent, lazily spewing smoke from their many exhaust pipes. This was the riskiest part—canalized into a narrow bridgehead, the vehicles backed up while they each crossed one at a time. Drivers' eyes fixed on the blackout lights of the vehicle ahead—no headlights to warn the Germans that a battalion was moving toward them. Assistant drivers and crewmen attempted to stay awake both to keep the driver awake and to stay alert for ambushes from the shadowy tree lines on both sides of the road.

Half a kilometer past the bridge, the scouts radioed back that they had found tank emplacements, fresh tracks, and cleared fields of fire on the far side of town. The Germans had hastily abandoned this position the night before as they set fire to their ammunition dump. Sam stiffened, suddenly more alert through his fatigue—realizing that if they'd tried to take the town during daylight hours, they would've faced a deadly ambush. All Sam could do was be thankful for that lucky break.

The giant armored gauntlets of the Third Armored Division moved on, pointed straight at the flank of five German divisions, the remains of the Fifth Panzer Army, headed east. The big picture showed Task Force Hogan guarding the right flank of this enormous force. To their left was Colonel Boudinot's Combat Command A, with Task Forces Kean and Doan under it. To their left was Brigadier General Doyle Hickey's Combat Command B, with Task Force King and Task Force Lovelady as left and right "fists." Fast-moving scouts from the Eighty-third Reconnaissance Battalion led the eighteen-thousand-man force, buffering against any unexpected ambush.[3]

Task Force Hogan rolled north through the early dawn, the excitement of expected contact and cups of black coffee the only things keeping tankers and infantrymen alert through the fatigue of two sleepless nights. They expected contact in the form of meeting engagements, where two sides do not know the location of the other and unexpectedly bump into each other. Whichever side sees, aims, and fires first has the advantage. Radio silence was in effect to aid in achieving the element of surprise.

A report came in from a French scout that mines awaited them on the road ahead, in front of a railroad underpass. The Germans, experienced as they were, intended to slow and then canalize the armored force into a preestablished kill zone. Sure enough, at the railroad underpass, Clayman's infantry managed to surprise an enemy PAK 43 cannon and knock it out. Several more enemy defenders scattered as the Twenty-third Engineers carefully but quickly removed the mines so that the column could drive on.

Approaching the small towns of Ohain and Trélon, more scattered German infantry and PAKs were awaiting the task force. Alert scouts, and small-arms and mortar fire, managed to scatter the ambushers before the main body could get in their range. Stopping in Trélon, Sam, Don Clayman, and Carl Cramer inquired of the townspeople: *Ou sont les boches?* (Where are the Germans?) Their response, pointing north excitedly: *En avant, à Solre! Beaucoup de boche!* (Up ahead, in Solre! Lots of Germans!) Checking their map board on the hood of a jeep, they verified that Solre-le-Château was about eighteen kilometers directly north along their route.

Rommel had passed through this town in 1940 on his way to the English Channel, after routing French and British formations. Now it was the Allies giving chase.

Sam radioed to the lead elements to prepare for heavy contact. The map showed a straight road leading to the town, with no danger areas such as river crossings or sharp bends in the road where an ambush possibly awaited. The terrain was flat and rolling but covered here and there in dense forests interspersed with fields of cattle forage. Beautiful farmland, thought Sam, thinking of the fertile Hudson Valley of his West Point years. Turning to Cramer and Clayman, Sam directed, "Let's keep them reeling back. Saddle up and we'll stop again ahead of the town to reconnoiter."

After traversing four kilometers, G Company and accompanying infantry came under fire from their front as the woods in the middle of the column also lit up with rifle and machine gun fire. Gunners in tanks, drivers, and their vehicle commanders in half-tracks and infantry trucks were startled out of their quasi-sleep state and into action. While G Company Shermans pumped suppressing fire into roadside positions to their front, infantrymen and several of C Company's light tanks opened up on the enemy to the west. One German vehicle was a Panther tank and the other an antiaircraft gun firing in a flat trajectory. Both withdrew after a withering return fire answered their shots.

As per the plan, the motorized infantry from the Ninth Infantry Division dismounted their trucks and pushed ahead in squads rushing from cover to cover on each side of the road. H Company, the "left fist" of the column, pushed Shermans to the west to flank the Germans firing near a small town on the map called Liessies. This flanking movement caught the Panther with a well-aimed 76-mm high-explosive round to the side of the hull, which disabled the tank in a violent shudder as crew in camouflage coveralls bailed out through hatches on top and underneath the hull, then hobbled toward the tree line.

Sam gratefully received reports from his commanders via radio that the attacks had been defeated with no casualties and several Germans captured—things were going smoothly. Maybe too smoothly. It was clear that Task Force Hogan was advancing alone on the extreme right of the Spearhead's giant formation. Solre-le-Château was a beautiful town crowned with a tall four-steeple church in the center of town. A half dozen buildings surrounding it spread out toward small farms and cow pastures on all sides for half a kilometer before the forests began again. Church bells began ringing—civilians came out of stone cellars with smiles on their faces, some in tears. A priest led the way as the crowd waved, smiled, and extended a friendly hand to the passing Americans.

For the first time, through the battle fatigue and sleepless nights, it dawned on the soldiers that the Germans had just left and that the Allies were liberating these villages. Tired looks gave way to smiles, and the tankers' exhausted bodies and spirits got a jolt of jubilant energy. As they rolled through the cobblestone streets, tank commanders in hatches stood a little taller, returning the smiles and waves with gusto.

No division reconnaissance had passed through here. Halting again, Sam addressed several villagers in his broken French, who replied in broken English and excited French that indeed, this was the first American column they had seen. Pressing on, the column passed two more villages without incident, Aibes and Rousies.

At Jeumont, the flags flown from balconies and windows changed from the blue, white, and red of the French to the black, yellow, and red of Belgium. Mons, and an anticipated big engagement with five German divisions, was twenty-five kilometers ahead.[4]

Across wooded acres to the west, Lieutenant Jake Sitzes, with two platoons of light tanks, was detached to guard the Third Armored Division command post. A strong guard for the CP was standard practice, since General Rose liked to be so close to the line, leading from the front.

The enemy began streaming toward them along secondary roads in the late afternoon of September 2. Jake and his agile little M3 Stuart tanks beat the bushes constantly over the next twenty-four hours, flushing out the German infantry like quail from a wheat field. Each time, they returned with twenty to thirty prisoners.

All was going according to plan, but a lack of sleep began to take its toll, as it does regularly in combat. Major Walker radioed Sam: "Six, this is Blue-five, we need to stop the march—over."

Sam growled. What now? He halted the convoy, with infantry dismounting and spreading out, guns at the ready.

Walker sprinted up to Sam's command tank: "Sir! We've lost Service Company." Service Company, with its maintenance platoon and supply/transport section, kept the task force's vehicles running and supplied. They also had the medics and their half-track ambulances. All unarmored trucks, trailers, and jeeps—not combat units. Their biggest weapons were three .50-caliber machine guns mounted on the 2.5-ton trucks, including the kitchen or "gut" truck. *Did we lose them to an ambush?* The task force would not be able to roll on much farther without their logistics tail.

Sam went on the command net, breaking the radio silence to his commanders: "This is Six. Coil the formation, company commanders up." Walker was still panting as they conferred on the hood of his peep. "The maintenance section, medics, and assault gun platoon apparently took a wrong turn, Colonel." The well-planned operation had just turned into a soup sandwich—military parlance for a complicated mess. Sam tried to keep calm—nothing was gained by losing control—but his expression was dour. "Well, we're in a friendly town. We'll send back a patrol to reestablish contact with them."

The truth was, they needed to stop anyway. Fuel tanks were getting below half full again. It would not be the last time that logistics—the ball and chain of mechanized warfare—took precedence over military goals. The entire division was running short, as they were now at the tail end of a 125-kilometer main supply route (MSR) that was not keeping up with the tanks. Movement was limited to a single road, and it was unsafe for fuel trucks to move on any of the side roads, which were not secure and likely to contain German patrols. It was getting dark on their second day of nonstop movement and battle. His main concern now was that the missing Service Company could not stand on its own against any significant enemy ambush, especially against tanks or determined infantry.

SOMEWHERE IN BETWEEN TASK FORCE Hogan and the division CP, and out of radio contact, the Service Company lead truck driver sat hunched behind the steering wheel, staring worriedly at the town ahead. After jolting himself awake, the driver had gazed wide-eyed at the fearful sight of nothing in front of him but empty road and woods instead of the comforting sight of the rear fenders and taillights of a column of armored vehicles and trucks loaded with infantry. Both he and his assistant driver had soundly fallen asleep and missed the front part of the convoy moving out.

Cursing, the driver stepped on the gas, with three half-tracks, four trucks, ammo carriers, the task force medics, and the M8 assault gun platoon in tow. He knew he had screwed up royally. Looking at his folded-up map, he remembered his platoon leader briefing the turn west at Givry. He glanced down the path and turned the steering wheel left. The column of cooks, mechanics, medics, and the assault guns were back on the right track for the moment. Five kilometers down, another fork in the road. *Did the lieutenant brief another turn?* The young private second-guessed himself and floored the gas with the steering wheel turned left—turning off the intended route and heading to the enemy-held town of Harmignies.[5]

Panic set in, and the driver felt a cold sweat on his neck. He was at an unknown town in the dwindling light of that early September day. He couldn't even remember what day it was, exactly. Dazed and exhausted, his lower back tight and aching, he stepped out of the cab of his 2.5-ton truck. He walked down the row of maintenance trucks, carbine in hand, ignoring the quizzical looks of several junior-enlisted drivers as he passed their cabs. He went straight to the third truck in line to talk to the senior noncommissioned officer, First Sergeant Hoyt D. Rogers.

"Top, we've lost the main body of the convoy," the driver managed to stammer out. Top Rogers's brow slowly furrowed, his eyes narrowing into a soul-draining stare at the soldier looking up wide-eyed at him.

"Whadya mean we've lost the main body?! Fuck! What town is this?! How did you miss the truck in front of you moving out?!"

The loud cracks of German rifles followed by the *BRRRRRRRP* of a machine gun interrupted the first sergeant's interrogation.

Calls of *"Get down!"* and *"Assault guns up!"* chorused down the line as First Sergeant Rogers scrambled for his carbine and some cover. Drivers were startled out of their daze as they sat in their truck cabs fumbling for their pistols.

The assault guns moved to each side of the parked trucks as they knocked down small saplings to climb over the shoulder of the country road and roared to the front, where they could shield the vulnerable trucks and return fire.

Inside the cramped turrets of the assault guns, crewmen were riding high on adrenaline, each tank commander yelling to his gunners to prepare for direct fire using their already loaded HE rounds.

Riding high in the gun turret ring of the second truck of the convoy, Sergeant John Robert Burns Barclay—no relation to Captain Barclay, H Company commander, but rather a battalion mess sergeant from Royalton, Illinois—sat wondering what in the hell he had gotten himself into.

A 1941 selectee and early arrival to Camp Polk, he had grown up poor, one of eleven children of a hard-drinking Scottish miner. He grew up cooking to help his mother feed the large family. After finishing school, he was the chef at a family restaurant, so it seemed surprisingly efficient that the army made him a cook after drafting him in the wake of Pearl Harbor. He loved to cook, and his mother felt it would be a safer job.

The twenty-seven-year-old Sergeant Barclay reflected on this as he stood in the gun turret of a 2.5-ton kitchen truck, a .50-caliber machine gun feeling like a foreign artifact in his hands. He began firing at the muzzle flashes coming from the hill ahead as occasional tracers zipped in green, blinding flashes overhead. *RATATATAT* came in the staccato response to his pressing of the butterfly-shaped, dual-thumb trigger. He heard the hot casings land with metallic pings on the bed of the truck behind him.

John kept the fire going until the barrel began to smoke. He had forgotten in the heat of the moment to keep his rate of fire down by shooting in bursts.

"Whelp, it's too late," he mumbled to himself as he felt the firing mechanism seize up and jam with the ejecting cases. He cursed and began taking it apart in the darkness as best he could, yelling to his buddy who was squeezing off a few rounds from his carbine in the back of the kitchen truck: "Slim! Bring me another gun barrel!" A response of "What?! Where's that?!" was discouraging to say the least.

The assault gun platoon aggressively fired at the muzzle flashes coming at them from the wooded area adjacent to the village, while the truckers sought cover behind engine blocks and kept an eye out for any flanking attempt by the German infantry coming out of Harmignies. The firefight lasted twenty-five minutes until the forceful fire of the assault guns convinced the Germans to pull back from what they thought was a strong armored force. If they had waited for a little daylight, they might have seen an opportunity to destroy a large US support convoy guarded only by three light-skinned assault guns.

The Service Company survived, but they still had to reestablish contact with friendlies, ideally their own task force, without being shot up by Germans or other Americans with itchy trigger fingers.

BACK IN THE MAIN BODY of the task force, at 3:00 A.M. on September 3, the column was low on fuel and their supply and mechanics were still missing. As if that weren't enough, there was an air liaison report that an enemy column that stretched for miles, composed of three hundred to four hundred vehicles, was moving in their direction.

The task force halted to set up ambush positions from their first bivouac inside Belgium. The large force coiled in a 360-degree perimeter, then set out roadblocks, observation posts, and ambush positions on the avenues of approach. Their next priority was to reestablish contact with the missing company.

Sam directed two Shermans from H Company plus infantry riding on top: "Clear the area one mile to their southwest, and find and retrieve the missing loggies." He then ordered the remainder of G and H Company tanks with their infantry to push their perimeter out with roadblocks at all approaches to their position, instructing them to hit hard but be prepared to accept surrenders. Across a five-kilometer front, Spearhead hunkered down, tensely waiting in ambush. The men were fatigued but unable to sleep, knowing that the enemy was coming their way—their numbers, aggression, and desperation as yet unknown.

All along the southern border of Belgium, the three combat commands of the Third Armored Division began making contact with German infantry, tanks, half-tracks, and self-propelled howitzers. It began with single potshots, as the antagonists blindly drew closer and then sighted each other. Radios blared, and the hoarse yelling of commanders began echoing through wood-lined firebreaks and tree-studded ridges.

"Shit, this is it. Red Platoon prepared to engage!" Jake Sitzes heard it like a tide rolling in and crashing on a beach. All around, the static of small-arms fire grew into a constant sound, interrupted only by the sporadic pounding of heavy artillery. Smoke began to rise over treetops to the west and radio sets blared transmissions with hardly a pause. The lieutenant dropped down inside the cramped turret of his light tank to load a canister round into the breech of his 37-mm cannon. Like a giant shotgun, the canister round exploded out 122 steel balls designed to cut down large formations of infantry. "Red Platoon, move forward one hundred meters," Jake called out, as machine gun fire began peppering his turret, bouncing off with a harmless metal-on-metal clang.

Across the division front, situation maps grew swathes of red "enemy" markers as the German wave crashed on the "breakwaters" set up by the Third Armored Division. The giant running battle began in earnest. Groups of German tanks and infantry rolled into kill zones and roadblocks set up all along the enemy's likely avenues of approach based on the intelligence available and the gut instinct of sergeants and lieutenants.

Combined with artillery and airpower, the Americans inflicted massive casualties on the German divisions streaming east trying to reach the relative safety of their West Wall fortifications. US howitzers and mortars rained devastating barrages of shrapnel, high-explosive rounds, with ear-bursting detonations that knocked out vehicles and shredded infantrymen.

One roadblock called in artillery on a long column of horse-drawn German equipment fifteen hundred yards away, wreaking similar havoc on the poor beasts and their drivers, but more important, on the howitzers and ammunition they were pulling.

The situation was so chaotic that rear-echelon units were engaging German infantry who were avoiding the stronger US formations to their front by crawling through dense wooded areas. Supply trucks and the tail ends of the armored columns were subject to sniper fire and hasty roadblocks.

Early on September 3, one supply truck headed to resupply the task force was informed by locals that the Germans had reoccupied Givry. The driver didn't hesitate to turn the truck around to head back to the division trains. Behind it, a German truck loaded with infantry gave chase. Passing a US roadblock at high speed, the supply truck driver slowed down enough to yell at the US infantrymen operating the machine gun position that the truck behind him was full of Germans. The GIs wasted no time in firing several well-aimed streams of machine gun fire at the oncoming truck, sending it careening into the woods in a shower of dust, fire, and shattered tree and human limbs.

Forward-echelon, heavier-armed buddies were holding their own—but meanwhile, several kilometers east, the members of the lost Service Company were still alone, unwittingly on Belgian soil, and in a fight for their lives. Sergeant Barclay shook his head awake as he scanned the unfamiliar surroundings ahead. He rubbed his tired eyes with one gunpowder-grimed hand as he continued to protect his kitchen truck and crew from his position behind the machine gun.

It was twilight, and early-morning fog shrouded the roadsides. The convoy slowed at a series of bends in the road. They fully expected enemy contact, so the drivers went as fast as they dared given the darkness and odds of flipping over a top-heavy truck.

Two of John's cooks sat clutching their rifles behind him on the bed of the gut truck among stacks of kitchen pots and boxes of canned goods. One, Private John Cambolito, yelled out, "Look at that fence!"

Barclay turned to his right front and his eyes widened as he swiveled the machine gun over, yelling, "Those aren't fence posts—those are Germans!" A five-round burst from his machine gun sent the Germans scrambling for cover as the kitchen truck roared through the kill zone. The other cooks, ammunition specialists, and mechanics fired rounds to the sides from truck cabs and beds. Squads of five to eight German soldiers popped in and out of the woods, lining the road. Each side were surprised and shocked to see the other.[6]

The little convoy pushed forward, continuing to fire as the Germans organized and streamed out to the front of the convoy, throwing grenades and rifle shots at the Americans. First Sergeant Rogers took some shrapnel but kept directing the convoy from the passenger seat of his deuce-and-a-half truck. Secrecy and stealth were lost.

"Keep trying to raise some friendlies on the radio," he called out to the soldier sitting in the middle of the cab. Several other men received shrapnel wounds from the grenades exploding outside their vehicles. Doc Spigelman and his medics bandaged what wounds they could, when they could, in between rushes forward.

The front truck sped up with crunching gears and loud cuss words emanating from the cab. Sergeant Barclay's "Roach Coach," one of the combat soldier's endearing nicknames for the kitchen truck, coming in second, accelerated past the bend. Soon the remaining vehicles cleared the curve and were on the straightaway. The fire of German machine guns died down as they moved farther from the enemy picket. Barclay wiped his brow with a shirtsleeve, looked back at his wide-eyed cooks, and managed to stammer out, "That was a close one." The ragtag caravan of mismatched trucks rattled down the road at full speed. Would they run into another German patrol or even a tank? Or would they run out of gas first?

Pushing on three kilometers farther as the sun climbed up, First Sergeant Rogers kept his radio microphone to his face, "Any Omaha element, this is Orchard Whiskey Seven—over." His voice was growing raspy and choked. The little convoy began cresting a hill, but had no idea what was on the other side. "Any Omaha element, this is Orchard Whiskey Seven—over." Nothing but static.

Rogers's truck had topped the small hill when his radio crackled to life. "Whiskey Seven, this is How One-Seven, read you loud and clear." The driver let out a whoop, "H Company tanks!" which resounded in every truck cab with a radio and spread to those riding in back. Top Rogers simply inclined his head and whispered, "Thank God." The missing convoy was finally able to raise friendly units on the radio. It was H Company that sent tanks to retrieve them. They followed the tanks back to the Task Force Hogan position, much to Sam's relief, but surely to the highest relief of the truck driver who had fallen asleep, and who shall remain nameless.

There was no tearful reunion when the lost convoy pulled into the task force coil at midday. There was a battle going on, ammunition and fuel were running low, and even the cooks were needed to help man roadblocks. However, news of the lost convoy had filtered to the tank and infantry pickets, who expected them coming in.

They arrived inside Task Force Hogan lines to cheers and pats on the back. There was always some good-natured teasing between the trigger-pullers of the first echelon and the rear-echelon "enablers." One tanker, as he saw Barclay spill out of the back of the kitchen truck, piles of spent casings toppling out behind him, teased: "Hey, Sarge! I heard Colonel Hogan is going to put you all in for CIBs [Combat Infantrymen Badges] . . . in your dreams!"

Everyone liked Sergeant Barclay—the only thing he loved more than preparing a hot meal was dishing it out to the bedraggled tankers and leg infantry. On the chow line, he would grin affectionately when the soldiers attempted some fake small talk in order to get that extra scoop of mashed potatoes. He always made sure they got their fill. However, a lot of the time the kitchen truck couldn't go where the tanks went due to the mud or lack of roads. In those cases, he tried his best to get food out to the soldiers.

John barked back at the grunt, with a tired wink, "It's okay, I'm in need of KPs for the next bivouac. I'll talk to your platoon sergeant."

Despite the ribbing, the combat troops respected and loved their loggie brothers. Even Spearhead's rear echelon was always far forward of 80 percent of the rest of the US Army. Unlike noncombat troops, Spearheaders—whatever their specialty—didn't benefit from the comforts of large rear-area camps, such as warm meals every day, showers, and visits by Hollywood stars or the brass. The GIs' response, repeated over the past weeks since the division got their new nickname: "Where there's a Spearhead, there's a shaft . . . and we're always getting it."

The shared suffering was a badge of honor to them, and it solidified their camaraderie.

Sergeant Barclay, Top Rogers (with his face bandaged up), and the others got right back to work after their warm greeting.

AT 7:00 A.M. ON SEPTEMBER 4, vehicles now fueled and ready to roll, Task Force Hogan received orders to clear the enemy out of southwest Mons.

Operating on their last reserves of energy, as well as ammunition and fuel, the boys saluted and mounted up. By this time, each man alternated between frayed nerves and a kind of numb exhaustion. Most everyone's backs were sore, knees, shoulders, and necks, too, from the constant bumping along trails and country roads. Dehydration headaches came and went.

Infantrymen took turns napping on the back decks as they rolled along, their buddies both pulling security and holding on to their napping friends' pistol belts so that a sudden turn wouldn't roll the slumbering soldiers off the deck to a seven-foot drop to the ground.

Drivers napped when they could, and so did Sam, taking turns for a thirty-minute catnap here or there while seconds-in-command monitored the situation. Another welcome adrenaline shot kicked in as they approached Mons. Tanks and infantry cleared the outskirts against light resistance, and a dozen more prisoners were taken.

The day's mission complete, the armored columns backtracked to their bivouac area one mile northwest of Givry. The First Battalion, Twenty-sixth Infantry Regiment of the First Infantry Division, the Big Red One, arrived to relieve the Ninth Infantry Old Reliables. This marked the beginning of a team effort between Task Force Hogan and the First Battalion of the Twenty-sixth Infantry, the "Blue Spaders"—so nicknamed for the wide blue spade on their regimental crest—with their outstanding commander, Major Francis Woodrow (F.W.) Adams, that would go on well into the German heartland.

The outgoing Ninth Infantry lieutenants, sergeants, and riflemen welcomed their Big Red One counterparts, showing them where the avenues of approach were, who was who among the tankers, and what could be expected of the Germans' continually surging into their positions. The Third Battalion, Forty-seventh Infantry doughs headed back to the rear to join their division. Watching Don take a single jeep and light tank into the woods to flush out German units south of Mons, Sam thought he was one of the bravest officers he'd ever seen. They parted with a handshake.

For the remainder of September 4, the task force sent out patrols from H Company to clear out the forests around Mons as the remaining Germans moved through the woods attempting to rejoin their front line, which was continually pushed farther east. It must have been extremely frustrating for the Germans. They continued to trudge along east, all the while running into American ambushes. During the day, ground and air artillery observers hammered them with fire while US fighter-bombers swooped down from the gray skies, raining rockets and machine gun fire on their convoys.

At the close of that long day, Sam and Travis Brown attended a commanders' meeting at the division CP to plan the capture of their next objectives. General Joseph Lawton "Lightning Joe" Collins, the VII Corps commanding general and future army chief of staff, and General Rose were almost as unrelenting on their subordinates as they were on the Germans. The next stop: capture Namur, capital of the Wallonia region, then Liège, with its bridges across the Meuse, clear across Belgium to the Siegfried line.

At 10:00 P.M., the task force refueled again at their perimeter. Relatively safe in their coil of vehicles, men napped while the refueling went on. Captain Barclay walked around the perimeter to check on his soldiers. The guards were alert and walking softly around the parked tanks and trucks. It was actually peaceful. A few crews milled about their tanks, belts of .30-caliber machine gun ammunition passed from one tanker on the ground to another kneeling on the hull, then through the bow gunner's hatch.

Jake smoked a cigarette and chatted with First Sergeant Filyaw about the latter's farm in Alabama. Inside tanks and half-tracks, some snored away while others wrote letters home under the feeble light of a red-lensed flashlight.

Sam reread a few of his letters from home. It was a quick escape and helped him wind down from the "fight or flight" highs enough to get some sleep. Even at home, though, there were worries. His father's health was bad, and money was still tight. He sent what he could every month from his earnings.

His wife Belle's letters were growing a little cooler whenever the topic of having children came up. Six years into their marriage, kids were not likely to happen. She didn't seem to enjoy giving or receiving affection. She found it "sinful." He lowered the letter away from the glow of the blue light inside the tank and rubbed his eyes. *Well, I can't worry about this now—things will work themselves out.* He needed to take advantage of the pause to catch a few hours of rest.

Inside Sam's tank, it was uncharacteristically peaceful. The temperature was cozy, and the tank bathed in the soothing low light coming from radio sets and the commander's station lamp. Clem Elissondo was snoring on the deck and driver Elmer Johnson breathed heavily, slumped over in his seat. The low hum of the radios was interrupted only by the occasional radio check with higher command. Not the usual panicky voices, but the steady drone of a combat unit in a tactical pause.

As a young lieutenant of horse cavalry, Sam had learned he could take naps on the saddle during long-range patrols along the Mexican border. He'd learned to do it in his tank at a halt as well: push the lower back up to the tiny metallic lumbar support on the commander's station, drape the upper body back, fold the arms across the chest, and tuck in your chin. Lean to the side a bit onto the smooth metal of the turret. His tanker's crash helmet provided a small cushion for the side of his head, and he could still hear the radio chatter.

As the early glow of fall sunlight rose to their front, the task force coil buzzed to life, hatches cracked open, oiled rifle bolts clicked forward, and coughs hacked up phlegm. The army rhythm of cleaning weapons, taking care of personal hygiene, and getting ready rang across the crisp fall air. It was time to continue the advance.

Past Jeumont, Task Force Hogan headed toward the hamlet of Paturages. Sam, Travis Brown, Carl Cramer, and John Barclay came up with a simple scheme of maneuver to clear the town and its surroundings. G Company would come up from the south while H swept down from the north. Sam, seeing how smoothly things were going, remembered why he liked his current higher-up, Colonel Bobby Howze. The no-nonsense officer let his subordinates operate with little micromanagement. He'd deliver the big picture and let his subordinates figure out how to accomplish the mission while standing ready to support them with any additional resources, shielding his battalions from unnecessary administrative tasks or visits from generals outside the division.

G Company had a tough time traversing the woods but arrived at their northern position after accepting the surrender of 250 prisoners and their colonel. Escorted by a light tank, the 250 were marched back to the division prisoner-of-war cages. In accordance with the Geneva Conventions, GIs pitched the German colonel a pup tent to sleep in next to Sam's command half-track. Military intelligence debriefed him.

He and other captured Germans lamented that they had "been abandoned" with instructions to "get back to Germany as best they could."[7]

BY SEPTEMBER 5, THE DIVISION prisoner-of-war cage was filled to bursting and was beginning to run out of food. No soldiers could be spared to guard the eight-thousand-some-odd prisoners. They were inspected for their ability to march on their own and, if able, were lined up on the road five abreast and 250 deep and told to march toward Mons, where a larger holding area was being set up at an old sugar refinery by the Third Armored Division's higher headquarters, the VII Corps. One C Company M3 light tank led the way slowly, its turret pointed menacingly to the rear to dissuade anyone from "skipping out" to the tree line. This was unlikely, though—these Germans' spirits were broken.

The rest of the Big Red One arrived behind the Third Armored Division to help clear the woods surrounding the approaches to Mons. The already-clogged roads became almost impassable inside the "kill zones" facing the Spearhead's roadblocks. Hundreds of German tanks, self-propelled howitzers, prime movers, and trucks littered the shoulders of roads and the farmer's fields where they had tried to break out cross-country.

The pretty country lanes were horribly soiled by soot-covered mechanical wrecks, grotesquely mangled, surrounded by the smaller detritus of abandoned ammunition boxes, helmets, and coats. The sight of the bloated brown lumps of dead horses saddened the farm boys and former horse cavalrymen—hooves and legs sticking stiffly to the side or crumpled up under their haunches as they lay where they had collapsed. Their leather harnesses still tethered them to wagons of upended ammunition and supplies.

General Collins ordered a further advance, sensing that the Germans were wobbling. Pursuit, pursuit, keep them reeling. Even the normally conservative First Army commander, and Collins's superior, General Courtney Hodges, opined to his staff that with "ten more days of good weather, the war could be over."[8]

Everyone was running on adrenaline and the hopes of dealing a knockout blow. Once at Namur they were well inside the Belgian Ardennes. It was time to repeat, in reverse, the German's own offensive plan of 1914 and 1940 by sweeping through this ancient forest region and then crashing like a tidal wave against the Siegfried line and on into Germany.

The boys of Task Force Hogan, exhausted but exhilarated by the feeling of having the enemy on the ropes, rolled on through rolling green hills, fruit orchards, and fields of dandelions—a beautiful tapestry of summer, and perfect tank country. On September 8, they received the order to liberate Liège. Crisp, cool days followed, with rapid advances. Sam's Texas flag and Jake's Missouri mule fluttered from their respective tank antennas during the fast march forward.

Advancing from Fléron, they reached their first objective, Chênée. There were no Americans killed in action, but one of the brave Belgian Resistance fighters died pointing out enemy mines and three Americans were slightly wounded in action. The armored columns liberated small, postcard-perfect towns as the next two days blurred together in heady advance. In each village, crowds of overjoyed Belgians came out to greet the Americans. Impromptu picnics of bread, champagne, and wine were spread out on the decks of Sherman tanks for the crews and GIs to enjoy.

The high point for TF Hogan was Liège. Belgium's fourth-largest city was the gateway to the tree-covered Ardennes massif, which loomed beyond to the east. The deep, blue-gray Meuse River bisected Liège's medieval old quarter. Stout maple and oak trees crowded its banks, shrouding it in fall colors of brown, red, and gold. Beyond the Ardennes, the terrain sloped down to the plains of the German Ruhr. The Americans were astride the historical invasion route that had taken German armies almost to the gates of Paris in the Great War and all the way to the English Channel in 1940.

TF Hogan split into two columns of tanks, supported by GIs from the Big Red One's First Battalion, Twenty-sixth Infantry. The German garrison fell back in disarray, surprised at the speed of the Americans' advance, as US tanks and infantry pressed them to the front, and Belgian

Resistance fighters sabotaged their flanks and rear. Past the industrial outskirts and into the old town the tank-infantry teams pressed on.

Cramer's team were experts at setting up roadblocks. Down a narrow country road on the outskirts of Liège, they set one up. One Sherman tank and an infantry squad backed them up. They maintained radio and wire communications with the company command post nearer to the town.

Suddenly, screeching out of an old stone farmhouse, a German staff car tried to evade the advancing Americans. The driver's panicked eyes scanned the sky for US aircraft, then back to the curves of the road. The speeding staff car turned a corner only to screech to a halt fifty yards from an American tank. There was nothing for the Germans to do as they stared down the barrel of the Sherman's cannon. Infantry sprinted up and leveled rifles at the occupants' heads. The German driver threw his hands up. Slightly more hesitantly, a German general in the back seat raised his as well. A couple of minutes later, the radio transmission got to Sam's tank: "Blue Six, this is George Six—we've captured a high-ranking prisoner."

Cramer's tank-infantry roadblock had reeled in a big fish. Flushed out and captured in his staff car trying to escape was the German garrison commander, General Bock von Wülfingen.[9] But there was no time to celebrate this victory—General Collins wanted Spearhead across the Meuse and probing the German defenses right away. The soldiers were slowed only by the joyous Belgian civilians who came out of each town to greet them—and that was okay by Sam.

Once in Liège proper, shells were still falling on the east side of town when villagers began leaving their cellars to meet the Americans. Dust floated over on the breeze from nearby demolished houses and began to settle on the cobblestone streets. Flags, folded and hidden for years, were suddenly unfurled from balconies in colorful swathes of black, gold, and red. The red, white, and blue of both French and American flags also unfurled and flapped in the wind. Cheers and laughter drowned out the distant *pop pop* of rifle fire coming from the direction of the German border. Crowds surged out of their hiding places, filling the sidewalks.

It was a grand day. Task Force Hogan took no casualties, and C Company, with Lieutenant Jake Sitzes's platoon in the lead, rolled through the cobblestone streets of downtown Liège—now crowded with hundreds of people, tearful with joy. There were friendly greetings, handshakes, hugs, and kisses. Some of the citizens scrawled the names of their town in chalk on the sides of the American tanks. Jake, smiling ear to ear, received kisses from beautiful burgundy-lipped girls as he stood almost hidden by a layer of flowers and champagne baskets piled onto the decks of his tank.

Captain Carl Cramer and his tankers followed close behind, their dust-covered faces peering up from tank hatches, confused at the sudden celebration. Carl managed to let his guard down a bit, letting his G Company tankers take in the festivities—they had just captured six hundred German prisoners, including their commander, General Bock von Wülfingen, as they cleared their portion of the outskirts of Liège east of the Meuse.

But the rapturous welcome did what the German army failed to do: slow down Spearhead's relentless advance. On the west side of the Meuse, Major General Rose lit up a few of the Big Red One units moving through town: "Get those women and flowers off our vehicles! Don't you know we're fighting a war?"

However, in the Task Force Hogan sector, Sam, Travis Brown, Stewart Walker, and the company and platoon commanders relaxed a little, letting themselves crack a smile and bask in the glow of the day—if only for this short rest before Spearhead started for the German border.

They set up a bivouac for the night one hundred yards on the far side of the town. Everyone closed the day with feelings of hope and optimism but knew in their hearts that the easy part of their advance was over. The German armed forces would now be fighting savagely—on and for their own soil. The war would continue on ground they knew intimately and had prepared to defend since the late 1930s.

But, just for that night, Task Force Hogan rested with broad smiles on their faces—their hearts full with the contentment of having spread joy and freedom to others.

6

★ ★ ★ ★ ★

ATTACKING THE
WEST WALL

SEPTEMBER 9–OCTOBER 22, 1944

On September 9, 1944, Task Force Hogan crossed the line of departure (LD) from their position east of Liège. Many of them wished they could just stay in Liège and wait for the Germans to fold. But they knew this was wishful thinking—the way home was through Berlin, and they would be damned if they let their buddies down now that it seemed they were halfway there and the Germans were nearly spent.

The going was smooth, and as they advanced the Belgian town names began sounding German—no longer French. More and more, the village doors and window stayed closed or displayed white flags instead of the Belgian tricolor and the Stars and Stripes. The villagers' body language also changed: indifferent, sheepish.

Initially, the waving from locals was simply less enthusiastic, but by September 11, signs were in German and the reception from the civilian populace was downright cold. Surely they remembered the back-and-forth of occupiers over the past thirty years and feared reprisals should the Germans go on the offensive again. Sadly, this turned out to be very prescient of them.

The war machine moved, set up roadblocks, cleared wooded areas or small towns, stopped for a couple of hours to refuel, then moved on to the next objective. All the while, they planned for the next big battle. Occasionally, each battalion came off the line and into Spearhead's reserve. This was the time to receive personnel and tank replacements and to keep their machines running with higher-level maintenance than the normal checks and services done in the field between battles.

On September 14, Task Force Hogan crossed the German border at 4:30 P.M., near the town of Langfeld.[1] Resistance was light—all the Germans who should have been manning this first belt of the Siegfried line were in POW camps or lying dead in the woods around Mons.

From the German border onward, the going got tougher. The Germans had placed whatever forces they could gather at the critical points on the front. They were disorganized and could not mass forces, but the Third Armored Division had been on the march for weeks, sustaining casualties and equipment losses. The task force was operating with half of initial effective personnel strength and functioning vehicles.

Spearhead, as part of the mighty VII Corps, was driving full speed into Germany proper, aiming to isolate Aachen—the ancient capital of the Holy Roman Empire. To isolate, then capture Aachen would strike a blow at German morale, showing how US forces could not only pass the defensive lines on the German border but also capture their first major city in the face of stiff, fanatical resistance.

To the city's southeast loomed the Hürtgen Forest. The little mining towns in between Aachen and the forest needed to be secured—thus the division's initial objective was centered around the main town of Stolberg.

In and around the small towns passed two defensive belts of what was known as the West Wall to the Germans and the Siegfried line to the Americans. The first, the Scharnhorst line, consisted of pillbox bunkers, minefields, and "Dragon's Teeth"—rows of concrete pyramids about one meter tall designed to flip a tank if a crew was dumb enough to try and drive over one. This was all covered by machine guns, artillery, and antitank guns, including the dreaded 88-mm antiaircraft cannon, or FLAK (in German, Flieger Abwehr Kannone). The defensive line followed and complemented the existing contours of the terrain: If a tank formation were to follow the path of least resistance, it would take them to predesignated kill zones. If they took a harder route through a narrow draw, they'd run into a minefield covered by antitank cannon. As the formation slowed or stopped, the guns would open up on them, with deadly effect.[2]

The second line, the Schill, was a deeper defensive belt nearly five kilometers thick, on the flats in front of Aachen. Task Force Hogan was assigned back under Colonel Boudinot's Combat Command B, and they received orders to plug a dangerous gap between the First Infantry Division and Spearhead at the objective town of Dorff on September 17. The little town sat astride the southern approaches to Stolberg, their springboard to Aachen.

As Task Force Hogan rolled out, from their turrets, tank commanders viewed a changing landscape. From the quaint forests and villages of Belgium, they were now entering a bleak industrial landscape. Gray factory buildings, gray roads, cleared fields among gray rock escarpments— this was mining country. Riding just behind the advance guard, Sam saw the white steeple of the St. Maria church in the middle of Dorff coming into view. He radioed a halt as the scout vehicle in front stopped outside of rifle or machine gun range. No sense blowing up a building for no reason.

But Sam knew in his gut that the high steeple spelled trouble. He radioed for his supporting self-propelled artillery piece: "Steel Three-Five, this is Six, move forward to my pos—over."

"Roger Six, this is Steel, moving." The open-top howitzer rumbled up.

"Guidons, move out," Sam drawled into his mic as he waived the formation on. The small tank column slowly rumbled forward, crews buttoned up in case a sniper was making use of the steeple. At two hundred yards, a German machine gun opened up. No surprise there.

"Steel, this is Six, light up that steeple."

"Six; this is Steel, roger wilco." A lung-flapping explosion followed the radio transmission squawk, sending a 155-mm artillery shell whistling toward the steeple, which crumbled in a cloud of dust and beige brick fragments. It was becoming too automatic—you almost did not think about the cultural landmarks being destroyed. Mass your firepower—air if you have it, artillery and mortars if you don't—leave nothing standing, keep the enemy on his heels, take no more casualties.[3]

Something was wrong on their right flank, and the forward momentum stopped. Word seeped back even before Sam was called to the division CP to get his new orders. The Spearhead's own grunts of the Thirty-sixth Armored Infantry Regiment were taking a licking near a small mining town called Diepenlinchen. Enemy veteran units from the eastern front, the Twelfth Infantry Division and two companies of the Ninth Panzer Division, were rushed forward after arriving by train. Poor weather prevented US airpower from harassing them, and they arrived at full strength.

They unleashed a powerful counterattack from Werth and Gressenic to the northeast, led by fifteen Mark V Panther tanks with infantry and artillery support, including the division's 150-mm guns. They caught E Company, Thirty-sixth Infantry in the open, and the fierce attack pushed back Spearhead's right flank one thousand yards. The US infantry, made up mostly of recent replacements,[4] lost their officers to tank fire and, with no friendly armor nearby, dropped their M1 Garand rifles and sprinted back toward friendly lines. Thirty men who didn't run, or who weren't fast enough, were taken prisoner. General Rose was fuming and wanted the town, the prisoners, and the rifles recovered at all costs.[5]

For the attack, Rose bolstered Sam's tanks with a battalion of infantry from the Big Red One, the First Infantry Division. The First Battalion of the Twenty-sixth Infantry, the Blue Spaders, was commanded by Major Francis W. Adams. He was tall and athletic, with a strong chin, high cheekbones, and steel-blue eyes. Captain America incarnate, thought Sam. Despite his super-soldier good looks, Adams's firm handshake and can-do attitude were telltale signs that he was no prima donna.

The tough major already held the Silver Star for actions in the Tunisian campaign, where he had singlehandedly navigated a path through a minefield after his vehicle was taken out by a mine.[6] On June 6, 1944, he celebrated both his twenty-ninth birthday and his wedding anniversary storming ashore on Omaha Beach, Normandy.[7] His wife, Jeannie, waited at home for word that he was okay, and was probably not as thrilled for that anniversary.

Sam was glad to work once again with this top-notch officer and his riflemen. In addition to Major Adams's infantry, Task Force Hogan counted on two battalions (thirty-six cannon) of 105-mm self-propelled artillery in direct support.

Sam and his command group checked their maps and planned. This part of Germany had been a mining area since Roman times. Diepenlinchen consisted of prefabricated housing, a handful of brick buildings, and a zinc-processing plant crowned with a forty-foot smokestack on their left. Mounds of sand and gravel rose up throughout the area.

Beyond the cluster of buildings was a clearing a half-mile long and about two football fields wide. The clearing stopped at a large pile of debris and mining by-products, or "slag." The pile was two hundred yards wide and forty feet high, dominating the view of the town.[8] A detailed look at the map showed that the area to the right was swampy, so a flanking movement with tanks was out of the question.

The attack order was for a 10:35 A.M. jump-off on the eighteenth. H Company Shermans would drive down the main road, while to their left B Company of Major Adams's 1/26 Infantry would maneuver through the woods along the approaches to the town in order to flank any German positions set up therein. [9] G Company would feint to the right to cover the approaches to the high ground. Once at the edge of town, the tanks and infantry would form up together to clear it, then move on to the high ground and slag pile. The tankers, Carl Cramer and Jake Sitzes, F. W. Adams of the infantry, and the supporting mortar and artillery lieutenants broke off to complete their own reconnaissance and prepare their commands for the battle.

After ensuring his command was ready to lead the following day's attack, Jake found some quiet time inside his command post—an abandoned German farmhouse. With his command tank parked next to the house and his ears open for any radio traffic, Jake leaned his carbine on the wall of the stone cellar and began to write a letter to his mother, Ann, back in Missouri.

It had been a long road from his commissioning at Fort Knox two years earlier, through all the training at Fort Indiantown Gap and then England—from pushing papers on the division staff to finally being honored with command of a platoon just before D-Day.

Jake was proud of all that his soldiers had accomplished. He had beamed a little to his mother in earlier letters: "The 3rd Armored Division has been first in every battle over here." His last letter had been less upbeat—he confessed to his mother that the grueling pace and the sight of several buddies dying inside their tanks was wearing on him. He asked about the farm. How were his brother, Robert, and his sisters, Rae Ann, Grace, and Marie? Had she heard any news about so-and-so from Sikeston High School who was serving in the Pacific theater?

Jake realized this letter was even shorter. There was no bravado in there to reassure her. A sense of foreboding enveloped him—maybe it was the fatigue. He closed his letter abruptly, telling his mother that he loved her.[10]

He snapped himself out of his funk by walking out to check on his tanks and chat with the crews. *Any word on tomorrow's fuel resupply? Ammunition racks replenished and ready? How is tank H-23 faring after getting its right sprocket replaced?* He loved breaking the tension with small jokes and anecdotes from back home.

"Did you see the look on that captured German general's face?" he asked, producing some chuckles. "There he was, going for a little drive in his staff car, when suddenly *screech* and he's in front of one of our tanks."

This lifted his mood a bit after the letter-writing. First Sergeant Ernest Filyaw, always looking out for "his LT," dropped in while doing his own checks and nudged Jake gently.

"Sir, you oughta catch some shut-eye," he said. Jake nodded in agreement and walked back to the command post with the stars shining brightly above the dark countryside. He wrapped himself up in his olive-drab wool blanket, stretched out on the floor, and fell hard asleep.

Sporadic gunfire broke the dawn's eerie quiet on the morning of the eighteenth. Jake and First Sergeant Filyaw had been up and about for thirty minutes by that point. There were always the final details before an attack: making sure canteens were topped off, maybe securing a little bit of hot powdered eggs in the soldier's mess kits along with a cup of coffee so they could fight on a full stomach, pulling any last bits of information from intelligence channels at division. They were up against the German Twelfth Infantry Division, recently redeployed from the Russian front, which was near full strength and supported by tanks and artillery. Not much else was known.

At 10:35 A.M., H Company, with Jake in the lead tank, crossed the LD. The infantry, as planned, maneuvered through the woods as the Shermans roared through the clearing in order to fire on anything behind the slag pile or in the town. The ground sloped up initially, and the little mining town came into view through Jake's periscopes.

The crack of rifle fire rang out from their left front. Jake called out over the radio: "Contact! Enemy infantry positions at one o'clock." They rolled on, Jake's tanks peppering the slope above with machine gun fire.

After ten minutes of movement, German artillery and mortars began falling around the tanks as airbursts hit the treetops on their left, raining leaves, branches, and razor-sharp metal shards like confetti from hell onto the ground below. The infantrymen of the Big Red One took cover and moved forward in short rushes from cover to cover, rolling left or right, then popping up out of cover to the next tree trunk or pile of bricks.

Jake's Sherman shifted suppressive fire to the factory buildings with their coaxial machine gun, on the off chance that they could force out whoever was calling in this artillery on them. As the formation approached the town, the fire slackened off a bit and the US infantry emerged from the woods to begin clearing the town's dozen or so buildings. Jake's tanks moved in among them on the streets.

A Sherman would fire into a building, the infantrymen would storm in to clear it, then on to the next one. Small-arms fire continued to dog them from the brushy areas in and around the slag pile as well as the woods to their left rear. Incoming artillery slowed the progress, forcing the infantrymen to take cover in stairwells and doorways. After an hour or so, they cleared the miners' housing complex of enemy soldiers. By the time they were halfway through the town, they had taken forty-nine prisoners without suffering any losses.

The prisoners were disheveled, dirty with coal dust, their eyes red around the edges and filled with defiance. This was their initial defensive line. They knew that, ahead, the German commander had prepared worse surprises for the advancing Americans.

The processing plant was next. They cleared the big building with difficulty, as it was full of nooks and crannies around heavy machinery and stacks of material.

Jake couldn't help feeling that they were being drawn into an ambush. He radioed in his reports and checked in with the infantry commander. It was likely that the clearing between the town and the slag pile was under enemy observation. It was also probable that the large force that had almost wiped out tanks and infantry the day before was somewhere behind the high ground.

Jake planned to minimize risk by crossing the clearings only with his Shermans. He hoped this would draw artillery fire away from the pinned-down infantry. The soldiers stood no chance in the open in the face of observed artillery and mortar fire. If they received heavy fire, his tanks would cross the clearing quickly under suppressive fire from the 105-mm howitzers, laid on and ready two thousand yards back. It was early afternoon—time to move on to the objective.

"Tank platoons, move out!" crackled his command over the company radio net. The Shermans emerged from the town and quickly assumed a wedge formation, pointing at the slag pile in an inverted V. They made good progress, crossing the clearing between the town and the high ground. Observed artillery fire fell in whistles and blasts as Jake ordered his tanks to keep going but stay buttoned up. Over his SCR 536 radio, he communicated with the infantry staying behind in the tree line due to the heavy artillery barrage.

Just twenty-five yards short of the debris pile, a heavily camouflaged German Panther tank rocked back—a muzzle flash and green tracer shot out from its position in the woods to the Americans' right. The armor-piercing round slammed into the side of the command tank with a sound like that of a sledgehammer against a grounded cathedral bell. Shaking off the concussion, Jake calmly ordered his crew to bail out as the vehicle lurched and began to fill with smoke. The Germans were using flashless powder—nobody saw where the fire was coming from. Watching from his own command tank at the edge of the clearing, Sam ordered H Company to fall back to the town—without infantry protection, they were sitting ducks for the hidden tank or marauding Germans armed with Panzerfausts. Better to call in air support and an artillery barrage on the hidden German positions.

The tank crews backed up to the line held by Major Adams's infantry, where the sloping terrain hid them from the German positions. The crew of the stricken tank made it back, but their report was dire—Jake was missing. They were sure he had bailed out right behind them, after making sure nobody was left behind. The word was that he was slightly wounded and was being treated by an adjoining unit.

For now, Sam and the task force needed to focus on taking out the enemy artillery several kilometers behind the slag pile to allow the tank-infantry teams to resume the attack. To that effect, the 105-mm howitzers attached to Task Force Hogan plotted counterbattery missions and began dueling with the German artillery. Everyone took cover where they could, though the piles of sand did not afford good protection and could bury a soldier if a round hit nearby.

Several of Adams's infantry soldiers had to help each other out of their positions after near misses toppled large piles of dirt onto the depressions they had taken cover in. *"Tom—help me out of here!"* Squad members pulled soldiers out by the shoulders or the end of their rifles. *"Shake it off—now let's go!"*

Darkness closed over the combatants facing each other across the small clearing and slag pile. The artillery ceased in the waning hours of daylight. Captain Barclay led a patrol to within twenty-five yards of German lines to look for Jake. First Sergeant Filyaw was one of the volunteers on the patrol. They returned safely.

But there was no sign of Lieutenant Sitzes.

The next day, September 19, the back-and-forth duel of artillery continued. Ammunition ran short and required General Rose's intervention with the VII Corps to send trucks on an overnight run with the much-needed 105-mm rounds.

Task Force Hogan was down to seven Sherman tanks from H Company and five medium tanks from G Company, plus two platoons of the relatively worthless M3 Stuart light tanks. The third platoon was absent, detached to guard Omaha Forward, the division command post.[11]

The infantry were hit even harder. Major Adams reported that his 1/26 Infantry would soon be ineffective after taking eight killed in action and fifty wounded. Most of his men showed symptoms of combat fatigue—what is now known as post-traumatic stress disorder (PTSD)—and he was at about 60 percent strength.[12]

Recently promoted Brigadier General Boudinot ordered a coordinated attack with neighboring Task Force Lovelady to their left while Task Force Hogan attacked down the center, plus a flanking attack on the slag pile with tank and infantry on the right prong of the fork. Sam protested—on reconnaissance the previous day, he'd seen with his own eyes that the ground to the southeast of the slag pile was boggy, making it a tank trap. General Boudinot nevertheless ordered the attack to proceed as planned. Other Spearhead units were also attacking and holding ground along this "Stolberg Corridor" in the VII Corps area.

The attack was set to jump off that afternoon. Before the task force set off, German fighter-bombers appeared overhead, and tankers and infantrymen gazed wide-eyed at a Hollywood-style dogfight as US P-47s pounced on them. The US Army Air Corps came out on top, but not before losing one of the P-47s. To Sam, the pilot appeared to have been severely wounded or possibly blinded—he'd flown his stricken craft in several flat, low triangles over both US and German lines. Suddenly, the P-47 nosed down straight into the ground, crashing in a fireball, to the dismay of the onlooking US infantrymen and tankers.[13]

At 2:00 P.M., with artillery and smoke to help conceal the infantry's advance, H Company launched toward Weissenberg in the center. Four

G Company tanks and the remnants of C Company, 1/26 Infantry advanced toward the slag pile from the right through woods and swamp.

As the Americans emerged from the town and into the clearing, German artillery fell again with deadly accuracy. To Sam, moving astride the road junction between his three maneuver units, it was the largest concentration of German artillery he had ever seen. Artillery and mortars of every caliber, plus at least one 20-mm automatic antiaircraft cannon, rained on the advancing Task Force Hogan. Nebelwerfers, six-barreled rocket launchers—nicknamed "screaming meemies" by the GIs—also rained down with a high-pitched screech as each seventy-pound warhead descended to earth before exploding in a concussive blast.[14]

The American supporting artillery was ineffective in suppressing its German rivals. The self-propelled M7 "Priest" howitzers, named for the pulpit-like machine gunner's position next to the cannon tube, sank in the mud, losing their ability to deliver accurate fire with every recoil of their 105-mm cannons. This also contributed to some of the US airbursts falling dangerously close to the Blue Spader doughs.

Hearing the frustrated transmissions from the Priest commanders, Sam clicked his microphone off and exclaimed to Sergeant D'Orio: "Damn! I told Boudinot the right flank was swamp!" It was an uncharacteristic outburst from the normally calm and collected commander. Sam halted the artillery fire so that the guns could register again and observers could keep up with the movement.

H Company, still without Jake, made good progress across the clearing until they reached the woods outside their objective, Weissenberg, where well-concealed antitank guns and at least one Panther tank knocked out two tanks. A third was destroyed by a Panzerfaust fired from the woods. Sam ordered H Company to pull back as G Company, on the right side, was bogged down in mud—as Sam had predicted. General Boudinot's overruling of Sam's advice had proved costly.[15]

Task Force Hogan regrouped in the early evening. German prisoners indicated that the Germans were planning a counterattack in the dawn darkness of September 19. They stated that Jake Sitzes's attack the previous day disrupted a counterattack by two hundred Germany infantry, when they were caught at their jump-off points by H Company's artillery preparation.

Sam lit a Camel as he looked at the map. He hated butting his head against the wall. If Task Force Hogan could not flank this strongpoint, they would storm it in a night attack—this way, they might foil any further enemy counterattack. He conferred with his assembled commanders: F. W. Adams; his S-3 operations officer, Captain Al Levasseur; G Company's Carl Cramer; H Company's John Barclay; the artillery liaison officer; and Sam's own trusty S-3 Travis Brown. Major Adams liked the plan. Even further, Adams and Levasseur suggested skipping the artillery preparation with only an initial volley of well-placed airbursts, after which the Blue Spaders would attack with fixed bayonets, hopefully surprising the Germans in their foxholes.

Early on the twentieth, it was foggy, cold, and dark. The light-blue glow of dawn was still at least an hour away when Major Adams and his doughs jumped out of their positions with gleaming bayonets fixed on their M1 Garands. One volley of 105-mm artillery whistled in through the quiet, graying sky, crashing with a *POP, POP, POP* and brilliant flashes of white, orange, and smoky gray behind the charging US infantry.

The artillery was calculated and executed perfectly, so that multiple rounds landed and exploded together at the exact desired moment. The doughs sprinted through woods and the open clearing, kicking up mud and puffing out condensation to the sound of the muffled stomps of their boots and the swishing of waterlogged pant legs. They surged past the silent ghost of the mining camp, letting out a murderous roar as they crashed into the German line, stabbing in flashes of bayonet steel at the figures in mottled camouflage.

Surprise was total—the few Germans on picket duty were bayoneted. Those caught sleeping, and those not killed by the airbursts, were taken prisoner. Adams radioed back that the high ground was secure. Sam, positioned at the edge of the clearing with his tanks, radioed them to roll forward and secure the objective.[16]

As they moved forward, Sam dismounted to survey the position.

The fog was lifting but still remained in cool, gray mists hovering over upturned dirt, shrubs, and bomb craters. Sam saw Jake's immobilized tank in a dark silhouette thirty feet away. He walked to it, .45-caliber pistol at the ready. It was an eerie dawn. As Sam walked toward the tank he could hear the faint commands of Adams's infantry as they consolidated on the objective—searching for surviving Germans, checking for wounded, and loading fresh ammunition clips.

Sam's tanks pulled forward, anticipating a counterattack. The fog was lifting, and Sam kept walking toward the empty tank. In a five-hundred-pound-bomb crater, about ten feet from the tank, a dark object drew his eye, stark against the grayish-brown dirt of the crater. He crept closer, swallowing hard with the initial, almost subconscious knowledge of what lay ahead.

It was Jake.

He was lying on the back slope of the crater, his body facing the slag pile. In the early light, Sam could see his youthful, calm face. There was a perfectly round bullet entry wound on his forehead. Jake was dead.[17]

Sam felt numb. He lowered his head and muttered, "Oh, Jake," then turned toward his soldiers consolidating on the objective. He began walking to the German positions as he holstered his pistol. There, waiting, were Barclay and Adams. The look on Sam's face told Barclay the bad news without a word spoken. Sam broke the silence: "He must've been observing the enemy line to see if he should make a run for it or wait until dark when some bastard shot him."

John Barclay stepped over to the bomb crater to check for dog tags, but they all knew it was the beloved lieutenant. They waited with Jake until a Graves Registration team came forward to pick him up. Top Filyaw wept openly at the news. There was little time to grieve or to process. *Just push it down deep.*

Sam walked on a bit, as if in a daze. Even through his grief, Sam was awed by the damage done to this area by the artillery duels—the lunar landscape of bomb destruction reminded him of pictures and descriptions he had seen of World War I's no-man's-land. Abandoned equipment and German corpses littered the battlefield.

Some dead Germans had an eerily peaceful look about them—as if sleeping quietly in their foxholes where the American airbursts had caught them. Others, surprised in the open, were mangled. Sam's eyes focused on one German caught outside of his hole by the US barrage. He had been cut almost in half by the concussive force and exploding shrapnel of a 105-mm direct hit. The main pieces of him were connected by a strand of gut suspended on some brush, along with his balls, which were intact. Sam couldn't help but hope that these were the remains of the sniper who got Jake.[18]

FROM THE HARD-FOUGHT BATTLE FOR Diepenlinchen, Task Force Hogan kept moving forward. There was no time to rest or to mourn Jake or the dozens of casualties incurred by Adams's infantry. Three task forces—Hogan, Lovelady, and Mills—pushed to conquer objective Stolberg on the afternoon of the twentieth. Sam continued in a sullen, mission-focused mood. He wanted to get payback for Jake.

G Company had lost two of its thirteen tanks, compared to H's six of fifteen, so they led the column as the task force entered the narrow river valley at the bottom of which sat Stolberg. Shaped like a kidney bean, with stout stone buildings and rocky cliffs to the east, the city was a hard nut to crack—its center dominated by a medieval castle on a stone promontory. Right away, enemy action sidelined another of Sam's seasoned commanders.

Captain Cramer, always leading from the front, encouraging his men, received wounds from artillery fire while outside his tank late on the twentieth. Before heading to the rear for treatment in one of Captain Spigelman's armored half-tracks, Cramer charged his platoon leader, Tom Cooper, in his soft drawl, "Take good care of my boys." Again, the echoes of training exercises that seemed an eternity ago. "Commander, you are out. Lieutenant, you're now in command." Little did they know at the time how often that one bit of training would resemble combat reality.

The attack resumed on the twenty-first and was the first indication of how hard urban combat in Germany was going to be. About half of Stolberg's population of thirty thousand had evacuated before the battle, their dwellings taken over by German troops. The task force made initial gains moving through the outskirts of town, attacking downhill. Once inside the built-up areas, German Panzerfaust and machine gun teams put up a wall of lead and rockets. Infantry took cover where they could, behind tanks, in doorways, and flat to the ground in drainage ditches as the tanks poured cannon and machine gun fire at the buildings on either side. Progress was measured in meters in the house-to-house fighting.

Sam, eager to get any advantage over the entrenched enemy of the Twelfth Infantry Division, requested a section of flamethrowers from B Company of the Twenty-third Engineer Battalion. Six soldiers, each armed with a flamethrower, a heavy fuel canister strapped to his back, divided up among the infantry squads. The advance resumed at 8:00 P.M., the streets lit up by tank cannon muzzle flashes and the orange glow of the flamethrowers pouring fire into cellars. This tactic helped the Americans advance into the central intersection of the town, where they halted.

Sam thanked the Twenty-third Engineers for their help that night. Their officer, a Lieutenant Eells, told Sam that to his knowledge that was the first use of flamethrowers in combat in the European theater to "encourage" an enemy to abandon their underground positions.[19]

"Thanks, Lieutenant, great job," was Sam's response. He was in no mood for pats on the back.

By the twenty-first, Task Force Hogan had secured central Stolberg. Pockets of German resistance continued to the north, so Sam enlisted the help of Stolberg's bürgermeister, or mayor—a Dr. Ragh—who surrendered, preferring captivity to an encounter with Lieutenant Eells's flamethrowers. Sam did not trust the doctor, but put him to good use at the head of the column, sitting on the hood of a peep. This way he was "motivated" to help identify mines and houses where German soldiers were hiding or where they tried to blend in with the population in order to ambush the Americans.[20]

An uneasy stalemate descended on the Stolberg corridor, but its capture helped VII Corps isolate Aachen and trap German forces in the Hürtgen forest. General Maurice Rose—always near the front line—stopped into the newly conquered towns and presented medals. Truman Boudinot officially pinned on the star of brigadier general. Major Adams's First Battalion, Twenty-sixth Infantry, was nominated for the Presidential Unit Citation for their valor and esprit, both at Diepenlinchen and Stolberg.

Since their first action on July 7, Task Force Hogan's parent regiment, the Thirty-third Armored "Men of War," had lived up to their name—and how. Up to that point in the war, the regiment had lost 133 Sherman tanks to combat action out of 162 assigned. They were the first to engage the Second Panzer Division at Mortain, first to link up with the British and close the Falaise pocket, and first to cross into Belgium and Germany proper.

The regimental coat of arms would soon incorporate imagery related to the liberation of Mons: two castle towers representing the medieval city and the two armored attacks, in the center, a Belgian lion standing over a broken German meat hook in the shape of a "7" at its feet, to signify the destruction of the Seventh Army.

Still, they were barely inside Germany; as Churchill might have said: "This was not the end. It was not even the beginning of the end."

But they were getting closer.

AFTER TAKING THE STOLBERG CORRIDOR, the entire regiment came off the line for a well-deserved rest and refit after the tough fight to secure Spearhead's jump-off point inside Germany. The Third Armored Division was down to seventy-five Shermans from its authorized strength of 232.[21] The armored regiments needed to await new tanks and personnel replacements. It was incredibly frustrating: the Germans were reeling like a boxer who had just taken several strong uppercut punches, his knees turning to rubber. One strong hit and the western front could collapse, leaving the road open to Berlin. But the Allies—both men and machines—were spent, too. Their supply line was stretched to the breaking point. They had to halt, knowing that the Germans would use the time to bring in reinforcements and dig in even deeper along the Siegfried line.

Task Force Hogan spread out around the industrial towns of Stolberg, Mausbach, and Büsbach—the gateway to the Ruhr region, which supplied the Reich with its steel and concrete. Tank companies and headquarters personnel took turns at roadblocks, for the front line ran through the northern edge of Stolberg, and they knew Hitler wanted it back. Main Street in Stolberg was still known as the "eighty-eight bowling alley," since the German FLAK cannon that sat on the opposite ridge plowed the flat stretch of road with heavy antitank shells at will.

On several occasions, task force soldiers repelled enemy probes and absorbed enemy artillery with no losses. C Company guarded the division command post at the Prym castle. Several times, H Company received alerts to prepare to fight off enemy counterattacks designed to break the encirclement of Aachen. One regiment-wide alert warned of a possible enemy parachute attack; all hands, including clerks and cooks, were to be prepared to fight as infantrymen.[22] To help preempt any counterattacks, the task force mortars stayed busy firing into the German lines and their possible assembly areas.

New personnel replacements arrived, as did some familiar faces—recovered from wounds received in Normandy and Mons. Sergeant Wilson Whitehead was one. Shot out of the tank in which Staff Sergeant James Curry was killed near Mortain, he rejoined Task Force Hogan at Stolberg.[23] General Rose made sure he visited each of his battalions during the three-day respite, awarding Purple Hearts and Silver and Bronze Star medals to his beloved tankers and doughboys. Several other men wounded at Mortain, including Corporal Robert Guy and Tech 4 Henry Hutchins of H Company, also returned to find they were under new platoon and company leadership due to combat losses. The capable Lieutenant Thomas Cooper had led G Company since Carl Cramer took shrapnel. The light tanks of C Company were under the command of Lieutenant Robert Resterer, formerly of the recon platoon.[24] The soldiers teased each other about all the action the convalescing soldiers had "missed" and the clean sheets, fluffy pillows, and pretty nurses left behind at the evacuation hospitals.

For many returning Spearhead soldiers, it was a matter of honor, but also a homecoming of returning to their close friends. They were back to watch out for them and help them finish the war alive. In this war, you fought until the Germans gave up or were wiped out. Nobody could guess when that would be. There was no rotation of units—Spearhead remained at the tip of every attack.

There were three ways a leader left the battlefield: either killed, wounded, or fired. Nobody elected for the last one by screwing up intentionally, though they could have in order to secure some safer staff job in the rear or even back in the States. But for officers like Carl Cramer and Sam Hogan, who helped found the unit and forged strong bonds with their soldiers, it must have been unthinkable, especially since nobody could guarantee that a good officer would replace them. They trusted their experience and tactical skills, and that they were the best officers to get their boys back home alive.

Doc Spigelman and the medical section stayed busy. Staff Sergeant Raymond Kuderka, Corporals Derrick Filkins and John Skuly, and a handful of privates drove around the different company bivouacs taking care of the task force soldiers. There were slight shrapnel wounds that wouldn't heal properly. There were new shrapnel and bullet wounds as patrols encountered enemy activity or received a volley of German mortar fire. Everyone had some sort of cold and cough, so the medics freely handed out sulfa packets and a pat on the back: "Drink lots of water and get on the chow line early for some hot soup—rest now while you can."

Already a medical doctor before the war, Doc Spigelman was the other "old man" of the unit, in which anyone over thirty was called "Pop." But none called Spigelman that, for he was a learned man—a "Doc." He had attended City College in New York before the war, then traveled to Lebanon, where he finished medical school at the American University in Beirut.

Young troopers respected his learning and experience and envied his full mustache. One time, back in the Mojave Desert during their four-month sojourn on tank maneuvers, soldiers were "smokin' and jokin'" after a day of chasing ghosts across the sandy expanses. Doc was listening in on their bull session when one recounted a newspaper article advertising plots of land for sale at a rest stop across the Nevada border called Las Vegas.

They turned to Doc and said, "Sir, why don't you invest?" Doc paused a moment, bent down to grab a handful of sand, then held it aloft solemnly, letting the grains slip through his fingers. He shook his head slowly, letting out an "I don't think so."[25] Now, after a dozen battles and with nobody knowing how many left to go, the soldiers hoped not to see him from the bottom end of a stretcher, but knew Doc would fight like the devil to keep them alive if they did.

During the Allies' tactical pause, Spearhead GIs profited from a visit by the roving bath and fumigation units that belonged to VII Corps. These units would set up shop in an abandoned warehouse, a bombed-out movie theater, or their own large tents where they set up communal, open-bay showers. For this operation, corps engineers set up large tents by the Inde River in the little town of Kornelimünster.

GIs trucked in thirty at a time from their camp or assembly area. They lined up, sometimes one hundred in a line, to enter the tents, where a heating system, water pumps, and pipes were set up occupying the entirety of the interior. Duckboards, beginning at the entryways, lined the dirt or concrete floors, allowing water to drain and keeping out the mud.

Once under the open-sided tents, the soldiers, many joking around but some sheepish, undressed. A few German civilians on the other side of the stream gawked at the tanned necks and arms contrasting with lily-white buttocks. Off came the shirts, pants, socks, and underwear they had been wearing for the past several weeks. The collars and cuffs had the appearance of dark velvet from filth and friction. It seemed like these garments really could stand up by themselves.

There were nozzles placed every three feet with steaming-hot water piped in. Soldiers moved through, factory-assembly-line style, for two minutes, then the water shut off for a minute to allow them to soap up. Another two-minute rinse off, and then the next soldiers moved forward.

The quartermaster units pitched smaller tents outside the shower area for the soldiers to receive new or newly laundered uniforms to change into. Troops needed no encouragement to dry off quickly, get clothed, and back in their trucks—the cold weather ensured that. "Shrinkage" jokes abounded. For the surviving old hands, it was only the second hot shower they'd had since leaving their barracks in England back in early June to load up onto LSTs for the trip to Omaha Beach. Many a GI felt like a new man after the invigorating shower and a clean change of clothes.[26]

The line soldier also took time to write letters home, clean his equipment, and prepare for the next move. The life of the majority of them was limited to the happenings of their tank crew, or infantry or mortar squad. Most knew only this: they would be "spearheading" again—and deeper into Germany—very soon. They knew they belonged to an elite unit that was always up front. They were proud of this but also knew the risks involved. In early October, VII Corps began its siege of the ancient imperial city of Aachen.

The first major German city in the Allies' northern advance held deep symbolic value for the German leadership. This was Charlemagne's capital of the Holy Roman Empire, where German kings and queens were crowned up until the sixteenth century. It was a large and expansive city with imposing stone buildings in the center ringed by hilltops, factories, and large neighborhoods of two- and four-story family dwellings, most of which were undamaged by Allied bombers.

Surrounded by woods and hilly terrain, Aachen anchored two defensive belts of the West Wall, the Schill and Scharnhorst lines, making the city the "sentinel of the Rhine." By taking Stolberg to the southeast, Spearhead had isolated Aachen and avoided frontally attacking its defenses. The city was in a plain that started at the foothills of the

Ardennes and swept east toward Cologne. Aachen sat surrounded by high ground—to the south, the Lousberg heights looked down upon the center of town, an ideal observation post for defender or attacker from which to call artillery. The high ground and key intersections below were defended by strong shelters called "pillboxes," with interlocking fields of fire covering their approaches. An aboveground railway line looped around the city, providing the equivalent of a medieval wall to thwart would-be invaders. Antitank obstacles, mines, and booby traps rounded out the defenses.

The *US Army Field Manual* discouraged the use of tanks in cities, forests, or mountainous terrain—so much for "schoolhouse," or stateside training, solutions. Once inside the center of town, most buildings needed to be searched, cleared, and marked by infantry.[27] Tanks, blind inside the narrow streets, would take care of pillboxes and antitank guns. The tankers and infantry mutually supported each other.

Although the majority of Aachen's prewar population of 165,000 people had evacuated, Hitler demanded that his soldiers and the remaining population fight to the death to hold it. In the first big Allied push into a major German city, First Army intelligence passed down a list of heavy-hitting SS and army units defending the city, so there was much colon clenching as both sides planned and prepared for a terrible urban slaughter.

VII Corps assigned two veteran infantry divisions to take the city after a preparatory bombing meant to reduce the enemy defenses. One of them was Spearhead's old partner in Normandy, the Thirtieth Infantry Division; the other was the redoubtable First Infantry Division, the Big Red One. For a week, the infantry divisions slogged through heavy urban fighting for the outskirts of "Fortress Aachen." Seesaw, house-to-house fighting between infantry yielded few gains for the Americans as the GIs crawled forward, having to fight for every pillbox and stone structure. After capturing the suburb of Übach, the US foot soldiers were subjected to fierce counterattacks by German infantry and armor supported by aircraft. Sherman tanks would be needed in what promised to be the largest urban battle for the allies up to that point in the war. Sam was alerted to reinforce a renewed push with his tanks and fight off any attempted counterattacks.

On October 17 at 9:00 A.M., he reported to the Big Red One's Major General Clarence Huebner for a briefing on the pending attack. A Kansan, Huebner had climbed the enlisted ranks from private to sergeant before receiving a commission prior to World War I. He was highly decorated for his participation in the St. Mihiel and Meuse-Argonne offensives. In this war, he had already participated in the campaign in North Africa and major battles in the European theater of operations since his division landed on Omaha Beach on June 6.

Huebner was gruff and to the point. Sam's tanks would play a key part, Huebner said. The enemy was dug in and fanatical. Facing the Americans were five thousand men, assembled under Oberst (Colonel) Gerhard Wilck from the 246th Volksgrenadier Infantry Division. Northeast of Aachen, elements of the First SS Panzer Division, Second and 116th Panzer Divisions, and the Third Panzer Grenadier Division, augmented by Tiger tanks of the 506th Heavy Tank Battalion (Schwere Panzer Abteilung), were positioned to counterattack against any weak spots in the US lines.

General Huebner directed Task Force Hogan to cut off the Aachen-Laurensberg highway, then, under cover of darkness, move into the outskirts of Aachen to a factory district, from which it would jump off at noon on the nineteenth. Objective "Red" was Lousberg Hill, the highest point in Aachen, and Objective "Blue," a railroad junction protected by a stone castle. The hill needed to be secured to control the high ground and push past the old city center. The tanks would act as the anvil to the Big Red One's hammer.[28]

From behind the hills ringing Aachen, elements of two dozen artillery battalions, each with eighteen cannons, opened up on designated targets. At the pull of one hundred lanyards, shells rained down in a crush of explosions. Buildings shook and spewed dust and smoke as windows shattered and the corners collapsed into piles of debris.

The artillery and bombing reduced some parts of the city into rubble, but most structures remained intact. Combat inside the urban area would require constant teamwork between the Sherman tanks and infantrymen of the Big Red One. German infantry occupied cellars, rooftops, and every nook and cranny of rubble.

It helped if infantry and tank commanders had worked together before, so Sam was happy to hear that Major F. W. Adams and his 1/26th Infantry were to his left. Sam saluted Huebner and departed to prepare the task force. Some parts of this war were becoming routine, but every mission was different, especially when his tanks supported commanders other than General Rose.

Upon returning to the TF Hogan camp, Sam, Travis, and the company commanders got to planning and preparation. Cooper, Barclay, and Cardon were apprehensive but excited.

"Taking down the capital of Charlemagne's First Reich will be the death knell of the Third Reich," Cooper chimed in, always the company historian.

"Maybe this thing can be won before Christmas," stammered a new lieutenant in between taking notes for his captain.

Sam burst the young man's bubble: "I wouldn't plan on it. All right, this is our first large-scale urban combat in Germany. We must have strong coordination with the infantry, and we also have to adhere to fire/no-fire areas." To prevent friendly casualties and make the best use of mortars and artillery in the constrained spaces of a city, they designated "no-fire areas" as well as checkpoints along their route of advance. Nothing was to be fired within one hundred meters of the forward line of troops.

Sam then released his company commanders to go over the drill with their infantry counterparts. Each tank would be supported by a platoon of infantry—the Sherman would light up the first building, driving the German defenders into the cellars and basements. They needed to avoid front doors. There would be no knocking, just blowing holes into walls with satchel charges and tank fire so the infantry could come in where least expected, staying clear of enemy kill zones. The infantry would then move up, using grenades or flamethrowers to kill anyone not surrendering. The infantry squad leader would yell or signal *Cleared!* And the tanks would shift fire to the next building. The advance would be very slow, but this deliberate, calculated system, combined with firepower, was intended to keep casualties light.

At least, that was the plan.

In the meantime, VII Corps' Lightning Joe Collins, call sign Jayhawk Six, sent an ultimatum to the German commanding the Aachen garrison. It read:

> The city of Aachen is now completely surrounded by American forces who are sufficiently equipped with both airpower and artillery to destroy the city, if necessary. We shall take the city either by receiving its immediate unconditional surrender or by attacking and destroying it.
>
> While the unconditional surrender will require the surrender of all armed bodies, the cessation of hostile acts of every character, the removal of mines and prepared demolitions, it is not intended to molest the civil population or needlessly sacrifice human lives. But if the city is not promptly and completely surrendered unconditionally the American Army ground and air forces will proceed ruthlessly with air and artillery bombardment to reduce it to submission.
>
> In other words, there is no middle course. You either unconditionally surrender the city with everything now in it, thus avoiding needless loss of German blood and property, or you may refuse and await its complete destruction. The choice and the responsibility are yours.
>
> Your answer must be delivered within twenty-four hours at the location specified by the bearer of this paper.[29]

THE DEADLINE FOR A RESPONSE to VII Corps' surrender ultimatum to the Aachen garrison came and went. Both sides prepared for the inevitable bloodbath. The gray industrial landscape matched the low gunmetal clouds drizzling cold, nightly rains through the eighteenth. Roads were slick with mud, and the overcast skies stifled US close-air support. The weather conditions favored Oberst Wilck's defenders. Axis Sally, the Nazi radio psychological operations propagandist, broadcast monologues prognosticating an "Allied Stalingrad" at Aachen.

Attacking from the north of town, John Barclay's H Company Shermans, with troops from F Company of Spearhead's own Thirty-sixth Armored Infantry, arrived at the Factory District, the jump-off point toward Objective Red, by 11:50 A.M. To their right, C Company light tanks and D and E Companies of the Thirty-sixth advanced against mortar and small-arms fire. Direct attacks with Sherman main gun rounds and artillery overcame the first pillboxes in view. Half-track-borne Thirty-sixth Infantry GIs took out two more with explosives and grenades. H Company moved forward in an inverted V-shaped wedge with the infantrymen following behind on their half-tracks. The first line of pillboxes gave way as the force moved toward Objective Red. So far, so good.

About a thousand yards in the distance, Sam spotted the elevated railway line through his binoculars. The railroad underpass formed a chokepoint in their advance.

"Move forward in column, artillery stand by to fire immediate suppression," hissed the radio. Barclay directed a narrowing of the formation. He ordered his tankers to keep eyes open for a possible ambush. Suddenly, there was a muzzle flash as a German assault gun loosed a 75-mm armor-piercing round toward the advancing tanks. Traffic lit up the company and platoon nets: "German assault gun, twelve o'clock inside the tunnel." The round missed its intended targets as the German vehicle backed up in a haze of diesel exhaust.

On the right leg of the wedge, eagle-eyed Lieutenant Robert Sleeth from Torrance, California, spotted a camouflaged antitank gun on their flank. He called out: "Gunner, target two o'clock, antitank gun, load HE!" The response "HE up!" resounded over the internal comms. The German antitank gun crew spread out in five directions as they saw the Sherman's turreted 76-mm cannon rotate toward them and lock on target. Staff Sergeant Seward W. Hull, filling in for the wounded gunner, replied, "I see him sir! On the way!" as his left boot pounded on the foot-pedal trigger.[30]

The Germans received a rude surprise: the Americans had seen their camouflaged gun first, fired, and exploded it into pieces, tires flying and barrel split in two. The gun crew threw down their rifles and prepared to surrender as the US tank formation cut off their escape path. The tank-infantry teams captured one pillbox, then stopped for the night to reconnoiter and look for six more antitank guns reportedly lying in wait ahead.[31]

It was a fitful night of shivering under GI wool blankets, either pulling guard, looking at maps under raincoats, or inside tanks preparing for the next day's attack into Aachen proper. The infantry sent out "listening patrols" and heard enemy movement to their front. Sam and his commanders studied their maps, confirmed what their trained eyes saw in the glow of fires and the coming dawn. The terrain flattened out past the railroad track. Beyond were the squat, wide buildings of the factory district, smokestacks rising here and there. Past this district began the cluttered confines of the city, with a half dozen steeples rising like menacing sentinels.

The horrors of urban combat loomed ahead, but first the scouts sighted several pillboxes in their path. They needed to deal with them first.

Pillboxes were reinforced concrete bunkers, the largest part of which went underground so that only the top vision slits and gun ports protruded. They looked like a round box of drugstore mints or pills. Most of them were built into hillsides or at the edge of copses of trees. They were designed to reinforce each other so that two or three could cross streams of bullets and cannon fire onto an oncoming invader. Over the previous weeks, US aerial reconnaissance had identified many, but others still lay hidden under piles of hay or mounds of dirt and leaves.

G Company, with Lieutenant Thomas Cooper in the lead, was released from supporting Major Adams's First Battalion, Twenty-sixth Infantry and rejoined Task Force Hogan for the day's attack. The task force would move on the right flank with the Third Battalion of the

Twenty-sixth Infantry on their left. Once in the center of the city, they would assault through the compound on the southern edge of the Lousberg heights, where two German headquarters sat inside the Quellenhof Hotel and the nearby Kurhaus—a three-story building used for community events.

Once that was taken, H Company would attack down the western side of the Lousberg heights, with G Company swinging around the hill to the northwest, the two armored formations emerging at the point where the tip of the hill slowly descended from ridge to flat ground and the railway junction named Objective Blue. C Company remained Task Force Hogan's reserve, to be used in case of German counterattack or at a critical time and place where Sam needed to bring a final jolt of mass and firepower to break through to the objective.

Sam rose early from a three-hour slumber and started his daily ritual of a cold-water shave, Camel cigarette, and cup of hot coffee courtesy of Phil D'Orio, who always had his little camp stove ready. Infantry and tankers were entering "stand to"—all soldiers up and ready to roll out at sunrise. Soldiers nibbled on canned biscuits washed down with instant coffee or a few spoonsful of the barely palatable "meat hash" in a can. Infantry grunts cleaned rifles and cartridge belts and verified that canteens were full. Coughs and colds persisted, and a cacophony of coughing and hacking up phlegm echoed among the clicks and clangs of weapons maintenance.

Sam barked the order: "Guidons, this is Six—move out!" At 8:00 A.M., the task force rolled forward, two lines of tanks in an echelon formation with the infantry and mortars in half-tracks and the assault guns in the second line ready to fire smoke or high-explosive rounds. Sam's command tank moved in between the two wings, Texas flag lazily fluttering on the radio antenna, wet with morning dew. Machine gun fire rang out from concealed pillboxes. The Americans knew the procedure like muscle memory. Tank gunners in the lead Shermans called out the target, then fired HE rounds into the pillboxes. Alarmingly, no antitank guns were in sight—were they well concealed, abandoned, or had the Germans pulled them back so they could support them with their own mortars?

Bigger bunkers lay ahead. To get at them, infantry identified the vision slits and attacked their blind flanks. When the bunkers supported one another, the technique developed by Major Adams was to bring up a "Long Tom"—a towed 155-mm howitzer—and blast away. The concussion was sufficient to bring down walls already weakened by bombardment. A hit by its ninety-pound round against a bunker resulted in massive headaches and bleeding from eyes, nose, and ears for the German defenders, who quickly thereafter surrendered.

Onward the task force churned, the tank companies advancing by bounds from one terrain feature to another, stopping only to blow up bunkers and obstacles and for the engineers to clear the lines of Teller mines. They advanced methodically and unrelentingly.

The two huge tank wedges split and narrowed into two columns, then broke off in sections as they advanced into the denser parts of town. They left behind the spread-out factory district. Just as planned, thought Sam as he motioned to his tank driver to stay down the middle with the mortars and assault guns in tow. Ahead, infantrymen dismounted at the first line of apartment and office buildings along a broad avenue.

They dashed from doorway to doorway, the tanks moving slowly for them to keep up. Gray stone buildings flanked the rain-glazed cobblestone roads littered here and there with rubble. No window survived on these four-story apartment buildings, and the shredded remains of white curtains swayed in and out, to and fro. The fifth story of a corner building puffed out gray-black smoke toward the sky. Flames licked the baroque masonry trim that topped the building. Aachen was a ghost town except for the enemy grenadiers waiting in ambush.

The Lousberg heights loomed ahead as the tanks idled, then roared forward in spurts as they kept up with US infantry darting in and out of buildings. Just short of the Lousberg was a park carved into a spur coming off the heights. Several large buildings and some smaller ones edged around Farwick Park. One was the Kurhaus, which served as a German tactical command post, and another the Quellenhof Hotel, which was a battalion headquarters. The area had changed hands earlier, when the Germans launched a counterattack, which recaptured the Kurhaus from the hard-fighting foot soldiers of the Third Battalion of the Twenty-sixth Infantry Regiment, First Infantry Division.

Sniper fire rang out. The infantry called out directions, their voices echoing in between the buildings along with the rifle claps. US doughs ran for cover in doorways as mortars whistled in, detonating among the rooftops and sending bits of mortar and hot shrapnel onto the street like a localized hailstorm. Sam looked at the church steeple halfway up the steep slope of the Lousberg heights.

"If I was a Jerry artillery observer, that's where I would be," he muttered to himself. So much for another cultural monument . . .

His tank crews knew what to do. Calls for fire went crackling out over the appropriate net as turret mechanisms whined and cannon tubes elevated in response. *BOOM!* Followed by *BOOM BOOM BOOM!* The steeple on the Salvatorberg exploded in a gray cloud of debris and shattered concrete as the first 76-mm tank rounds, then artillery in direct-fire mode, reduced the German observation post to a clump of dust and rubble.

To the left of the tanks, Sam's West Point classmate and commander of the Third Battalion, Twenty-sixth Infantry, Lieutenant Colonel J. T. Corley, had infiltrated his L Company into the Quellenhof hotel compound's tennis courts at first light, and these doughs were now clearing the outer buildings. The Big Red One brought up the Long Tom. The giant 155-mm towed howitzer paid dividends as its crew moved into the tennis courts to begin firing on the Quellenhof and the Kurhaus.

The gun's ninety-pound round, the length and girth of a traffic cone, had been used earlier with success against some of the bigger bunkers. Now it poked gaping holes into the façade of the elegant hotel. The battle increased in tempo as the rate of fire grew from a steady *pop pop pop* to multiple cracks, the ripping of machine guns, and the heart-vibrating detonation of tank main gun and artillery rounds leaving their tubes.

G and H Companies pressed on, isolating the hotel compound as the terrain began climbing more. Behind their columns, the accompanying infantry heard heavy fighting as J. T. Corley's doughs exchanged grenades inside the hotel lobby with German infantry holed up in the Quellenhof basement. Tank engines roared as they struggled up the northeastern slope. They passed the smoking ruins of the Salvatorberg church to their left. The top of Lousberg Hill, Objective Red, lay another two hundred yards up. Sam radioed: "Press on to the rally point past Objective Red." To everyone's surprise, the top was lightly defended, and Sam's infantry reached the crest by 10:45 A.M.[32]

The task force surged over and around the hill, pausing only to mop up a squad of German infantry. Before moving on to Objective Blue, Sam called a halt in order to evacuate fifteen infantrymen wounded on the move through the town and onto the heights. Doc Spigelman sent two armored ambulances forward and got to work patching up the wounded troops—always reassuring them with his warm smile that they would pull through, no problem.

On the reverse slope of the captured hill sat a German supply unit attempting to surrender. John Barclay radioed Sam that a logistics train wanted to surrender to him.

"Let's roll," said Sam, as tank driver Elmer Johnson stepped on the command Sherman's gas, sending the Texas-flag-laden antenna sagging backward.

On approach, Sam could see a long column of thirteen horse-drawn vehicles and seven half-tracks. The German supply lieutenant in charge looked very young and scared, his little unit cut off and surrounded. US tankers and grimy-looking infantrymen leveled carbines and Thompson submachine guns at them. Sam stood on his turret and motioned the lieutenant forward.

"You are now prisoners of war, understand?" The lieutenant nodded his understanding and handed over his Luger sidearm. "I want you to march back toward my rear carrying your white flag. I'll radio back that you are surrendering—the war is over for you."

The German lieutenant seemed relieved. Sam did not have time to deal with the dozen teamsters, supply clerks, and their wagons—plus they posed no threat. Their cargo was probably rations or ammunition. The sad column trudged back toward the First Infantry Division command post. Stopped by a picket of Big Red One doughs, their wagons and half-tracks were searched—and it was all booze! Sam would never live it down among his Big Red One brothers like J. T. Corley and F. W. Adams. At least the infantrymen could celebrate once the town was theirs. The hometown headline a month later would read: "Colonel Passes Up War's Biggest Hangover."[33]

Sam's two columns continued, blissfully ignorant of the booty the unit had passed up. Yet there was more. On the reverse slope of the Lousberg sat an abandoned German half-track, probably left by the surrendering lieutenant for lack of fuel. H Company first sergeant Ernest Filyaw, from Warrior, Alabama, approached suspiciously after dismounting his tank. Inside the open bed under some tarps were several cases of cognac. What a score! The salty Filyaw looked around, then gingerly walked back to his tank with a grin on his face to get some help unloading it.

Suddenly—*BOOM!*—a flash and another crashing explosion as the enemy half-track went up in flames. Filyaw's grin disappeared instantly, the column of fire, smoke, and cognac vapors rising behind him. He slowly turned around to watch his score evaporate in the inferno with an indignant shake of the head. An H Company tank had fired an HE round at it, the gunner thinking he saw movement in the waning hours of daylight. Such are the fortunes of war.[34]

After the day's loss of ground, Oberst Wilck moved his headquarters to an air raid bunker on the Lousberg Strasse. He issued a communiqué exhorting the remaining German defenders to fight to the death and not yield any ground.

"The Defenders of Aachen will prepare for their last battle. Constricted to the smallest possible space, we shall fight to the last man, the last shell, the last bullet in accordance with the Fuehrer's orders."[35]

Sam's two columns converged on the reverse slope of Lousberg and headed downhill with the sinking sun. Sam directed G and H Companies to occupy the small schloss, two hundred yards from Objective Blue. The stout building dominated the approaches, a perfect position to block possible German counterattacks down the Aachen-Laurensberg highway. It was the end of another long day, October 19. One last disappointment occurred at the schloss. Tankers and infantrymen searched the building and found stocks of ammunition in one part of the building. But in another were several cases of whiskey bottles—all empty.

Sam, with prose inspired by Oberst Wilck's order to his troops to fight until the last round, sent up his report to Huebner's CP: "Objective Blue secured—looks like they fought to the last drop."

The American force settled in for another night of patrols and nighttime exchanges of gunfire. The Germans could no longer call in artillery or mortars from the heights. Their defense was crumbling. Task Force Hogan tanks stayed on guard all night with artillery prepared to fire at the approaches of the Aachen-Laurensberg highway. Unbeknownst to Sam, the First SS Panzer Corps had been directed to give up relief of the Aachen garrison.

DAWN GAVE THE BIG RED ONE'S infantry another push into the German garrison's final redoubt. Lieutenant Colonel Corley called up his 155-mm Long Tom and began pounding the air raid bunker. At 10:26 A.M., the garrison commander, Oberst Wilck, disobeying his own orders to his command, decided to save his eardrums and surrender. It was October 21, 1944. The assistant division commander for the Big Red One, Brigadier General George A. Taylor, came forward to the house on Roland Circle to accept the surrender and the ceremonial handing over of Wilck's sidearm.

Sam was sitting in his command tank, on the far side of town and facing the front line, when he got the news from friends in the 1/26th Infantry. His brave friend and battle-buddy, Major F. W. Adams, was killed by a mortar round as he stood outside the pillbox he was using as a command post atop Crucifix Hill, overlooking the old town of Aachen. Adams last letter to his wife, Jeannie, was full of foreboding. Adams had written, "The fighting was so fierce and the casualties so heavy" that he wanted her to be prepared for "what looked like the inevitable." Other old hands likely shared Adams's sense of resignation with the question *how much more of this can we take?* Adams was thirty years old.[36]

Task Force Hogan casualties were several wounded in action but none killed, for which he was thankful. His burdened soul seemed to be releasing some of the load. But was he getting too used to all the carnage? Adams's death proved otherwise, jabbing at his heart once again.

Any man, no matter how tactically skillful—and, yes, lucky—could only face enemy bullets for so long before one got him. The law of averages had caught up to this brave officer. He had fought in North Africa and Sicily, waded ashore on Omaha Beach, and now paid the ultimate price in Germany. If the enemy could kill such an experienced, physically strong officer, they could reach out and kill anyone. Sam had already resigned himself to his fate, whatever that might be. But how many more friends and soldiers under his command would have to die? And why wouldn't the Germans give up? Pushing those thoughts aside, he focused on getting his people back safely. Nothing else mattered.

On October 22, Task Force Hogan was released from attachment to the First Infantry Division and headed back to Stolberg as Spearhead's reserve to rest and prepare for whatever came next. Beyond Aachen was Cologne, then the industrial heartland of the Ruhr, and on to Berlin.

But Hitler had one last ace up his sleeve . . .

7

★ ★ ★ ★ ★

NOT A QUIET CHRISTMAS

NOVEMBER 1–DECEMBER 22, 1944

The end of October and first half of November saw the Ruhr turn into a quagmire as persistent rains saturated the soil and grounded the Air Corps. German *Landser* and American GI settled into an uneasy stand-off to Spearhead's front. Before the Americans could even think of taking Cologne and its bridge across the Rhine, they needed to conquer a crossing on the tributary shielding it, the Roer. Third Armored Division units fought hard for every inch of ground, much of which was mined. The Germans then blew a dam on the Inde River, flooding the battle zone with up to five feet of water in some places. With the First and 104th Infantry Divisions also bogged down in the Hürtgen Forest, the stalemate held.

Frozen turkeys arrived at the front line ahead of Thanksgiving as Task Force Hogan paused to rest and refit after the grinding slog toward the Roer River. The objective of capturing Cologne was forgotten for the time, as the allies were forced to stockpile fuel and ammunition in preparation for the last big push. Units settled in for an expected quiet Christmas. The hope remained among some troops that the Germans might even surrender, that the GIs could still make it home for Christmas. But this soon proved overly optimistic.

The companies spread out around the recently liberated towns of Büsbach, Mausbach, and Stolberg. Soldiers kept to their roadblocks and occasionally exchanged gunfire with German patrols. The tense deadlock continued between the exhausted men and machines facing off under the low, gray clouds that portended a frigid winter.

On December 10, Task Force Hogan, with G Company in the lead and H Company in support, attacked the German town of Geich. From pillbox positions hidden within a barn and covered with hay, the Germans waited patiently for the advancing Americans to get in range. The platoon of tanks moved quickly but slowed down as alert tank commanders sighted the dark gray splotches of a minefield. "Minefield ahead, get ready for contact—over."

The German gunners opened fire from two directions, tracers crossing toward the Sherman tanks. With a series of loud crunches, the well-emplaced mines covered by antitank fire took out five G company tanks in the space of minutes. Radio queries of "What's going on, George element?" went unanswered as crews rapidly bailed out of smoking tanks. Miraculously, nobody was killed, but spalling fragments wounded Tech 5 Harold Stearns and Lieutenants Fred Matzenbacher and Robert Miller.[1]

Sam, situated between the two columns in his command tank, advanced to the sound of explosions and the last position of G Company. The radio traffic reported mine strikes ahead when, thirty seconds later, Sam felt a loud explosion and crash of metal but with no obvious penetration of the armor. The tank shuddered as driver Elmer Johnson attempted to steer, with no effect. Two mines ripped out both of the Sherman's tank treads. Sam knew from experience that the explosion was not from an antitank gun.

He slowly popped his head outside, looked around to see smoke coming from the front wheels, and pressed the intercom: "Mine strike—is everyone okay?" Johnson, closest to the explosion, complained only of ringing in the ears.

Clem Elissondo and the others exited the tank with grunts and cusses. At least they were all uninjured—although gossip spread among the soldiers that they were beginning to think it was unlucky to go "Spearheading with the colonel." Once again, Sam emerged out of the smoking tank without a scratch. How much longer could his luck last? Sam shrugged it off. He would face that damned law of averages again, and whatever it brought with it. Geich fell, thankfully, with no US soldiers killed in action.

Another pause to wait for replacements followed the short, sharp action of December 10. Of the original tank unit commanders that charged up the hill at Hauts Vents, only Sam and John Barclay remained. Only nineteen of the original fifty-four tanks were still rolling. The rest were replacements or overhauls. Both sides needed to lick their wounds, but the Germans clearly used the time to settle into their defensive belts of the West Wall. The occasional artillery duel produced a half dozen casualties—slightly wounded—but mostly it seemed that this quiet would hold.

Back in Berlin, accosted on eastern and western fronts, and slowly losing his remaining objectivity and wits, Adolf Hitler regained his fighting spirit in a manic incarnation of his hero, Frederick the Great. Germany would go on the offensive again. The Reich would muster all remaining resources to the western front, moving armored divisions and Panzer grenadiers on straw-covered roads at nighttime; assembling the Luftwaffe's reserve of trained pilots and jet fighters; and positioning stocks of fuel and ammunition in the strictest secrecy.

A special commando unit, Panzer Brigade 150—led by the scar-faced Austrian commando Otto Skorzeny, infamous for his daring glider-borne rescue of Benito Mussolini from an Italian hilltop fortress—would sow confusion behind US lines. Made up of English-speaking commandos using captured US equipment, the unit's mission was infiltrate by land and parachute among the unwitting Americans to tear down road signs, capture bridges, and ambush lightly armed convoys.[2]

The ultimate goal of all of these preparations for a giant offensive was to cut through the green units guarding the Ardennes, then drive on to capture the major supply port at Antwerp while splitting the British and American forces in two. The capture of all that fuel, ammunition, and supplies needed for the drive into Germany would stop the western Allies for months, giving Hitler more time to field his wonder-weapons.

To achieve this, the Germans needed to cross two major rivers—the Ourthe and the Meuse. The dense forests and hilly, broken terrain meant that they also needed control of the few roads and the high ground that dominated them. The inexperienced American units would be bypassed, then defeated.

After such a loss, and without their closest and largest port, Hitler gambled that the western powers would sue for peace. The scheme of maneuver had already worked in 1940, when the panzers outflanked the vaunted French Maginot Line. Across the already-frozen Ardennes Forest of Belgium and Luxembourg, three German armies, two of them armored, moved to jump-off positions opposite the US First Army—of which VII Corps, the Third Armored Division, and Task Force Hogan were a part.

Back at the task force command post in Mausbach, all were blissfully unaware that a giant German armored formation was massing in secret for an all-out offensive. Sergeant Phil D'Orio, Sam's inseparable orderly, looked in through the flap of the tent covering Sam's command half-track.

"Sir, I picked you up some Spam and eggs. All the troops have been through the chow line." Sam didn't feel very hungry but accepted a bit on his tin mess pan and ate the warm powdered eggs. By now, they had all learned to eat the hot food quickly, as the cold turned it into a lump of chilled gel within a few minutes, especially if you placed the metal tin onto the frozen metal surface of a peep hood or fender.

Sam thanked his sergeant warmly. D'Orio was a companion; his personable nature and his skill at caring for people—he'd been a page at New York's Algonquin Hotel—were always welcome and comforting. He was a small antidote to the constant activity, loneliness, and stress of command. Phil also had a good feel for the morale of the troops. The sense was that it might be a restful Christmas and that the war would soon be over.

Later that morning, December 16, those high hopes of D'Orio and others were shattered as news filtered in that the Germans appeared to be attacking to their north and behind Spearhead's forward position. The official radio transmission came in: "Enemy units have broken through US positions on the Belgian border, prepare for movement."

Task Force Hogan was alerted, but without any specificity—only alarm and confusion. The general order was "be prepared to move as soon as possible to meet the German thrust," wherever that might be. There were rumors that German commandos, dressed as American military police, were guiding columns into ambushes or in the wrong direction. That the same commandos' mission was to assassinate Eisenhower himself. Over the next forty-eight hours, reports confirmed via radio and at the regimental commander's meetings that paratroopers had landed in eastern Belgium in the American rear and that several US units had been overrun, with the survivors executed.

Across the front line to the north of TF Hogan's position, artillery opened up a gigantic barrage on the sleepy front, thinly held by green units of the US First Army. Platoons and companies were cut off, their communications wires cut by exploding German artillery. Low cloudbanks and winter drizzle grounded all Allied aircraft, from fighter-bombers to observation planes. In the enemy's path, the newest US infantry division, the 106th "Golden Lions," first arrived into the combat zone of the Ardennes on December 10, ostensibly to acclimatize and gain experience. They were immediately cut in two and encircled, the Germans bagging six thousand US prisoners in the first seventy-two hours.

The German offensive achieved complete surprise. Among the Allied leadership, there was shock and confusion. The First Army commander, Lieutenant General Courtney Hodges, seemed overwhelmed and practically incapacitated. Still, his deputies at First Army headquarters in Spa immediately alerted and prepared their two uncommitted units to rush into the fray—the Eighty-second Airborne and Combat Command Reserve of the Third Armored Division. They then packed up the field army headquarters to move thirty miles back to the relative safety of Liège.

With two-thirds of its valuable armored combat power assigned else-where, Spearhead began disengaging from its forward position to move "toward the sound of the guns"—something they were not accustomed to—as they normally *were* the "sound of the guns." Falling under XVIII Airborne Corps, their orders were to establish a defensive line from Grandmenil to Melreux.

Combat Command Reserve, with Sam's task force and two others, was the only uncommitted armored force in the northern shoulder of the German penetration. The only veteran unit in the area, it was ex-pected to hold a twenty-mile front against an enemy force of over one hundred thousand until the arrival of reinforcements from other sec-tors of the European theater of operations. The initial German "bulge" into the US line cleaved General Bradley's Twelfth Army Group from the First Army, resulting in Eisenhower's grudging decision to place the First Army—and thereby the Third Armored Division—under none other than Field Marshal Bernard "Monty" Montgomery. To say that the situation was fluid was a gross underestimation.

Orders reached Sam to send C Company to guard the division com-mand post in Spa and to detach H Company to the rear to search for the enemy paratroopers and commandos.

What was left of Task Force Hogan prepared to move southwest from their forward positions in Germany, backtracking to assembly ar-eas in Hotton, Belgium, by December 19. There was the headquarters, G Company (down to eight Sherman tanks after losing seven in the Roer offensive), and the supply clerks, cooks, and mechanics of Service Company. To make up for the loss of H Company and the lack of in-fantry support, Sam received some additional help: A Company of the Eighty-third Reconnaissance Battalion, A Battery from the Fifty-fourth Field Artillery, and a section of quad .50-caliber, half-track-mounted guns from the 486th Anti-Aircraft Artillery Battalion. From Hotton, they would attack to secure Houffalize, about fourteen miles north of Bastogne.

Sam's friends and fellow commanders Lieutenant Colonels William R. Orr and Matthew Kane moved their task forces to Sam's left, while

Task Force Hogan's own right flank was covered by the River Ourthe. They formed the southern boundary of the XVIII Airborne Corps. Despite Sam's having two task forces to his left, they could not mutually support each other due to the hilly, forested terrain. If they were lucky, they could reach each other by radio when cresting a hill—otherwise, they were without communication.

The Americans were truly heading into the unknown. Not only was the Third Armored Division being committed piecemeal (in violation of the principle of war that a force should mass for an attack) and with one-third of its combat power, but the information available to commanders from army HQ down to the battalion and company level was nil.

Rumors abounded, but nobody knew exactly where the enemy forward line of troops was. The few units in contact had either been overrun or fallen back in disarray. To complicate matters even further, fuel resupply was late in arriving, so the US task forces moved out with fuel tanks only half full.

Task Force Hogan rolled shortly after midnight on December 20 and headed back toward the towns it had liberated in Belgium a couple of months earlier. Dreams of a quiet Christmas faded in the roar and fumes of two dozen engines driving southeast toward certain contact with the enemy. Temperatures were freezing and ice covered the roads as drivers squinted hard to see the blackout lights on the vehicle ahead. Drivers posted assistants outside the cab, sitting on the fender, to help steer.

Most soldiers were fighting off chronic colds and coughs they'd suffered since early November. Extreme cold was a potential enemy, too. Chilblains, the precursor to frostbite, began just minutes after exposure to the freezing air. Fingertips turned red and swollen, and felt as if dozens of tiny needles were stabbing them. Half-frozen, numb, and stiff fingers became clumsy at even the simplest tasks, like opening a can of rations or loading bullets into rifles. Toes in boots no longer felt like flesh and bone, more like wood—numb and stiff.

These were hard conditions under which to lead men: exhaustion, cold, lack of information and supplies, and the enemy ahead in un-known numbers or locations. Backtracking away from Berlin was killing the troops' morale. Would they have to recapture the hard-won ground in Germany that they were leaving behind? All any reasonable human would want to do is curl up in a foxhole or tank and not come out. They rolled on anyhow. The situation weighed on every commander's mind as the column moved into the unknown—deeper into the thick, snow-covered Ardennes Forest under pewter-gray skies.

The terrain began to rise toward the plateaus and hills of the Ar-dennes. Eerie glows in the distance portended brutal combat. As the column climbed along the dark sliver of road, the front vehicles disap-peared into the mountainous and densely forested folds of the earth, like a black carpet laid out ahead and around the column. Every so often, the overcast sky glowed with a dull orange flare, droning across the sky in the opposite direction of their march—German V-1 rockets on their way to explode at US supply dumps in Liège and Antwerp.

Another of Nazi Germany's wonder-weapons, the V-1 (V for ven-geance) was the ancestor of the modern cruise missile. The "flying bomb" carried almost one ton of explosives, pushed through the air by a pulse-jet engine, to which it owed its pulsating drone. An internal gyro-scope steered it in the direction of its intended target.[3]

Clem Elissondo, gazing up through the darkness out of his gun-ner's hatch in Sam's tank, heard a jet engine cut off and go silent. Did that mean it was about to dive down and explode on the hapless ar-mored column clanking through the empty countryside? None of the Americans had any idea of the weapon's capabilities. He cast a worried glance at Colonel Hogan, who seemed unfazed as he stared straight ahead at the darkness of the coming battle. There was no explosion. Only the rumble of engines and the rhythmic pounding of tank treads broke the still of the night.[4]

Once onto the colder, higher elevation of the Ardennes plateau, the terrain changed constantly. From one kilometer to the next, the column rolled up steep inclines, then down into tight river valleys. Tank treads struggled to grip the ice-encrusted roadway.

Lieutenant (and later Captain) John Barclay of Task Force Hogan (*center*) spots tank targets at a range near Warminster, England, on February 25, 1944, as General Dwight D. Eisenhower and Field Marshal Bernard Montgomery look on.

Captain Louis "Doc" Spigelman during the train-up, early 1944, carrying his medical-aid bag under his left arm. Sam's intrepid battalion surgeon showed unflagging bravery and dedication to his patients, placing their care above his own safety many times throughout the war.

Company commanders during a break in training, early 1944: Captain William Talley, Headquarters Company (*left*), and Sam Hogan's superb G Company commander, Captain Carl Cramer.

The calm before the storm: key leaders gather prior to the attack on Hill 91, Hauts Vents. (*Left to right*) Colonel Dorrance Roysdon, of the Thirty-sixth Infantry Regiment; Sam Hogan; Captain Edwin Gunderson; and Captain Norbert Horrell of I Company.

Hellish bocage: Sherman tanks make their way through the dense walls made of packed earth, vines, and trees—called hedgerows—that divided every little Norman field and made US offensive action costly and slow.

A dozer-blade-equipped Sherman plows through a Norman hedgerow in the bocage. These improvised devices are a shining example of US ingenuity on the battlefield and allowed the Sherman tanks to avoid using often-perilous main roads.

Pictured here in the bed of his M3 half-track mortar carrier, Sergeant John Grimes (*left*) leads his mortar section. Covering fire from mortars was instrumental in the advance of the troops.

Sam Hogan, Camel in hand, and his loyal orderly, Sergeant Phil D'Orio, rest in an open-topped peep during a pause on the march to the next objective.

After helping to expel the Nazi occupation, an M3 Stuart light tank, with attached hedgerow prongs, moves through Liège, Belgium—with locals flooding the streets to express their gratitude—in September 1944.

A local woman celebrating the liberation of Chênée scrawls a greeting on a Task Force Hogan tank on September 7, 1944.

Sam Hogan's command tank moves through the outskirts of Liège in September 1944.

Into Germany: a task force Sherman fires its main gun at point-blank range on the streets of Aachen, October 1944, while accompanying infantry peers out from cover.

US soldiers inspect a dreaded enemy Panther tank, knocked out in the heavy fighting for Hotton on Christmas Eve 1944. Behind the Panther is an enemy Panzer Mark IV.

Soldiers of Hogan's 400 chow down on their first meal back inside friendly lines at a farm in Soy after a daring nighttime escape through enemy lines, December 26, 1944.

Staff Sergeant Lee B. Porter, whose quick action during a nighttime escape through enemy lines at Marcouray saved over four hundred men from discovery by the enemy surrounding them.

A disheveled Sam Hogan (*left*) reports to Major General Maurice Rose, commanding general, Third Armored Division, immediately after Sam's arrival back inside friendly lines after their daring Christmas retrograde.

Task Force Hogan tanks scan the snowy roadsides for enemy ambushers near Fraiture, Ardennes, on their way to push back the "bulge," January 7, 1945.

Lieutenant John Modrak of C Company inspects one of the captured Shermans, turned against their former owners and knocked out during the battle for Hotton in January 1945. Shortly after this photo was taken, Modrak was captured by SS troops during the US counteroffensive, shot, and left for dead.

Staff Sergeant John Robert Burns Barclay, Task Force Hogan Service Company, poses next to a line of antitank obstacles— "Dragon's Teeth"—on the Siegfried Line / West Wall between Stolberg and Aachen.

Lieutenant Jake Sitzes, company executive officer / platoon commander, selflessly led the fateful attack on the slag pile at the gates of Germany's Ruhr.

The crew of Sam Hogan's third command tank, the previous two having been "shot out from under them" during the fighting in France. (*Left to right*) Elmer Johnson, driver; Edward Ball, loader; and Clem Elissondo, gunner.

Colonel John C. Welborn, Thirty-third Armored Regiment commander (*left*), after presenting the Silver Star Medal to Sam Hogan for gallantry in action against a German counterattack during the breakout from Normandy. Büsbach-Stolberg, Germany.

(*Left to right*) Captain Edward Price, Major William Walker, and Captain Ted Cardon share a rare moment of relaxation during one of the tactical pauses to await supplies and/or replacements of men and equipment. Büsbach-Stolberg, Germany.

Task Force Hogan crosses the Weser River using a pontoon bridge erected by the Twenty-third Engineers, April 6, 1945. A T26 Pershing tank leads the column.

A Task Force Hogan mortar track enters a German town near Paderborn in spring 1945. Note the candy-cane-striped aiming stakes for ensuring the mortar stays on target despite recoil. A captured Panzerfaust antitank rocket can also be seen poking out of the back.

A Third Armored Division medic views the foul room where prisoners too weak to work were sent to die in the concentration camp at Nordhausen, liberated by the Third Armored Division in April 1945. The aftermath of the cruelty witnessed at Nordhausen haunted Sam Hogan for life and shook his faith in a higher power.

Task force commanders (*left to right*) Lieutenant Colonels Walter Richardson, William R. Orr, and Sam Hogan in Germany, 1945.

An older Sam Hogan (*left*), during better times, with his son and author of this book, Will Hogan, during a family cruise circa 2000.

Each curve was a possible ambush site. The high of expected contact cut through the fatigue as every set of American eyes scanned the woods surrounding them for enemy positions. Plateaus opened into small clearings for livestock, then turned into dense evergreen forests for miles around. The ridgelines gave way to ravines as the one-lane country road snaked dangerously close to twenty-foot drops into creek beds full of rocks, dead wood, and ice.

The cold, eerie night ended up resembling a tactical road march like the dozens conducted back in the US and England during training. The enemy was nowhere to be found. At 9:00 A.M., the red-eyed tankers arrived at Hotton—a quaint farming hamlet sitting astride the Ourthe on a slight ridge running northwest three miles to another village, Soy. There the combat command CP was going to set up in order to control the three task forces and any reinforcements, including the occasional stragglers from overrun units.

Hogan's mission was to recon in force, find the enemy, and hold until reinforcements could arrive. Thus, the task force had to travel light, especially in the narrow and winding roads ahead. Sam directed the Service Company to keep going west to Soy to team up with the regimental supply trains. The task force mortars would stay at Hotton, where they could support nearby units and help Colonel Howze hold the town.

After leaving the mortars, cooks, and clerks, Sam's column continued toward the objective of Houffalize. At 12:15 P.M. they arrived at the village of La Roche, again without contacting any enemy. La Roche (The Rock) was not as defensible as its name implied. At the bottom of a U-shaped bend of the Ourthe, the collection of stone houses around a tall church steeple looked to Sam like a miniature version of West Point. Overlooking the town and the bend in the river, a feudal lord had built a stone castle on the rocky foothills of the ridge. Behind the town and the ruined castle, the ridge steeply rose up three hundred meters. A one-lane country road snaked up the east side of the ridge, leading toward Houffalize twenty miles away.

The deserted center of town lay littered with abandoned trailers left behind by retreating US units upon learning that the Germans were coming in strength. Cartons of K rations and cigarettes spilled out of olive-drab trailers onto the cobblestone streets. The supply units from the Seventh Armored Division were still in town and greeted Sam's tankers with surprised looks. "Where in the world did you come from? Don't you realize the entire German Army is around us?" a frazzled troop guarding the center of town called out.

"Sir, are you here to relieve us?" was the optimistic greeting by their officer in charge, as his outposts were already receiving German incoming fire at the outskirts of town.

"Nope, my objective is Houffalize." The lieutenant's face sank as Sam continued: "You're going to hold this town as long as possible. I'll leave some help." To do this, and reassure the Seventh Armored loggies, he directed two of his attached M7 Priest howitzers to remain behind to bolster the little force—this would keep his own supply route to the rear open. Sam then instructed his key leaders to have their soldiers load up on the abandoned rations and cigarettes. After all, the vehicles' gas tanks were now below half-full, the enemy locations were still unknown, but definitely closer, and resupply seemed like a pipe dream under the circumstances.

The reconnaissance company (A, from Spearhead's own Eighty-third Reconnaissance Battalion) moved out ahead in a small combat patrol of nimble M8 Greyhound six-wheeled armored cars, with a Stuart light tank in the lead to check the route toward the objective and try to locate the enemy.

About a mile outside of town and heading up the steep incline out of the valley were felled trees blocking the road. The scout patrol slowed down as the roadblock came into sight. Out of the woods to their right and left, bright flashes and a *swoooosh* greeted them as Panzerfaust warheads left their tubes. Small-arms fire opened in staccato pops that echoed through the woods.

The Americans had found the German line.

In a matter of seconds, a Panzerfaust warhead hit the Stuart tank in the turret with a sickening pop, killing the artillery forward observer and wounding two more. Unbeknownst to the scouts, they had just run into leading elements of the 116th Panzer Division on their dash to their assigned river crossings of the Ourthe and Meuse on the way to Antwerp. The undergunned scouts returned fire—but their position on the narrow road, blocked by a rock wall cliff on the left and a twenty-foot drop to the river on the right, made it impossible to flank the road-block. The scouts pulled back.

Sam met the scouts to get the report. Doc Spigelman and his medics sprinted to the vehicles carrying the wounded. Puffs of condensation blew out of their mouths as they panted under the exertion of loading wounded men onto stretchers in the winter cold. Doc was in his element, calmly assessing, then directing his young medics where to bandage to stanch the bleeding and where to immediately start intravenous fluids.

Sam radioed back to report the casualties and was instructed to hold fast until morning, when he would receive further orders at 8:45 A.M. It was apparent that Colonel Howze had his own hands full fighting off enemy probes to Hotton and Soy. G Company and the recon elements set up a counter-roadblock, and Sam established his command post in an abandoned hotel on the banks of the Ourthe on the side of La Roche facing the newly identified enemy line. They waited at full alert for the dreaded sounds of the enemy's tank engines.

Against all expectations, the task force and Seventh Armored supply trains spent a quiet night guarding the 360-degree perimeter. The next morning, Sam swallowed some coffee before loading up in his peep with Sergeant Phil D'Orio and Private First Class Charles F. Gast at the wheel. Major Travis Brown followed in another peep with the recon platoon leader, Lieutenant Clark Worrell. Ted Cardon led a third peep with the extra firepower of three more riflemen aboard. Due to the chaotic and evolving situation, Stewart Walker took command of the perimeter while the little command group left to reconnoiter and receive their orders.

The trip started inauspiciously enough: "Sir, the battery on your peep ran down overnight," stammered Gast. The peep's radio battery was dead after being left on. But there was no time to waste, so Gast jump-started the vehicle and the little three-car convoy headed out, leaving their bedrolls behind with the expectation that they'd be back after a short meeting.

At the edge of town, a US picket called out to the three peeps, "The Germans are rolling grenades down the hill ahead from the bluff above!" Sam ordered them to push on as he lit another cigarette and cinched down his steel helmet. The peep drivers stepped on it, not just because of the supposed grenades, but because the task force needed to get its orders forthwith. The little convoy drove fast without encountering any grenades. To Sam's relief, the peeps cleared the outskirts of La Roche and the portion of road under the bluffs supposedly occupied by German infantry.

They were five miles out of town on their way to confer with Lieutenant Colonel Prentice "Iron Mike" Yeomans, the intrepid commander of the Eighty-third Recon Battalion.[5] The windswept road sloped upward, away from the depression occupied by La Roche. The Americans could only see fifty meters or so ahead as the road snaked around bends where the cliff dropped twenty feet into a creek on their right side and the upward slope of the ridge formed a wall on their left. Trees and a blanket of snow stood tall and thick to either side.

Could this road even hold tanks? Ice? Forget about it. It was a gloomy and cold morning, but it was light enough that Sam could discern tracked-vehicle marks on the dirt road ahead of them. He began wondering what could have made them when Clark Worrell's peep ahead of them ground to a gravelly halt.[6]

Twenty-five yards in front of Worrell's peep was a group of twenty soldiers standing around two American M3 half-tracks and a jeep chowing down from boxes of K rations. Two of the soldiers were wearing US-issued greatcoats—but the others wore German uniforms.

Worrell's peep was so close, he could see the Germans go wide-eyed. He mouthed the words *They're Germans, Colonel!* Sam clenched his jaw in a loud whisper: "Turn this thing around, Gast!" Gast slammed the peep in reverse and the little vehicle attempted to turn, lurching forward in the narrow confines of the road. The Germans, as surprised as the Americans, dropped their cans of looted US franks and beans to grab their weapons and attempt to destroy this little American patrol.

The peep stalled with a crunch of gears as Gast frantically attempted to turn it around, his turning radius limited by the narrow road bordered by thickets of evergreen trees covered in snow.

Meanwhile, Worrell, Travis Brown, and their driver abandoned the peep in front as the Germans peppered it with machine gun fire. Sam's peep emptied out, too, but his fleece-lined, British Royal Air Force boots slowed him. Stumbling and tripping, he managed to lunge into the woods, bullets clapping the ground hard on the tail of their mud-and-ice-encrusted tracks. The third peep in the line succeeded in driving off, bullets zipping after it.

The Americans sprinted into the woods for cover, where they continued until a ledge got them out of sight of the Germans on the road. D'Orio, Gast, Brown, and Worrell all arrived at the same drop, panting in misty clouds of warm breath. The Germans fired several machine bursts in their direction, but high over their cover of the earthen drop.

The crack and zip of rifle rounds going over their heads gave the Americans another jolt of adrenaline. They rushed up to push on into the woods and away from the Germans, who miraculously did not pursue them. Perhaps they feared an ambush. But most likely, they wanted to loot the Americans' belongings left in the two peeps. Sam felt a sting of anger as he realized his peep's back seat contained not only the cigarettes and extra rations they'd found along the way, but also Sam's bourbon-soaked Christmas fruitcake—only recently arrived in a care package from the United States. But he reckoned it was a fair trade for their freedom—maybe even their lives.[7]

"They were bad shots, weren't they?" panted Sam. "Let's keep moving." The five Americans pushed out and didn't stop until they arrived at the edge of the woods by a stream. They stopped and tried to listen for the sounds of a pursuing enemy over the sound of their panting and chronic, raspy winter coughs. The only sound was the twinkling, soothing stream flowing by.

Sam looked around at their flushed, worried faces. There's nothing like discovering early in the morning that the enemy is between you and the next unit, and that they're wearing American uniforms and driving around in US equipment, he thought to himself. Sam decided the best course of action was to continue cross-country and try to get around the Germans to reach Hotton or possibly Mike Yeoman's unit and some functioning radios.

The five Americans continued slogging through the woods in the direction of Hotton, away from the German roadblock they had run into. Suddenly, at a small clearing, they found that a mountain barred their route. *Keep moving.* They progressed in fits and starts, since they had to move with caution and the hilly woods and underbrush made the going very slow.

The sun dipped behind the mountain, beginning to darken the woods and make them even colder, when an explosion to their left rear startled them all. Machine gun rounds began flying high over their heads from the area of the explosion, but also in counterfire to their front. The five moved quickly, stooped along the bank of the stream until they reached its head. The shooting stopped and the five could hear voices in the distance that carried over the small cliff sheltering them.

After a few minutes they were able to make out that the voices spoke in English, but before they could call out to them, they heard the sound of a peep driving off. Soon after, they heard sounds of leaves crunching and digging on the cliff above them. Somebody was digging in. The five looked at each other.

"Brownie, what do you think?" They whispered ideas about what they should do. Was that a German patrol digging in after driving off the Americans? Was the American peep being driven by Germans posing as American GIs?, Or was it a US patrol? The questions were swiftly answered when German voices rang out above the cliff.

"Fritz?"

"Ja?" the digger responded.

"Was hast du da?" the first voice asked.

"Ich habe Panzerfaust," Fritz responded.

The Americans froze in place and waited.[8]

The presence of dismounted enemy infantry likely meant that the Germans were using their foot soldiers to move through the woods and cut off the American units. This was the 560th Volksgrenadier Division, supporting the panzers of the 116th Greyhound Division. "Fritz," digging a foxhole eight yards from the hiding Americans, was called back by his sergeant to another position twenty-five yards farther from Sam's hiding spot in the creek bed.[9]

This German outpost was a fraction of the force that swarmed the Belgian Ardennes around the small groups of isolated tankers holding the towns. Again, chidings of the *US Army Field Manual* rang in his ears: *Armored troops, when restricted to roads and defiles, unless frequent "turnarounds" are available, are particularly vulnerable to attack . . . defending towns with only tanks should be avoided.* Without US doughs to chase the Germans back into the woods, the US tanks were sitting ducks for enemy Panzerfausts. The game was on, and the Germans were moving pawns, knights, and rooks quickly.

Now, in the early full darkness of winter—a few dozen yards from a well-armed, entrenched enemy—the five Americans tried their best to stifle their coughs. Each one seemed louder to his comrades than their own and resulted in dirty looks from the non-coughers. Cold and hunger set in. Under cover of night, and not hearing any more voices, they quickly conferred and decided to leave their noisy steel helmets and move out with a thirty-second spread between them. Once out of earshot of the German position, they planned to reassemble and get back to friendly lines.

After about thirty minutes of stumbling through the darkness, boots catching on tree roots and faces scratched by tree branches and brush, Sam, Gast, and D'Orio met up and waited for Brown and Worrell. They waited, and waited some more. Something was wrong. Sam, Gast, and D'Orio huddled up under Sam's trench coat. The woods were quiet and cold, with only the occasional whistle of a shell flying overhead. The three fell into a shivering, broken sleep.

The sun rose, and there was still no Brownie or Worrell. Sam, Gast, and D'Orio moved out toward what they thought was the task force's last assembly area. They plodded through deep woods; Gast was on point, a pistol at the ready.

Gast halted and took a knee. Sam, at a low crouch, moved up next to him. "Sir, I just saw an American wandering through the woods back there." He pointed in the direction they had just come from. Was that another German saboteur? It was more likely that it was one of the stragglers of the Seventh Armored Division or 106th Infantry, separated from his unit and not captured or killed in the initial battle. If so, the sad sack was probably just as worried that the three Americans were Skorzeny commandos.

"Roger, let's keep moving," Sam replied.

The trio finally came upon a clearing on some high ground overlooking a battery of US M7 Priest 105-mm self-propelled howitzers. They descended from the ridge, always staying near the tree line and out of sight in case the men in the clearing were Germans with American gear. After a short walk, they came upon the edge of a Belgian village named Marcouray, where they found Task Force Hogan.

Major Stewart Walker, in command until Sam returned, was relieved to see his commander alive and walking toward him. It almost didn't work out that way: a task force tank had nearly shot at the trio as they looked down on the battery of howitzers from the tree line above.

Worrell's driver had made it back to friendly lines the day prior and informed Walker and Iron Mike Yeomans about what had happened to the command group after they ran into the German roadblock.

While Sam and his little group were on the run, Walker had received orders to move the task force back three hundred yards out of La Roche, as the Germans began surrounding the high ground, firing Panzerschreck rockets and machine guns at the US positions. The firing was the battle the five Americans had heard while hiding out in the woods.

After getting caught up on the action, Sam reported, "Major Brown and Lieutenant Worrell are still out there."

Were they already prisoners . . . or dead?

AFTER THE TWO GROUPS SPLIT up, Brown and Worrell had stumbled across a road, only to be fired upon by a German patrol. They ran back into cover, then made their way on a parallel route through the woods.

After a while of trudging through the woods, they stepped into a clearing, where Worrell heard voices in English. The two officers raised their hands, saying, "We're Americans!" The US infantrymen rushed the two officers until they had the muzzles of their rifles pressed against Brown's heart. The operations officer and scout platoon leader had found the US lines, but these were not Task Force Hogan soldiers.

Suspicious, the US sentries tried to quiz Travis on American popular knowledge.

"Who led the Yankees in RBIs?"

Brownie, one eye injured from running through the brush, hungry and exhausted, had had enough.

"You lousy, no-good, gaddam sonafabitch, tender-footed, dumbass Joe—we're Americans!"

The infantry sergeant lowered his rifle slowly, stiffened, saluted, and replied, "There's no way a German could cuss that well in a southern accent."[10]

SAM SAT IN HIS OWN little corner of the fog of war, mixed in with a dose of Murphy's law. He was witness to a fraction of the chaos that was happening within the fifty-mile-wide front that would become known as the Battle of the Bulge. They did not know it yet, but the close calls were just starting.

Task Force Hogan received new orders to move around the strong German positions in and around La Roche by shifting north toward

Amonines. But it was too late—the Germans already controlled the high ground on the hilltop village of Beffe. Again, this illustrated the problem of not having infantry to secure the tree line surrounding a position.

A thick, fluffy blanket of snow fell overnight on the twenty-second, then hardened. The battalion radio net reported that the headquarters mortar troops in Hotton were under attack. This meant that Task Force Hogan's enemies were to their northwest as well. Sam ordered everyone to mount up and move out as they tried to find a weak spot in the ring of German tanks that was closing in around them.

At 2:00 P.M., with G Company in the lead, they began the slight climb toward Beffe. Securing the hilltop crossroads at Beffe was key to any advance toward Amonines to reestablish contact with the Spearhead line that ran from Hotton to Spa. Fire greeted the Americans as they encountered an entrenched German force. Tank and machine gun rounds poured down at the advancing Shermans. Tom Cooper's lead tanks fired their 75-mm main guns at the muzzle flashes ahead, knocking out two American 57-mm antitank guns and an M3 half-track used by the enemy infantry.

Several of the German dismounts were in US uniforms, and the three tanks of G Company were not able to hold the ground gained without infantry support. A German counterattack of infantry led by two M4 Sherman tanks, presumably captured from overrun units of the Seventh Armored Division, pushed the Americans off the hill. Task Force Hogan pulled back to the only high ground left to them, six kilometers back at Marcouray—the hilltop crossroads village they had just left.

While the task force attempted to fight its way out, the enemy swarmed into the villages of Cielle and Marcouray's twin village on the other side of the Ourthe, Marcourt. A vise of Krupp steel, bearing the markings of the 116th Panzer and the 352nd Volksgrenadier Divisions, snapped shut around the outnumbered task force.

8

★ ★ ★ ★ ★

NEVER SURRENDER

DECEMBER 23–26, 1944

Task Force Hogan set up roadblocks at the seven roads leading into Marcouray, each composed of a Sherman tank and a scout machine gun nest. Three M7 Priest howitzers occupied a small plot in the northwest quadrant—in a pinch the artillery system could fire like a tank, but with a less accurate sight. They reestablished radio communications with Colonel Howze's command post at Soy and the mortars and assault guns at Hotton. Sam and his lieutenants took stock of what they had at their disposal to fight their way back to friendly lines. One member of the task force had been killed in action and seventeen wounded, under the care of Doc Spigelman. Medical supplies were running low. Doc especially needed O-positive blood as he tended to several jagged shrapnel wounds in arms and legs. Ammunition and food were at "yellow"—not critical, but in need of resupply within seventy-two hours.

The fuel situation was worse, at about one-third of a tank for each Sherman, half-track, M7 Priest howitzer, and scout car. Dividing the fuel between vehicles gave the task force a ten-mile range—just a hair under what they needed to make it back to their starting point. Even if they tried it, they would not be able to maneuver if engaged by a large German force like the ones already controlling the roads back to friendly lines.

The hilly terrain was key in the Ardennes. The side that controlled a hilltop crossroads dominated all its approaches. Sam decided to stay put and block the advancing Germans.

Marcouray, a village of about 140 residents, sat on an ideal defensive position overlooking the Ourthe, protected by the river on one side, woods on the other, and low, sturdy stone houses looking out for a thousand yards over most avenues of approach. The only weak spot was to the south and southeast, where the sloping terrain prevented overwatch from the town. Sam mitigated this weakness by pushing out a roadblock of scouts.[1]

Hogan reckoned it would take at least a regiment of Germans to drive them out. He gathered his commanders: "Gents, we have plenty of weapons, ammunition, and a good defensive position here—if Jerry wants it, they'll have to come and take it."[2] Sam inadvertently harkened back to Texas frontier days, when a Mexican army demanded Texas settlers surrender their little cannon, which they used to defend their town from Comanche raids. They'd hoisted a flag with a Lone Star, a cannon barrel, and the fighting words "Come and Take It." Thus started the territory's path to freedom and eventual statehood in the United States of America.

It was not bravado—Sam had learned that a calm confidence projected onto his troops was contagious. Soldiers look to their leaders, especially during times of uncertainty, fear, and stress. They would do their duty; he was confident in his boys—however, without resupply, they would not be able to hold off the Germans for very long.

Sam's faith in his troops was well placed. Around the perimeter, the soldiers were not idle. The sergeants and soldiers improved their defensive positions and were already engaging Germans on the other side of the Ourthe River. Sergeant Shorty Wright of the recon platoon lit up a German convoy with artillery as it tried to bypass the American position.

"Fire for effect!" crackled from Shorty's radio, and high explosives arced high through the crisp winter air, then descended before puffing in muffled explosions of hot shrapnel over the enemy convoy slightly over a minute later. Twelve trucks and Kubelwagens (the German jeep equivalent) went up in smoke and fire, to the cheers of the onlooking Americans.

Sam observed a turkey shoot as the Germans kept trying to reach a Kubelwagen. Every time they approached, Shorty dropped some steel rain on them until there was not much left of the little Kubel and whatever maps or codes the Germans were trying to salvage. After dark, the clearing skies and moonlight allowed the Americans to call in artillery as well as direct fire from tanks and M7 Priests on any sorties of the Germans advancing on their flanks.

At first light, Sam stepped out of the stone farmhouse to the heart-stopping sight of two German eight-wheeled armored scout cars loaded with troops screeching by his CP. He jumped back inside to radio the tank at the roadblock in the direction the German scouting party was headed, then he radioed the roadblock from which the Germans had just driven. The tank crew had been alert and ready, but condensation overnight had caused a mechanical failure.

"Sorry, sir, the turret froze up on me," Gunner Clem Elissondo radioed back. He had been unable to turn the turret to fire at the fast German scout cars roaring by. Scouts with the roadblock fired off a few rounds, but the enemy cars got through. The normally calm Sam let out a few expletives that might have thawed out the turret ring, then returned to the task of dealing with "enemy in the wire."

"South Roadblock, this is Six, prepare to engage enemy scout cars—over." The response came back crisp and clear: "Roger, Six, we're ready for them."

The G Company roadblock at the south end of the village was prepared. Inside the tank, the gunner aimed for the road that led down the hill from the CP. Suddenly the tall and fast German scout car came into view. "Hold . . . hold." If they fired too soon, the round could go through the scout car and into the US positions. The gunner turned the turret and aimed at the scout car, several German troops clinging to it. Some held on, while some jumped off and spread out in all directions. "Hold!"

Rifle fire began to rip as the German and US scouts exchanged potshots.

Once the scout cars cleared the friendly-held buildings, the tank commander ordered, "FIRE!" The breech rocked back and the round shot out and impacted the German scout car on the side, sending it rolling into a field.

"Load high explosive!"

"HE up!"

"FIRE!" A second round exploded out of the tube, hitting the crippled scout car again for good measure. The dozen or so German soldiers who'd been riding on the outside of it were dead or sprinting down into the tree line.

Sergeant Shorty Wright and Captain Ted Cardon took a patrol out and engaged the German dismounts, killing several more. Another patrol found five lying prone in a ditch near the road. Before anyone could stop him, a recon lieutenant drew his .45-caliber pistol and began firing at the incapacitated Germans. One was killed outright and a second was nicked before the lieutenant was stopped and disarmed. The remainder of the Germans were taken prisoner.

Sam was livid. Besides one of his men acting with inhumanity—the same inhumanity they were supposed to be fighting so hard against—now the task force was surrounded, in danger of being overrun, and there was a German corpse with a gunshot wound to the back of his head.

Things looked grim.

TEN KILOMETERS BACK, INSIDE FRIENDLY lines at Soy, were Task Force Hogan's own Service Company—where Mess Sergeant John Barclay, survivor of the "lost" supply convoy south of Mons—was becoming an expert at the traditional army game of "hurry up and wait."

It was a cold, dark night. Barclay and his two permanent KPs, Privates John Cambolito and Macario Candelaria, had just finished unloading a truckload of frozen turkeys; the captain wanted to cook up a Christmas Eve meal for the task force and get it through once the supply line was reopened to Marcouray. A dozen fifteen-pound turkeys were lined up in large field sinks thawing out to be cleaned, when the shouting started: *"The Germans are coming!"*

First Sergeant Rogers called out: "Barclay, load up and be ready in fifteen minutes. We're pulling back." Fifteen minutes later, having emptied out the pots and loaded up the wet, cold turkeys, they were waiting in their kitchen truck panting when the call went out: *False alarm.* They unloaded the turkeys again from the gut truck.

Twice more that night the alarm rang out—*"The Germans are coming!"*—and twice more Barclay and his KPs loaded and unloaded the frozen turkeys.

Cambolito and Candelaria got on each other's nerves, with the Mexican American venting at the Italian American, "Cambolito, you heel-beely," to chuckles from everyone.[3] By midnight, the little team was finally able to set up long enough to cook up roasted turkey with local brussels sprouts and fruitcake. Anyone who came through Soy on the twenty-fourth and twenty-fifth was fed—there was plenty of food, yet the cooks were aware that they could not push it through to their buddies sitting surrounded in Marcouray.

The other part of Task Force Hogan, the headquarters assault gun and mortar platoon, wasn't in the same predicament but still had their own hands full. They were up twelve kilometers northwest of Sam's position, on high ground among the hamlets of Hotton and Melreux, and Staff Sergeant Slack Schlaich and Sergeant John Grimes knew they were in trouble from monitoring the battalion radio net.

They also knew the Germans wanted Hotton—or, more accurately, its bridge over the Ourthe. Since dawn on the twenty-second, they'd fought off repeated probes as enemy units surged forward. Looking out the window of a small stone building the mortars were using as their fire direction center, Sergeant Grimes experienced the colon-clenching sight of a Panther tank three hundred meters away, advancing toward Hotton. The tank was astride railroad tracks leading straight to the little mortar section.

Grimes called out to his two section leaders: "Kozloski! Svoboda! Get your gear! Enemy tanks coming up!" But Charles "Dick" Svoboda and Kozloski were veteran hands from Mojave Desert maneuvers and were already moving.

The mortar crews clutched carbines and hugged the stone walls close as they tried to get back to their half-track.

"Ozark this is Hawk Seven, we have enemy tanks approaching our pos—over."

The call came back: "Acknowledged."

Svoboda looked at Grimes. "That's it?! Where are our tanks?!"

Grimes put a finger to his mouth. They heard the deep growl of the Panther's engine getting closer. Outside, shouts among the engineers and infantry rang out. "He's coming up the main road!" "Bazooka team up!"

"Get ready, we're going to make a run for it. I have one of those Jerry Panzerfausts in the track." Svoboda and the rest of the section lined up behind him. The staccato of the Panther's hull-mounted machine gun rang out like a typewriter from hell. "Get ready . . . GO!" The little section sprinted out of cover one by one, crouching low along the stone buildings to their waiting half-track.

Mortars weren't much use against a tank close up, so the Panzerfaust inside the half-track was their only hope. One more corner to turn, and the mortar section could fight back on more even terms. But suddenly there were two loud swishes and then, in quick succession, two dull explosions as several intrepid combat engineers ambushed the tank, taking it out with bazooka fire from the rear.

Sergeant Grimes's little section, Kozloski, Svoboda, and Debone (invariably called "Da Bone"), didn't end up having to use their souvenir Panzerfaust. They spent the remainder of the night firing flares and high explosives when the flares illuminated any enemy advance.

Even so, the Germans were somehow able to slip past Hotton through an enfiladed position, skirting the town to cut off the assault gun platoon in Melreux. They met stiff resistance from Schlaich's lightly armored, snub-nosed howitzers shooting in direct-fire mode. The uneven duel went on into the twenty-third. As Germans got closer, Schlaich called in artillery and mortars on them, disrupting their attack.

That night, Texan John Dozier—another cook from Headquarters Company—served up a Christmas Eve-Eve dinner of cold spaghetti noodles (no sauce, no meatballs).[4] As the frigid dark of evening grew near, the men in Melreux solemnly prepared to destroy their assault guns, now almost out of fuel and ammunition, and move by foot to rejoin their comrades in Hotton under the covering umbrella of their mortar fire.

BACK IN BESIEGED MARCOURAY, Task Force Hogan continued to exchange fire across the forested hills and fields surrounding the little town. Each time Shorty or Ted sighted German patrols, or checkpoints heard attempted probes of the perimeter, they received a volley of artillery fire. The Germans moved along the roads circling the US position. Just as the Americans had eyes on them, they could see the little stone houses on the hilltop, too.

German artillery fell on Marcouray, terrifying the few residents, made up of families of farmers and lumberjacks, who hadn't had time to evacuate. The able-bodied younger men were all off fighting in the Resistance or had left at the beginning of the war. In a few sturdy stone cellars, the remaining sixty civilians cowered. There was unspoken worry about the bloodshed that a strong tank assault, supported by German infantry coming out of the woods and artillery to keep the Americans pinned down, could do to the civilian population inside the little task force perimeter.

Colonel Bobby Howze's command finally got through on the radio after many replies of "Wait—over." Colonel Howze commanded the three task forces, several paratrooper units from the Eighty-second Airborne, as well as handfuls of stragglers from the Seventh Armored and 106th Infantry who had worked their way back to US lines.

Howze's headquarters started with what initially sounded like good news: "Two companies of paratroopers are fighting to clear the road in your direction." The radio operator smiled as he deciphered the message and handed it to Sam. But then the letdown: "They are proceeding on the line Soy to Hotton."

As the second part of the message was decoded, Sam sighed. US troops were trying to clear what had been Task Force Hogan's starting line two days earlier. That meant the enemy not only had them surrounded but surrounded in force. Ripping up the message, he called a leadership huddle.

No units were fighting their way toward Marcouray. They had their own battle to wage holding back the enemy in their own sectors. Artillery support, outside of the three howitzers on the perimeter, was stretched to the maximum. There was no word on resupply.

Doc Spigelman and his senior noncommissioned officer, Staff Sergeant Raymond Kuderka, ran the infirmary out of a farmhouse belonging to the Delcourt family. They were running out of medical supplies, especially plasma. For some of the wounded, all they could do was keep them warm in their stone basement aid station. Loss of blood and no plasma meant that several of the wounded men would only be able to survive a few more days.

In a sign of desperation, logisticians at division came up with the idea to attempt delivery of medical supplies via artillery shells shot into the perimeter. Their plan was to take special artillery canisters designed to carry propaganda leaflets and, instead of leaflets, to load them up with bandages, cotton, and plasma.

The Fifty-fourth Armored Field Artillery, A Battery's parent battalion, fired half a dozen shells into Marcouray—with everyone taking cover to avoid getting hit in the noggin with a thirty-pound shell full of meds. The artillery net radioed, "Medical shells on the way!" followed by "Shot out!" when the rounds left the tube. The rounds whistled in, landing with dull thuds after several minutes.

Troopers on the perimeter excitedly emerged from cover to find the rounds outwardly intact. After fumbling with frigid, gloved fingers and improvised tools they opened the canisters to reveal compacted pucks of gelatinous, wet cotton.

Doc and Sergeant Kuderka looked down at the useless contents and shook their heads. Shooting plasma-filled propaganda leaflet canisters into the perimeter had seemed like a good idea—but, sadly, the contents were shattered by the firing charge and ensuing G-forces necessary to shoot them out of the howitzers with enough range to reach the surrounded Americans.[5]

More mouths to feed trickled into the surrounded town during the evening hours. A tanker from H Company (which had been detached earlier from Task Force Hogan to support Bill Orr's First Battalion, Thirty-sixth Infantry) straggled into the perimeter—disheveled, dirty, and cold. The company had expended its two remaining tanks—the command tank and a bulldozer tank—on an attack, which prevented the encirclement of Bill Orr's command. The tankers, operating as foot soldiers alongside doughs of 1/36th Infantry, were isolated and pushed back into Sam's perimeter by the relentless enemy advance.

On Christmas Eve, in place of Jolly Old Saint Nick, appeared a young German lieutenant in a staff car bearing surrender demands. He drove up to the picketing tank astride the road to Beffe under a white flag of truce.

The sergeant of the guard, Clem Elissondo, radioed back to Sam: "Six, this is Security Post 4, you're not going to believe this, we have a German officer here under white flag demanding to see you."

Sam grabbed the microphone on the tank outside his command post: "SP 4, this is Six, I want you to blindfold him, drive him in circles around the village, then to this CP—over." The guard sergeant did just that. He blindfolded the German, then drove him around in a few circles to confuse him before escorting him in to meet the Task Force Hogan commander inside the stone farmhouse basement.

The staff officer announced, "I hef bin shozen for my English-speaking eh-beeleety"—and that was the extent of his English-speaking ability. He condescendingly presented a note signed by a German colonel-general (three-star equivalent) demanding surrender. It stated that three German panzer divisions surrounded the Americans and that their situation was hopeless. Doc Spigelman helped bridge the language gap with his Yiddish and Sam's meager German. Out of "a desire to avoid unnecessary bloodshed," the general offered to accept their surrender.

There was tension in the air, an uncomfortable pause. Now I know how the Texans felt at the Alamo, thought Sam. For the colonel raised on Lone Star lore and descended from frontier lawmen, soldiers, and pioneers, thoughts of the Battle of the Alamo surely surged up—uninvited, unwelcome.

Sam looked the German in the eyes, saying: "We have orders to fight to the death, and as soldiers we will obey those orders."[6]

Sam lit a Camel off the butt of his previous cigarette, partly to calm his nerves and partly to deceive the lieutenant that they had plenty of supplies to hold out. He exhaled the tobacco smoke. "All right, Sergeant, blindfold this gentleman and take him back out to his staff car." The young German looked down his nose in a sneer as he was blindfolded and escorted out of the perimeter.

Incoming radio transmissions from Colonel Howze's headquarters broke the tense quiet after the German departed back to his staff car. The Army Air Corps would attempt an aerial resupply of fuel and plasma. Sam advised the perimeter guard to keep an eye out and be prepared to send a patrol to recover the supply canisters—provided they didn't fall squarely within German lines.

Later that afternoon, seven C-47 cargo planes flew over La Roche with their cargo bay doors open. The Germans eagerly waited behind the sights of their 88-mm cannon until the C-47 crew chiefs pushed out the cargo. Once they saw the parachutes open up over the supply crates, they blasted away.

A massive FLAK barrage opened up. The German LVIII Corps headquarters, the 116th Panzer's parent unit, occupied La Roche, and immediately all but three of the cargo planes went down in smoke and the occasional bloom of a crew parachute. The GIs on the ground looking up booed and cursed angrily at the sight of their Air Corps brothers being hit so badly while trying to help them.

The planes flew so low that most soldiers looking on assumed the distance to be too short for a safe parachute opening. Still, two fliers—Staff

Sergeant Andre Mongeau and Sergeant Earl Mayo—eventually walked into the Task Force Hogan perimeter, scratched up and sore but unhurt.

Mongeau had jumped out of his stricken plane at 350 feet and his chute caught the top of some pine trees. The dense forests had broken his fall, but he was trapped in his harness hanging several feet off the ground when he heard German voices nearby. Releasing his harness straps, the twenty-three-year-old Mongeau stealthily dropped to the ground, then ran off into the woods, where he bumped into his fellow crew chief, Earl Mayo. The pair avoided German patrols and headed in the direction the V-1 rockets were flying, figuring that would lead them toward friendlies.[7]

After skirting some woods and crawling through a clearing, they came to a slope rising toward a hilltop town. A sharp command of "HALT!" froze the two fliers, who immediately threw up their arms. Two unshaven GIs approached them menacingly with carbines leveled. A check of Mongeau's dog tags earned the two fliers relief.

"Arms down, boys—you're in the hands of Task Force Hogan." The disciplined sentries didn't shoot them on sight, as less-methodical soldiers were doing across the front after hearing all the stories about the German commandos dressed in US uniforms.

GIs led the airmen back to the stone farmhouse-turned-command-post, issued them carbines, and allowed them to catch a nap in the CP. Lying in the safety of the farmhouse cellar, Mongeau felt safe despite knowing the unit was surrounded. He was impressed with the disheveled-looking soldiers, how they did not complain or fear the outcome. They had full confidence that their commander would get them out of this mess.[8]

As for the supplies, none landed anywhere near the task force perimeter. Four thousand gallons of fuel, rations, and medical supplies drifted away from the American position toward the enemy lines. The supplies landed in German-held Marcourt—an unfortunate spelling similarity with Marcouray. The airplane crews had taken off from England earlier in the day with only vague instructions about where on the map to drop their supply canisters. Sometimes, bravery is not enough to overcome the fog of war.

There were two more heroic attempts to resupply the task force, with similar results—the Germans receiving a Christmas bonus of fuel and medical supplies from the sky. With irreverent good humor, on the twenty-fifth, Sam had his radio operator send in the transmission: "Everything quiet. Request SITREP [situation report]. Request Xmas turkey be dropped by parachute."[9]

Patrols sent out on Christmas Eve returned with more bad news. There were no passable firebreaks or roads out that weren't saturated with Germans. Even if they could get through a roadblock, regimental-sized units of the 116th Panzer Division choked up all lanes as they streamed around Marcouray toward Hotton. Sam dutifully relayed this intelligence to higher headquarters via encrypted radio message.

Monty allotted General Rose a regiment of the Seventy-fifth Infantry Division and told him, "This is it"—there was no other Allied reserve. Every combat unit was committed. Sam sent up, in code, "Tell them to be aggressive." Two hours later, the troops from the Seventy-fifth's attack stalled out against the superior numbers surrounding Marcouray. Unlike the 101st Airborne, also surrounded twenty kilometers away, no help was coming for Task Force Hogan.

They were on their own.

IT TURNED OUT TO BE a white Christmas, but not one that evoked fond memories. Many soldiers, including Sam, would never be able to hear the Bing Crosby song again without feelings of isolation, cold, hunger, and impending doom.

Sam walked the perimeter to check on his soldiers, but also to clear his mind. It was bitterly cold outside. At least the wind's died down, thought Sam. Stars poked through the overcast sky here and there.

Whether on radios calling in artillery or walking the perimeter to check any enemy probes, the soldiers felt cold and lonely—cut off from friendly units, they thought of previous holidays spent with families in the warmth and safety of home.

Several soldiers coming off a guard shift took a little time to eat a

Christmas Eve dinner of cold K rations, sharing it with a few of the local villagers who were trapped with them. Twenty villagers sheltered at the Techy farmhouse, and twenty more in the sturdy home of Valère Raskin.[10]

Sam nodded at the local parish priest, Pastor Chariot, who was also making his rounds offering comfort. His little church had been devastated by several German artillery hits. "O Holy Night" sprang up in a haunting chorus from the lips of the villagers.[11] The Americans within earshot whispered along or said a Christmas prayer for salvation and protection for the civilians left behind in the little town. Everyone knew the danger to life and limb posed by the coming German assault on the town.

Sam followed the cobblestone road, paying special attention to his footing so as not to twist an ankle on the slippery stone. Explosions on the horizon looked like far-off lightning. He checked up on the roadblock. Watchful and pensive were Shorty Wright, Ted Cardon, and Rob Resterer. He walked farther.

"We can take 'em, sir," said a chatty Clem Elissondo, watching from his gunner's hatch as he munched on a cold biscuit. No frozen turret ring this time—he'd procured a small blowtorch, and used it periodically to warm the seam where the turret met the hull. Morale was high despite the circumstances. The commander was proud of his men.

Out on the perimeter, it was impossible to see anything past the dense woods that surrounded the little town. A couple of hours after dark, the US roadblocks shot up German patrols probing for weak spots. The machine gun fire lit up the cold night for a few brief minutes, then died down as the enemy probes pulled back. Tanks exchanged potshots and the American artillery remained sighted on all roads coming into Marcouray. Artillery missions were fired "in the blind"—aiming as best they could where the scouts heard the heavy clanking and diesel motors of enemy tanks.

They spent the rest of Christmas Eve in an unnerving wait for a German attack. For those resting, the cold made sleep almost impossible. Involuntary shivering clashed with fatigue as soldiers tried to catch some shut-eye and teams took turns on and off guard.

CHRISTMAS DAY WAS CLEAR. THERE was an inch of snow on the ground, and the crisp cold held the promise of a fresh start. A message came in around noon—once decrypted, it spelled out an order signed by General Rose. It ordered the task force to destroy all heavy equipment and make their way back to friendly lines as best they could, and wished them good luck. Sam gathered his commanders and their sergeants—they would take the rest of the daylight hours to destroy equipment and documents and prepare to move.

The plan was to move out in groups of twenty soldiers as soon as it got dark. Every thirty seconds one of the groups would march into the woods.

"Scouts will lead the way, but it's imperative that each soldier keep visual contact with the fella to his front and the one behind him," Sam guided his men. "Otherwise, we'll be like a herd of housecats out there going in different directions, lost in the woods."

All soldiers were to leave their helmets behind and darken their faces with burnt corks, ash, or axle grease. Drivers and track commanders moved swiftly: pouring sugar into gas tanks, then running engines a few at a time until they cracked up and shut down. Weary soldiers slashed tires and jammed handfuls of dirt and sand into transmissions.

Tank main guns were harder to destroy without explosions alerting the enemy of what was happening. The discreet method was to remove the breeches (the back part of the cannon that closes behind the round) and drop them in the nearest well, or bury them in the hard ground. This worked too with their individual firearms—once the soldier took out the firing pin or trigger assembly, a pistol or rifle became useless as a firearm.

The lead scouts would have their full load of ammunition and weapons. Trailing elements would keep only their sidearms with a few rounds of ammunition. One accidental discharge of a rifle or pistol would doom the entire exfiltration, resulting in their death or capture.

The orders from Sam filtered down—nothing was to be left for the Germans to loot. He invited the Belgian civilians to help themselves to the remaining rations, extra coats, and any scrap metal they could salvage.[12]

What to do with the seventeen wounded soldiers, including those hit in the initial ambush on A Company of the Eighty-third Recon Battalion? Doc Spigelman, Staff Sergeant Raymond Kuderka, and a handful of medics volunteered to stay behind with the wounded. Sam and Doc fully knew the risks of a Jewish doctor being captured by the Germans, but Doc refused to leave his wounded behind. They had a plan to get out, but it was very risky. There was no guarantee of success, and in the case of failure, there was no guarantee that the hell-bent-for-leather Germans wouldn't execute prisoners—as they'd already done in nearby Malmedy.

The seven enemy prisoners captured after their scout cars entered the perimeter were another headache to deal with—not to mention their comrade now in full rigor mortis with a .45-caliber entry wound to the back of the head. Several of the less-wounded soldiers guarded the German prisoners, who were loaded, along with the non-ambulatory US wounded, onto the last remaining motor vehicle—an ambulance. The unwounded German prisoners were to be released into the woods at sunup.

The German corpse was buried as deeply as possible in the frozen ground, then covered with brush. The dead US artilleryman was given the regulation burial, with location information recorded for his eventual recovery and exhumation.

Slightly wounded soldiers who could walk without assistance—such as Sergeants Luis Alamea and Everett Bunker of G Company, their shrapnel wounds to the head bandaged up—joined the main body drawing up to escape the German encirclement.[13]

The preparations made, the task force waited until full darkness embraced the surrounding woods to make the estimated ten-mile trek back to Spearhead lines. It was colder than hell. Sam walked over to the battalion infirmary to say goodbye to Doc, his medics, and the wounded.[14]

Back at the command post, radio operators sent and received a final transmission before smashing the radios and coding devices to pieces at the end of a rifle butt. The decoded reply had been long and ominous: "All preparations made—acknowledged. A patrol from the

Eighty-second Airborne will guide you into friendly lines. Challenge and password are 'Final'—'Edition'—out."

Some GI at headquarters had a macabre sense of humor.

Colonel Howze added a personal note to the transmission: "Good luck. God bless you." As nighttime cloaked the forest, amplifying every sound, sentries heard the rumble of German vehicles on the roads around the perimeter to the south. It was time to get moving.[15] The long column, over four hundred men—scouts, tankers, and artillerymen—spread out and took a knee in their respective squads. The last man in the group that just moved out tapped the kneeling point man of the following squad. This started another thirty-second count, then the point man rose, hand signaled his group to move, and began their march quietly out of the shadows of the stout stone buildings that had protected them and into the blackness of the forest, bathed in dark-blue moonlight.

At the head of the column was a Missouri woodsman turned army scout named Lee Brenson Porter. Staff Sergeant Porter was a master huntsman and survivalist. He had helped raise his siblings after his mother died in childbirth, and his skills traversing woods and fishing in rivers put food on the table. In his element, he glided through the forests of southern Missouri with the stealth of a mountain lion on the hunt. Never was there a better man for a job.

For most everyone else, it was hard going following the uneven, frozen terrain. The cold numbed their feet and hands, making it harder to sense the folds of the ground under an inch of snow. Men twisted their ankles in the brush or tripped on tree roots they couldn't see. Little sleep or food over the past forty-eight hours made everything worse.

After a handful of squads had moved out, and with the majority of "the 400" still inside the perimeter, one of the tanks they'd heard moving around the perimeter fired a main gun round within view of the wide-eyed soldiers trudging through the woods. The round crashed into Marcouray and got the column shuffling quickly through the woods, some tripping and picking themselves up or helped along by the buddy behind them.

Once clear of the perimeter, the 400 were now in enemy-held territory. They stumbled down a ridge cut through by intermittent streams. Sam had lost his regular combat boots to the Germans who looted his peep. Instead, he was still wearing the heavy, fleece-lined RAF aviator boots that he used for long wintry rides in the open. They were great for keeping warm while flying in unheated bombers or riding in the turret of a tank or passenger side of the peep, but terrible for hiking. The terrain descended and then ascended so steeply that most soldiers got on all fours to get a grip, feeling their way and attempting to not slide backward. Sam's heavy boots meant two steps up, one step sliding back. On the downhill part, you slid on your ass, feet first.

The ground leveled off a bit, then rose again as the column weaved its way across the various streams crossing the ridge.

The streams or any clearings were—in tactical parlance—"danger areas" that needed to be crossed carefully. The leading scout, the point man, would arrive at the edge of the clearing and signal a halt by raising his right hand above his head. The second man moved up to cover the clearing opening while the point man dashed forward to check the other side. Once there, the point man signaled back across the gap to the second trooper that all was clear. In this way, the squads began crossing one by one. Each man moved up and took a knee, awaiting a signal from the point man to sprint across the open area and back into the cover and concealment of the woods. The last man, or "rear guard," must have been very lonely. The process was dangerous and time-consuming.

At about midnight, the head of the column passed by German troops digging in. Commands rang out in German, with soldiers grumbling in guttural German as they labored with entrenching tools, sounds common to any army in the field. The only difference was the language spoken. It was too late to move the route of the march, but the point man steered away from the sounds of spades hitting frozen ground and the German sergeants barking instructions to their squads.

The march continued, unending. Sam would look at the stars above and think, One foot in front of the other—that's all you have to do. The night was eerie. At times, fog cloaked the low folds in the terrain.

As the squads ascended from the depressions, they looked like ghosts. The only sounds were the occasional exhalation or crunch of branch underfoot.

Toward the front of the long line, a horrible screeching startled everyone as a wild pig darted in and out of the column, even more frightened than the soldiers. The marching continued, with thick brush scratching faces as the men struggled to move forward through the shadows of the dense forest. They encountered another German unit off their flank, this time an artillery battery. The GIs could hear the staccato of firing commands in the enemy's language.

On they moved through the moonlight, the scouts leading the way. At about 3:30 A.M., the column spread out wide and the lead element of scouts reached yet another German unit. This time, a sentry heard the trudging of feet and challenged into the darkness: "Halt! . . . *Wer gehts?!*" The silhouette of a large figure in a trench coat and distinctive German coal-bucket helmet was the source of the challenge. A machine pistol appeared in the shadows in front of him. The Americans within earshot froze and swallowed hard as they considered their options . . .

If anyone fired a shot at the sentry, it would alert whichever unit he was guarding. A firefight in the middle of the woods with an enemy in unknown numbers was just what Sam wanted to avoid. The tension in the air was as thick as the hot, visible breath puffing out of the German's mouth.

Without wasting another moment, Sergeant Lee Porter sprang into action. As the German sentry squinted into the darkness and repeated his challenge, the lithe and tall scout stepped out of the column and sprinted—full of adrenaline—around a tree and behind the sentry.

Several bounds and only a handful of seconds later, Porter was behind the German, covering his mouth with his left hand while plunging his bayonet into his throat with his right. The German kicked, emitted a gurgling sound from his punctured esophagus, stiffened, then went limp. Porter lowered him to the ground gently, then signaled the men to keep moving. The column marched on, speechless. They had gotten lucky.[16]

Nobody but the first half dozen soldiers in the column realized how close to discovery they'd come. They slogged along, "accordioning" as the distance between each man increased or shortened depending on their level of fatigue and the roughness of the terrain.

Back near the tail of the column, Sam, D'Orio, and Gast slowed down significantly. Their commander squinted in the dark, trying to keep visual contact with the others. *Keep an eye on that silhouette in front of you.* Every so often, the silhouette ahead suddenly vanished and there would be a short second of panic. Then a crunch of snow and brush, a whispered curse: *Fuck!* The shadow ahead had only tripped and fallen. Catching up, Sam helped Gast to his feet. Onward they moved.

The trio stayed together but drifted more toward the back of the column. Close to dawn, Sam's feet—always suffering from fallen arches—gave out. Sam gave his two companions an understanding look and a fatigued grin that intimated wordlessly his desire for them to keep going with the formation. The two soldiers looked at their commander and shook their heads in refusal. D'Orio and Gast refused to go on without him, and the three again took shelter under Sam's trench coat for an hour or so of rest.

The azure glow of the coming daybreak woke them out of a restless slumber, with teeth chattering and uncontrollable shivering in the bone-numbing cold. The beauty of shimmering ice reflected the first golden rays of dawn and were lost on the fatigued, nearly hypothermic men. The trio resumed the march. They came across abandoned equipment, patches of dirty olive-drab and field gray spoiling the lily-white blankets of snow—a unit, defeated there, had left their equipment behind. Spent shell casings twinkled here and there like fallen Christmas ornaments. The three moved past with only slight interest.

At the edge of a field, they saw a little village in the distance. There was a voice cutting through the crisp air. It sounded like English, but they couldn't be sure. They crept closer to get within earshot.

"Down Five-Zero—fire for effect," a radio squawked, the commands echoing on the other side of a radio.

American troops!

As they got closer to where the voices came from, the trio froze at the yelled command: "Halt! Put down your weapons." They did as they were told. "Come forward with your hands up." Sam, Gast, and D'Orio complied.

Two sergeants from the Seventy-fifth Infantry—a fresh outfit, recently rushed to the front—leveled their carbines at them.

Sam identified himself, but the sergeant hardly needed the introduction: "Sir, we've heard all about you all. Welcome back." The three got a ride back to a command post, then a waiting jeep took them to the division headquarters, recently emplaced at Soy. On the way there, the sergeants said they saw the three at the edge of the field and figured they were Germans. One wanted to light them up but the other wanted to find out who they were first. Sam's group had been lucky that the second soldier won the argument.

IT'S TOUGH TO OVERSTATE HOW difficult it is to move four hundred soldiers through wooded, snow-covered terrain at night—a feat that would be difficult enough in peacetime, much less through a gauntlet of German tanks and infantry. The main body of "Hogan's 400" came out of the woods on a road between Hotton and Soy, in an area controlled by the US Seventy-fifth Infantry Division.

The units on the front had been notified overnight that Task Force Hogan would be passing into friendly lines. Unfortunately, one machine gunner from the 290th Infantry Regiment, Seventy-fifth Infantry Division, carelessly propped up his Browning automatic rifle (BAR) on a tree. In the rush to greet the Hogan's 400, the BAR fell over and shot out a stray round. The slug hit one of the Task Force Hogan soldiers in the thigh as they limped into the perimeter. The BAR gunner cursed himself and apologized profusely to the wounded man. But, miraculously, that was the only casualty of the Christmas Day retrograde.

At Hotton and Soy were the task force mortars, the assault gun crews (sans vehicles), and the Service Company, each with their own tales to tell of German attacks stopped by barrages of artillery and mortar fire. A jeep pulled up and radioed back for trucks to take the exhausted troops back to Soy for their first hot meal in days. Sergeants John Grimes and John Barclay were only too happy to be drivers in a group of a dozen 2.5-ton trucks sent to pick up their lost brothers, now safely back within friendly lines.

In the afternoon of the day after Christmas, the entire battalion, Travis Brown and Clark Worrell included, finally reunited at a stone farm compound in Soy. Cooks dispensed cups of hot coffee and soup into canteen cups or empty ration tins. Exhausted smiles abounded.

A little while later, a peep pulled up—it bore a small red plaque with two stars on its front bumper. Sharply dressed as always, General Rose leapt out of the cab toward the gathered officers. Sam, with his men around him, face still camouflaged, his head bundled against the cold, stood tall in front of General Rose. Sam didn't know if he would get dressed down, relieved of command, or congratulated.

Immaculate in riding breeches, tie, and a polished helmet, in front of his disheveled subordinate, his hands on his hips, General Rose reassured Sam that after a couple of days of rest, his unit would be outfitted with new tanks. He then asked Sam in his businesslike, commanding voice why he was the last one out. Sam thought of several heroic things to say and finally elected for the truth: "My feet hurt." General Rose cracked a rare smile, patted Sam on the back, and returned to his peep. After a short tactical road march, Hogan's 400 camped at Barvaux, where they remained through the New Year to reequip and reorganize.

BACK IN SURROUNDED MARCOURAY, Doc Spigelman and Staff Sergeant Ray Kuderka awaited daybreak. The ruse had worked. The Germans still believed the town to be occupied. As planned, Doc and Kuderka assembled their motley crew of wounded soldiers and, under Red Cross flags and impromptu white flags made from ripped bedsheets, began marching out of town to reach the US lines themselves.

They were a sorry sight—the limping, bandaged soldiers supporting each other, several medics and the less wounded slipping and struggling with the litters. After a short march, they reached the first German roadblock, where astonished sentries did not know what to make of them.

Doc summoned his best "command voice" and, with his Yiddish and pointing to the Red Cross flag, stated, "*Rot Kreuz!* This is a group of wounded under a Red Cross protection. You must let us through per the Geneva Conventions." The German wounded—inside the trailing ambulance—stayed put, under guard of other US wounded laid out on the suspended bunks inside. The German guards lowered their weapons and made way for the little caravan.

Spigelman and Kuderka flashed tired smiles at each other as they rounded the bend of the little country road headed west toward Hotton. They trudged along for another kilometer, with some of the wounded grimacing in pain but with nobody moaning. They were moving, and toward friendly lines at that, so there was hope.

They approached another checkpoint, this one manned by soldiers and a grizzled-looking sergeant. A machine gun position covered the roadblock, composed of a half-track and staff car. Again, Doc confidently approached, pointing to the Red Cross flag above his head, and Kuderka pointing to his armband.

"Geneva Convention! *Rot Kreuz!*" The grizzled sergeant looked skeptical, but let them approach. At about twenty-five meters, the sergeant gave Doc a look of pity, then waved his soldiers to let them through.

After this second roadblock the group was feeling optimistic. Maybe another couple of hours' march and they would come up to a US picket, where they could get water, food, and morphine. Doc and Kuderka could set up some plasma flows for the worst of the wounded. This hopefulness caused the pace to pick up just a little despite the fatigue.

Kuderka and Doc took their turns carrying the heavy litters. Around yet another bend in the dirt road, they laid eyes on a menacing group of figures in winter camouflage gathered around a towed antitank cannon. Doc swallowed hard in his parched, achy throat. This time *"Rot Kreuz!"* came out in a scratchy, low-pitched croak. Still, pointing at the Red Cross brassard on his shoulder, Doc stepped closer to the German position. Assault rifle barrels trained at Doc and Ray's midsections. The German in charge called *"Halt!"* then reached for his radio. Crackles of static followed by a brief exchange of angry radio chatter. The German motioned for Doc to come closer. In broken English, he explained that they must wait at this roadblock until "completion of our upcoming attack."[17]

The Americans collapsed in heaps by the side of the road. Doc and Ray checked on them and offered what they could. A short while later, the German marched up and angrily ordered the group to their feet. The German attack had not gone as planned—by then, word got back that the American fighters holding up progress at Marcouray had exfiltrated back to their own lines.

"AHP! STEEND AHP!" bellowed the German sergeant, brandishing a machine pistol at the exhausted Americans. Doc and Kuderka exchanged glances of sadness mixed with faux encouragement. *We were almost there . . . almost . . . but we will survive.* Spigelman, his medics, and the ambulatory wounded slowly got to their feet and raised their hands. They were now prisoners of war.

To the south of the Spearhead positions—thirty-six miles away—the 101st Airborne Division's acting commander in Bastogne, Brigadier General Anthony McAuliffe, made history with a succinct reply to German demands for surrender: "Nuts!" The day after Task Force Hogan's return to friendly lines, Sam's friend from the Academy, Creighton "Abe" Abrams, in command of the Thirty-seventh Tank Battalion—a part of Patton's Third Army—was able to break the ring around Bastogne, saving their paratrooper comrades-in-arms.

For Task Force Hogan, it was a Christmas miracle—evacuating four hundred men across ten miles of enemy-held forest, covered by parts of three German divisions. Their nighttime escape captured the front page of the *Stars and Stripes* under the headline: "From Mouth of Hell Came the 400." Stateside news outlets picked up the story as well, and the band of exhausted, grit-faced soldiers became minor celebrities to their families, friends, and neighbors back home. After a few hours of shut-eye in the large stone barn at Soy, the Spearhead GIs only wanted some warm chow, a change of clothes, and a few functioning vehicles so they could get some payback.

9

★ ★ ★ ★ ★

THE SCOTCH BET AND
THE ROSE POCKET

The Ardennes counteroffensive (remembered in history as the Battle of the Bulge) took place during the bitterest winter to impact the region in a hundred years. The US Army was surprised by the enemy and was beaten back violently, but it held and then fought back. It was the largest battle involving US forces in the entire war. Spearhead sustained battle losses of 125 medium tanks, 38 light tanks, and 1,473 casualties, including 187 killed in action. The battle began on December 16, 1944, but the Germans would not be pushed back to their starting positions for another six weeks.[1]

TF Hogan paused for a few days to reintegrate its three tank companies, reequip, and welcome back soldiers wounded since July. Carl Cramer was among them. He returned to duty on December 29, after recovering from the wounds he received fighting for Stolberg. He'd been itching to get back to his company, who welcomed him with tired smiles and good-natured teasing that he "missed a big one."[2]

Somewhere within the haze of cold, tiredness, and the whirlwind of tasks to get the battalion ready, 1944 had become 1945. Sam shared a sip of bourbon from his flask with Brownie, D'Orio, and Gast and toasted a new year that might end in peace and homecoming.

The Americans struck back on January 3, 1945. It was time to "wipe out the Bulge" and retake the Belgian towns that had changed hands repeatedly in the Great War, and in the current one at least three times. The Germans had expended their last reserves of men and materiel gambling on their failed offensive. Still, they held an edge in advanced equipment, fanatical ideology, and the advantage of interior lines (the concept of being able to shuttle a smaller number of troops along the interior of your defensive lines, while the attacker is forced to move along a wider front). More vicious house-to-house, hand-to-hand fights for major German cities loomed large ahead.

Rumor was also already circling that Spearhead was to ship off to the Pacific theater of operations as soon as Berlin capitulated, in order to lead the way across the Japanese home island to Tokyo. How did any of these soldiers expect to survive another year of combat? For Sam, he maintained his confident calm. Take the days as they come. One at a time. Just like on the twenty-five-mile marches at Camp Pickett and Fort Indiantown Gap back stateside.

Put one foot in front of the other—get to your objective.

On January 7, 1945, Spearhead elements liberated Marcouray—or "Hogan's Crossroads," as it had been christened by division troops. The Germans were not able to use any of the equipment that'd been left behind.[3] Doc Spigelman and his medics were still gone—for all their friends knew, taken prisoner by the Germans, or possibly worse. Sam could only hope they were alive and marching east toward the relative safety of a Stalag Luft, a German Air Force POW camp.

But the odds weren't entirely stacked against the Americans.

New tanks arrived on low-bedded tractor trailers ("low boys") and the crews got busy unloading them. Fresh coats of olive-drab paint, but no white star to serve as aiming points for the German cannon. Clem Elissondo and Elmer Johnson happily clambered onto their new ride. This was an M4A3E8—an "Easy Eight" Sherman, with a bigger turret and a slightly larger gun, at 76 mm. It could definitely hold its own against a Mark IV at any distance. The slightly bigger diameter than the 75 mm was good, though the powder charge remained small, so fighting face-to-face with a Panther or Tiger was still a bad idea.

Sam strolled up to the formation with a brand-new tanker's helmet on. He set foot on the Sherman road wheel, then vaulted up to the hull. With a grin, he greeted Elmer Johnson, whose head poked out of the driver's hatch, then he slid up onto the turret and into the commander's hatch. Though the tank smelled new, it felt somewhat like home. Sam reached down for the microphone cable, plugged it in to his helmet, and called out, "Clem, Elmer, how do you read me?"

Task Force Hogan rolled again—rearmed, but with only twelve medium and ten light tanks. GIs of the Eighty-third "Thunderbolt" Infantry Division fell in for support. C Company, still riding the lightly armed and armored M3 Stuart tank and untouched by the previous weeks' heavy fighting, would bear the brunt. The columns moved across roads choked with German vehicles destroyed by US artillery in the preceding weeks. But the enemy was not in a disorganized retreat. Rather, Hitler ordered two SS panzer divisions to cover the withdrawal—the Ninth and the Second (nicknamed "Das Reich," which had been their deadly opponent at Mortain). Sam, Carl Cramer, John Barclay, and many others must have wondered how much longer they could go on. *One foot in front of the other.*

The Nazi war crimes continued as the SS units fought fanatically to cover the enemy withdrawal. On January 7, C Company was hit hard when one of its platoons, led by Lieutenant John Modrak, a replacement officer only with the unit since early November, hit a mined intersection near the crossroads town of Fraiture. The mine's blast penetrated the hull, shredding the metal inward. The command tank filled with smoke as a recently concussed Modrak dragged his driver out of the stricken light tank. Tech 5 Joseph Gorczyca's right foot was dangling at a ninety-degree angle, held to his leg only by some skin and tendon.

But the crew managed to exit the tank, as did Modrak with the wounded soldier in tow. Once out and on the sludgy ground, the lieutenant fashioned a tourniquet out of his belt to stop Gorczyca from bleeding out. Suddenly, the tree line exploded with small-arms fire and rockets. It was an ambush, and they were in the middle of the kill zone. Modrak fired his .45-caliber pistol until an enemy bullet shot away his index and middle fingers. Panzerfaust rockets hit their wingman tank, also injuring its crew.

SS infantry rushed out of the woods, surrounding the wounded tank crews. They strode purposefully, leveling their StG 44 assault rifles at the dazed and injured Americans lying on the ground. *BRRRT*—a burst of fire at almost point-blank range, as a wild-eyed SS sergeant strode about shooting the wounded Americans. Joe Gorczyca, Private Ralph Baker, and Tech 4 Waitman Simons were executed as they lay on the ground.

Modrak, clutching his injured hand, shouted at the Germans: "Don't kill my men!" One walked over menacingly, machine pistol in hand.

"You are an officer, yes?" asked the German.

"Yes!" Modrak replied. "And I demand you give my men the treatment accorded prisoners of war!"

Modrak's reaction stopped the Nazis' bloodlust. Instead of killing Modrak and Private First Class Wilbert Forsythe, the Germans began searching the Americans, taking their watches, compasses, and billfolds. Modrak's wallet contained a picture of his wife and baby.

It was 4:00 P.M., and the sun was going down as the SS dragged the surviving Americans into the woods to their command post. A little while later, the SS returned with the commander of the second Stuart, Sergeant James Clark. Modrak's shock wore off and turned to anger. He demanded that his men be taken to a hospital. The demands fell on deaf ears.

By nightfall, Modrak heard the sounds of approaching US tanks punctuated by rifle fire. The Germans began packing up as they prepared to retreat. Modrak asked again of a German medic to be taken to a hospital. The medic replied coldly that the Americans were to remain in place.

At 9:00 P.M., the SS squad began moving out. Modrak thought that maybe they would let them be. The last one out, the SS sergeant, coldly walked up to the semiconscious Forsythe, drew a pistol, and shot him in the head. Another shot rang out near where Sergeant Clark lay.

Modrak closed his eyes and turned his head. Then the SS man walked to Modrak, fired, turned around, and strode into the dark woods.

Modrak woke up a little later in a pool of blood. The blood was coagulated and freezing. It was pitch black in the woods. *Was he dreaming?* He couldn't believe he was alive. The bullet was a low shot that passed through his groin, coming out at an angle that almost severed his private parts.

He felt the anger surge back. He refused to die in those cold woods. He had a wife and child to get back to. Crawling, gripping bushes and tree trunks, he made his way back to the road. Adrenaline and anger kept him going. He crawled several more feet—his hands were numb and his body shivered from blood loss. Surely, the road they were ambushed on was ahead. Keep crawling, he thought.

He crested out of the woods onto a road shoulder. One last push with his tired legs and he'd be able to see the ambush site. He heard chatter in English and an idling tank engine. He heaved himself up out of the ditch and onto the country road.

That's when he saw "the most welcome sight in the world"—a Task Force Hogan tank. The crew was securing the area and recovering the bodies of the American dead. Modrak was soon safe and on his way to the field hospital for treatment.[4]

One foot in front of the other.

AT THE HAMLET OF BIHAIN, Belgium, a sharp skirmish pitted the other platoon of C Company against a German counterattack. At 8:40 A.M. on January 11, three Panther tanks and infantry charged at the town. C Company and its attached tank destroyers from the 703rd Tank Destroyer Battalion stopped the attack in its tracks. If it were not for the lightly protected, heavily armed M-36 tank destroyers (armed with a 90-mm cannon; the 703rd was the first unit to receive them), the Panthers would have made short work of what remained of C Company. They knocked out one Panther and took fifty prisoners.[5]

Next, Hogan received the objective of linking with Task Force Kane at Vaux to secure the flank of the Eighty-third Infantry Division and then move on to Cherain to cross the river that bisected the town. The Germans had blown the bridge and covered all approaches by antitank and artillery fire. The task force was down one-quarter of their infantry support. Between the combat losses at Bihain and several cases of frostbite, it was not likely that they their numbers could withstand another counterattack by German armor and Panzer grenadiers.

Colonel Howze radioed Sam to hold on and alerted A Company of the Eighty-third Reconnaissance Battalion to be prepared to assist. Thankfully, the night remained quiet, with both sides thinking it too cold to do anything other than hunker down for the evening. A Company was probably relieved to stay away from the hard-luck Task Force Hogan this time.

Finally, after a short but brutally fought counteroffensive, the battle was over. They restored the original front line of December 16 as the last German unit was pushed back near its starting point on January 25. Task Force Hogan had lost thirty-four killed in action and eight tanks since rearming and going back on the attack three days into the new year. Ten miles away from Task Force Hogan, the north and south Allied pincers linked up to "pinch off" the bulge. The lost ground had been regained and the "bulge" eliminated.

Field Marshal Montgomery sent the following secret cable to Eisenhower:

"I have great pleasure in reporting to you that the task you gave me in the Ardennes is now concluded. First and Third Armies have joined hands at Houffalize and are advancing eastward. It can therefore be said we have now achieved tactical victory within the salient. I am returning First Army to Bradley tomorrow as ordered by you. I would like to say what a great pleasure it has been to have such a splendid Army under my command and how very well it has done."[6]

After linking up with Patton's Third Army to the south, Spearhead stopped to let the snows melt and to rest and refit. The tyranny of distance and a long logistical chain were both a blessing and a curse as the Allies used up and outran their supplies. The higher-ups were busy planning and lining up the supplies for the drive into Germany, where the First Army would help take Germany's industrial heartland, the Ruhr. This would destroy the Reich's ability to wage war and put the Allies on the doorstep to Berlin.

The regiments spent the next two weeks conducting maintenance and integrating replacement personnel in marksmanship and tank-infantry cooperation. Sam, through a haze of fatigue and fever, instructed the first sergeants receiving the replacements: "Make sure they're put on supply duty until they're acclimated." Barclay's H Company, down to seventy-three soldiers from its authorized strength of 112, received thirty replacements. So did C and G, both hit just as hard. The replacements needed additional training in combat drills and how "we really do things over here, unlike at the schoolhouse." There were also classes to familiarize the soldiers with enemy mines and booby traps, large numbers of which were expected as the Allies entered Germany.[7]

After over two years of hard training followed by six months of brutal combat, Sam was physically and mentally at the end of his tether. He still functioned, but it was obvious to everyone that he was very sick and run-down. One morning, Sergeant D'Orio was taken aback by the sight of his colonel's face as he pored over some maps. Sam looked ten years older than twenty-nine. His usual pink cheeks were pale and gray. Even his normally excellent posture was stooped over just a bit.

He took one look at Sam and, in his pull-no-punches Brooklyn accent, told his commander: "Sir, all due respect, you look terrible. I'm taking you to the aid station." The chronic cough, aggravated by two nights spent in the woods outside of Marcouray, had turned into a high-fever pneumonia. He's right, Sam thought. Now's the time to heal up, before the push into Germany. Sam checked in with Doc Don Drolett, the new battalion surgeon, who promptly ordered him off the line for a few days.[8]

CHARLIE GAST STEERED THE PEEP ten kilometers back to the Forty-fifth Field Hospital. There was not much chitchat, but Gast was pleased that his commander was getting some rest and recuperation. He only ever saw Sam eat after his men had eaten, or sleep only after his men had slept. This meant only catching a nap or a bit of food here and there for weeks on end. The colonel's body was calling for the check.

"Sir, I'll be back for you in a couple of days. Don't worry, we won't roll out without you." Sam managed a flash of his trademark grin, shook Gast's hand, and bade him goodbye.

Sam's body was spent. His spirit, too. He lay a dozen kilometers back from the front lines in a field hospital, on a firm cot with clean sheets. The first good sleep he'd had since England.

During his intake, he shaved with running water for the first time in what seemed like months. There was a full mirror mounted over the washbasin. Sam was taken aback by what he saw.

Staring back at him in the mirror was not a twenty-nine-year-old but a tired-looking man of forty. His hair had turned gray. His light-blue eyes still had a spark in them, but they had retreated into his eye sockets from malnutrition and the wear of sleepless nights and pneumonia. No wonder D'Orio had sent him packing. Sam's mother probably wouldn't recognize this skinny, ashen man.

Warm food, sleep, and some sulfa drugs got his fever down, and coming up from one of his delirious dreams he woke to the sight of a beautiful, petite army nurse lieutenant from Pennsylvania. Her name was Virginia "Gina" Gough, and she lit up the general-purpose medium tent like a spring day in Texas.

Gina thought the tall, gaunt officer looked old and weary. Still, his bright Irish eyes were full of life, and his courteous but flirty grin took her breath away. For Sam, Gina's sweet and caring demeanor cut through the emotional void he'd been feeling. They experienced a slight romantic tension in a handful of passing encounters that made Sam feel alive and human again. The realization—or maybe it was acceptance—finally set in that there had been a distance between Sam and his wife back home, Belle, which had grown over the months of separation and war.

Sam finally had time to reflect on the events of the past months. For a while, he observed that he was losing his humanity and becoming hard-hearted. In a few letters, Belle had made it clear that she didn't want children. Sam knew he still wanted to be a father—and that desire lifted his spirits above his worries that he'd become distant from everything, too hard-hearted. He didn't want to come home with that ice in his veins, like he'd felt at the slag pile and at Aachen.

Over the next three days, a welcome friendship blossomed between the salty officer and the young nurse. On his last day, dressed in crisp fatigues and clean polished boots, Sam thanked her and bade her farewell with the words: "I'm heading back to my unit and the front line, where my boys need me. I hope our paths will cross again. May I get your address so I can write to you?"

He signed himself out. Walking out of the field hospital tent, folding a notecard into his chest pocket, Sam found the tune "We'll Meet Again" playing in his head. He whistled it as he waited for his peep ride back to the front. *We'll meet again, don't know where, don't know when. But I know we'll meet again some sunny day.* For now, it was back to the line after those three days of rest. A peep pulled up containing D'Orio and Gast's smiling faces. They took him back to the battalion laager.

Back in the saddle among his boys, dozens of wide-eyed, rosy-cheeked new faces awaited him. Replacements had arrived to make up for the battalion's heavy losses since Mons. Sam made time to meet and greet the new soldiers and make them feel welcome. Nineteen-year-old Tech 5 Henry Elefante from Pennsylvania and his M5 tank crew were sitting around a small fire with their tin canteen cups warming up some water for coffee. They saw the colonel walking up and sprang to their feet.

"As you were," Sam said, removing his gloves and shaking each of their hands. He told them how important their light tanks were and how glad he was to have them in the outfit.

Sam continued checking on his troops. The day was cool and crisp, with the bright blue sky that promised an early spring. The sound of an accordion humming a polka greeted Sam and Captain Barclay as they rounded a copse. In an adjacent field was another tank crew relaxing while the driver checked the track tension with a crowbar. Private Vernon Sechrist, a new replacement from Baltimore, Maryland, slowed his accordion playing, then picked up the beat when Hogan waved away calls to attention. Looking on was Tech 5 Lloyd Dixon from Dallas, Texas, a solid veteran soldier since Camp Polk days. On that sunny day, the normalcy of Sechrist entertaining the fellas, smiling behind his wheezing accordion, was one of those memorable and pleasant moments in between the tragic hazes of war—like the sun coming up after a slumber filled with nightmares.

Sam felt a pang of concern in his heart. Maybe the numbness was coming back? Something told him that he should not get too close to these kids. There was plenty of fight left in the Germans. There were more hard calls to make in the future. Sam thought about Ed Wray back at Mortain—his apprehension about the attack Sam had just ordered. Ed had known his chances of coming back were slim, and he went forward anyway. Moving along to another crew, Sam thought to himself, Focus on the battle ahead. Let's get as many of my soldiers back home alive as possible.

The task force was still waiting for supplies to reach the front. For the last push into Germany, they could not go at it with ten rounds of artillery per day or fuel for just a few dozen kilometers, so there was a bit of time for rest and relaxation while the "loggies" figured it out. When not training or on frigid guard duty, Hogan's heroes relaxed watching a Hollywood movie inside a warmish warehouse taken over by the United Services Organization (USO). Parked outside was the rare sight of a "Clubmobile"—a large bus converted and outfitted like a giant food truck with windows on the sides from which friendly women of the Red Cross service dispensed hot coffee, doughnuts, and a warm smile or flirty banter.[9] Another morale booster.

Spearhead was one of only two divisions in the entire US Army to receive the new T26 Pershing tank. Finally, a tank that could stand up to the enemy's Tiger and Panther tanks.

The "guidons call" had gone out early that morning. Rumors preceded it. The call summoned the tank battalion commanders to the outskirts of town for an orientation to some new equipment.

Sam, Brown, Gast, and D'Orio pulled up to a football stadium outside Stolberg. As they rounded the great building, their eyes widened at the sight of three olive-drab giants, long-barreled 90-mm cannon pointed menacingly to the sky. A crowd of gawking officers already surrounded the beasts.

Sam and Brownie looked at each other, then cracked smiles like boys seeing a new bicycle under the Christmas tree. The group drove up and all jumped off quickly, eager to take a look. There were distracted handshakes among fellow commanders. General Rose arrived, leading a delegation of brass, including the First Army's General Hodges and VII Corp's Lightning Joe Collins.

A crew of civilian technicians cranked up the powerful Ford engine, all eight cylinders, packing five hundred horsepower of wallop. The normally conservative officers gathered let up a cheer. Sam looked at D'Orio and Brown. "Now this is a pleasant surprise!"

Each medium tank company in the division would get a Pershing. Better armored, it weighed in at forty-three tons of tank compared to the Sherman's thirty-three and the Stuart's seventeen.

"Brownie, these will lead our attacks," Sam continued, his eyes fixed on the aggressive lines of the turret. "Cramer and Barclay can handpick the crews." Maybe things were looking up.

The next handful of days' respite from combat served to acclimate a new crew in G and H Companies to their new tanks. To the veteran tank crews, many of whom (in old horse cavalry terms) had had their Shermans shot out from under them or seen 76-mm rounds bounce off a Panther's sloped armor, it was like getting a new toy for their birthday.

BY FEBRUARY 10, SPEARHEAD UNITS had integrated their replacements and were back to a semblance of their organizational strength. An alert came down sure as the shadows of night—they would attack across the VII Corps line into Germany on the twenty-sixth. The 104th "Timberwolves" Infantry Division and Spearhead faced the well-developed defenses on the German side of the Roer River that had caused so many

US casualties before the Battle of the Bulge. Three German divisions—the 352nd Infantry, 363rd Infantry, and Twelfth Volksgrenadier Divisions—occupied the defensive positions.

The Rhine and several tributaries loomed ahead. The Rhine, swift and wide, was the moat to the Reich's medieval castle. The massive river had presented a problem for armies since Roman times and is a major reason Latin-based languages stopped being spoken east of its banks. By February 1945, the winter's historic levels of precipitation made the water barriers even more swollen and swift. Spearhead objectives were to secure crossings on the Roer and Erft Rivers first, then on to the Rhine. Once past Germany's third largest city—Cologne, straddling the Rhine—they could move on to the Ruhr to fulfill Ike's master plan.

A division liaison officer arrived at Sam's CP with an interesting encouragement from General Rose. Most of the commanders and staff in the division were familiar with the friendly rivalry developed in the two years of training between Sam and fellow Texan Lieutenant Colonel Walter "Rich" Richardson. They both commanded the Third Battalion of their respective tank regiments—Rich commanding in the Thirty-second Armored, Sam in the Thirty-third.

General Rose's carrot: the first battalion commander to place troops across the Erft wins a bottle of scotch whiskey. Sam dragged on his Camel and leaned against the map board behind him. Richardson was looking on, having arrived for a quick visit to his friend.

"Well, Rich, what do you think?" asked Sam. The two looked at each other with mischievous grins.

"Let's make it a case of scotch, and may the best tankers win," replied a grinning Rich. They would cross the canal, and if the scotch came Task Force Hogan's way, then great. If not, Sam's good friend would get it.

The Erft, although small and seemingly inconsequential, was vital to the Allied plan of attack. In one of the intelligence successes of the war, corps personnel had captured the engineering schematics for the dams upstream. What they saw dropped jaws and redirected First Army and VII Corps priorities. The danger to the entire Allied effort was that the Germans, by their system of locks and dams on the Erft and Roer, controlled over one million cubic meters of water. At the turn of a valve, they could flood the rivers and make them overflow their banks, creating a massive obstacle that would slow the entire western front's advance for weeks, or maybe months. This led to General Rose's desire to get control of the river by sending two of his best task forces after it.[10]

The Germans emplaced an obstacle belt in front of the Erft canal, the canal itself forming another barrier covered by guns in even more bunkers and pillboxes. Obstacles on both sides of the river served to slow down an attacker, channeling forces into prepared kill zones. Task Force Hogan—augmented by their infantry comrades of the Third Battalion, Thirty-sixth Armored Infantry Regiment, a platoon of tank destroyers from the 703rd Battalion, and the reliable bridge-layers and mine-clearers of the Twenty-third Armored Engineers—prepared to attack on the left, with Task Force Richardson on the right.

The race was on.

Task Force Hogan's lead elements reached Glesch on the Erft and prepared to force a crossing. The existing bridge, capable of holding tanks, had been blown, but reconnaissance showed that the Germans had neglected to blow up a footbridge downstream. Sam ordered a company of infantry across, occupying the far side without incident. Now it was the turn of the Twenty-third Engineers to lay down another bridge to bolster the Americans' precarious hold on the far side of the Erft. Sam's mortars and supporting artillery laid down suppressive fire and smoke. Infantry and the tanks prepared to lay down a wall of fire on any muzzle flashes coming from the enemy-held high ground across the river.

But when the Twenty-third Engineers approached the banks with their bridging trucks and half-tracks, they received heavy direct fire from well-camouflaged machine guns and antitank guns on the other side. Just approaching the bank was difficult—setting up a bridge was suicide. Sergeant Grimes's mortars fired 81-mm shells one after another to suppress the dug-in Germans. Despite their best efforts, German direct fire, mortars, and artillery destroyed two of the bridge trucks and pinned down the infantry on the far side of the Erft. Things were hairy.

Sam radioed the infantry and engineers to stay put and await nightfall before making another try.

Meanwhile, to their right and down the river three kilometers, Task Force Richardson fought past enemy resistance near Castle Paffendorf to find an intact crossing by nightfall on February 27. However, on approach, they lost five tanks in a blaze of 88-mm fire coming from dug-in FLAK guns. The rest of Rich's command withdrew, also to await the cover of darkness.

Early the next morning, February 28, at 2:40 A.M., through skillful night maneuver, Hogan's doughs of the Third Battalion, Thirty-sixth Armored Infantry moved to the banks right behind the engineers, who worked all night to emplace an infantry footbridge. The nighttime provided concealment from German snipers on the opposite bank, who constantly fired at any American soldier who happened to stand up or step outside of the cover of the tree line.

The scouts watched the opposite bank, searching for signs of enemy counterattack. They strained their eyes to see artillery observers or snipers hidden among the trees and bushes.

Captain Barclay keenly watched, too. "Come on, boys—get the Bailey bridge up," he whispered to himself, unable to influence what was a time-consuming process.

Dawn was due in another hour, and Barclay felt a wave of relief as the last segment of the eighty-foot bridge was muscled into place with crowbars and elbow grease. Two scouts crossed the bridge at a sprint, then took position on the far bank. Five tense minutes later, two red flashes of light indicated all was clear. The infantry squads began hustling across the bridge in shuffles that barely echoed over the river, as worn leather boot soles struck treated wood planks.

Things were finally moving along, and half of I Company was across. One of the scouts on the far bank—Private First Class Robert M. Cassady, twenty-five, of Lafayette, Indiana—began moving out to expand the perimeter. However, to the Germans, dawn slowly revealed the bridge and the olive-drab figures hurtling across. Cassady moved at a crouch, from cover to cover, but suddenly he jerked back and dropped to the ground, instantly dead, his arms and legs splayed out. A crack of rifle fire from a hidden German sniper echoed a few seconds later.

The I Company GIs reacted automatically almost in chorus with calls of "Sniper!" and "Medic up!"

But before the sniper could be located or medics brought up, enemy mortar fire whistled in, splashing on the Erft and among the treetops of the far bank. There were shouts of "Incoming!" as the Americans dove for cover. The bridge quickly emptied.

Ted Cardon called in for immediate suppression with mortar and artillery, and those whistled in three minutes later from behind the friendly side of the Erft. Under cover of the barrage, the GIs of I Company advanced three hundred yards from the east-side bridgehead. Ted's fire mission silenced the sniper, but the crossing was costly. Private Cassady was dead, and the enemy mortar rounds wounded a handful of the infantry. Cassady was one of the scouts who had survived the Christmas night trek through the Ardennes—the young man left an equally young widow behind.[11]

Sam ordered the high ground east of the bridgehead seized to deny the enemy observation, impeding the Germans' ability to place direct and indirect fire on both of Sam's and Richardson's crossings. The aggressive move by two tanks with infantry support took away the enemy's overwatch without further casualties.

A cycle ensued where the engineers methodically moved forward with heavy sections of bridge for the tanks to cross, received fire, took cover, then awaited the Americans' suppressive fire in the direction where the German fire was coming from. Once things quieted for the moment, the engineers dusted themselves off and resumed preparing sections of bridge to enable it to bear the weight of a Sherman.

Downstream, Task Force Richardson doughs on the east bank confronted a strong German counterattack from a battalion of enemy infantry supported by two tanks. The small infantry force radioed back to Colonel Richardson that they could not hold much longer. At 9:40 A.M., as soon as engineers placed the last treadway on their own bridge, Task Force Richardson crossed tanks on their bridgehead, moving swiftly across to meet the incoming attack.

A flight of two P-47 fighter-bombers zoomed in from behind the wedge of tanks.

Tankers and piggybacking infantrymen looked up to see the awe-inspiring sight of a stream of rockets swishing out from the P-47's wings, then a trail of smoke toward the unseen enemy line. The tanks, supported by the Thunderbolts' strikes and artillery, drove back a counterattack without losing any of the ground gained. Two hours later, G Company finally crossed the existing Paffendorf Bridge and rejoined Task Force Hogan in attacking the German positions.

Back at Task Force Hogan's bridge site at Glesch, the attack out of the footbridge moved forward after two replacement bridging trucks arrived to maintain the pace on a second bridge capable of holding forty-ton vehicles. By early afternoon, the G Company tanks threatened the enemy flank from the Paffendorf crossing as I Company doughs surged forward from the bridgehead at Glesch. By later afternoon, the task force occupied a trench system that covered the entire river frontage across the task force's axes of advance.[12]

That night, the Luftwaffe bared its teeth again with an attack on both bridgeheads and the tentative crossing at Glesch. German night fighters flew bombing runs guided by their nose-mounted radar antennae. They were often equipped with radio-controlled bombs, precursors to modern "smart bombs."

Not tonight, thought the crews from the 486th Anti-Aircraft Artillery Battalion (the Anti-Anything Battalion, as they liked to be known, for they were often pressed into action against all manner of ground targets, too). They opened up with blinding streams of red tracers, shooting up at 120 degrees from their quad .50-caliber machine gun mounts. The stream of fiery red bullets lit up the sky like Fourth of July fireworks, moving faster than the speed of sound toward the dimly lit gray shadows droning above.

The massive rounds flashed as they met their mark on the fuselage of a German bomber. The flash grew into a fire on the starboard wing, and the dark-gray bird suddenly became illuminated as it leaned over and began diving to the ground, its struggling engine shrieking in vain to generate enough lift. A yellow plume and streak of light-gray smoke chased the stricken bomber on its collision course with earth. There was a fireball and an explosion thirty seconds later, followed by cheers and hollers from the American artillerymen and other onlooking GIs.

The American gunners brought down three more German bombers before the enemy air raid turned back. They hunkered down for another night on watch, with movement to follow at dawn.

ON MARCH 1, TASK FORCE Hogan was engaging with the enemy before the bridgehead. The footbridge had collapsed overnight, along its far side abutment, from the relentless bombing and indirect fire. Nevertheless, the other bridge emplaced by the engineers got all of the armor across, and the tireless engineers got to work making any repairs needed. This was crucial in keeping the task force lines of supply open as they advanced into the Rhineland.

The onward movement continued out of the bridgehead. Task Force Hogan passed through Auenheim, moving all night and into the morning. It was so dark that Sergeant Grimes, the mortar section leader, helped his half-track driver Dick Svoboda not only to stay awake but to see the blackout lights of the vehicle in front.

"Dick, swallow this coffee. Now I'm gonna help you see the road and direct you." Grimes peered above the open cab of the half-track, squinting ahead. When the sergeant saw the blackout light ahead move to the right, he would firmly tap the driver's right shoulder. Similarly with a left turn. A sharp tap to the helmet indicated a stop.[13]

Stopping only to refuel and overcome pockets of resistance, the armored column kept going, with Sam and Travis Brown keeping in constant contact with TF Richardson to their left. From Auenheim it was on to secure a jumping-off point at Rheidt, where the task force would link up with adjoining units. Somewhere ahead was the German 301st Heavy Tank Battalion with its behemoth Mark VI Tiger tanks.

West of Rheidt on March 2, the volume of mortar and machine gun fire increased. G Company, in the lead, soon reached an antitank ditch covered by indirect and direct fire.

Out of the shattered landscape of felled trees and urban detritus, a camouflaged antitank gun fired a round into the wedge of tanks. The phosphorus-lined round left the tube in a spinning bolt of steel, light, and heat. It connected with a dull crunch on one of the US tanks. The G Company tank staggered to a halt and spewed smoke as hatches opened and the heat inside built up. Smoke spewed out of two holes in the turret where the round had plowed clean through the armor and beyond.

The crew made the most of their six seconds, scrambling out with the almost superhuman speed afforded by fear and adrenaline. Tanks looking on saw the drama unfold.

Sergeant Emmett Tripp, searching in his gunsights for the source of the fire, couldn't help but count one crewmen, two, three, then nothing. One remained inside. Sergeant John Wolf of Faribault, Minnesota, commander of the Sherman, was killed.[14]

Carl Cramer, always thinking on his feet, moved his tanks aggressively to flank the ditch. His radio transmissions were calm but directive: "White platoon: move left and hit 'em in the flank—over."

The Shermans swung wide away from the antitank cannon position just as two Mark VI Tiger tanks on overwatch pulled up out of their defilade, opening fire on the American tanks. Their tank turret scanning from side to side, Sergeants Ellis Butler and Emmett Tripp couldn't miss the sight of the sixty-eight-ton tanks—twice the weight of a Sherman—moving into firing position. It was a hair-raising sight, even for the experienced veterans.

"Tiger tanks! Two o'clock!" echoed over the radios.

The first volley of 88-mm antitank rounds shot out behind puffs of smoke from the long barrels of the hunting Tigers. The shells whined out in two streaks of burning green, flying so fast that all you could do was look at them, thankful not to be in their paths. Tripp let out a grunt as he saw the green lighting zoom past his optics. Somebody was about to have a terrible day.

BOOM, BOOM as two Shermans were pierced. Cramer's command tank, G-6, filled with smoke. "Bail out! Bail out!" sounded over the intercom, followed by the gasps of the wounded. "Immediate suppression!" "Six is hit!" Turrets zoomed to the called-out direction and drivers began to zigzag their tanks—anything to make a harder target.

Inside G-6, the seconds ticked away before the Sherman ammunition would catch fire, incinerating everything and everyone within. Tech 5 Robert Creviston and Private First Class Walter R. Schmidt—bleeding, uniforms torn and scorched—helped each other out of the stricken tank.

Cramer's entire right side from neck to leg was covered in shrapnel cuts, staining his coveralls crimson with shades of ash. The second tank was also knocked out, leaving platoon leader Lieutenant Joe Lukowski badly wounded and with two of his crew—Sergeant John Delahanty and Corporal Robert Rainey—killed in action.[15]

Captain Cramer had been seriously wounded yet again. He'd had multiple narrow escapes, including a previous combat wound near Mons (his second Purple Heart award). He was rushed to a field hospital and ultimately wouldn't return to battle.

Lieutenant Thomas Cooper once again assumed command and requested immediate suppression of the Tiger tanks and covering smoke from the mortars. At the same time, Ted Cardon was calling on P-47 fighter-bomber support. Mines knocked out three more Shermans as G Company encountered the first line protecting the German defensive belt. Mortar smoke obscured the kill zone enough to allow armored ambulances to meet up with the wounded and take them back to the battalion aid station. A few minutes later, P-47 fighter-bombers roared in and destroyed the Tiger tanks and the camouflaged antitank guns that had withstood Grimes's 81-mm mortar volleys.

Captain Ted Cardon—the Arizonan jack-of-all-trades—proved invaluable again, bringing aerial firepower to bear when and where it was needed with an accuracy that prevented friendly casualties. Forty-eight hours later, all enemy resistance ceased in the task force sector. On their right, the Ninety-ninth Infantry Division moved through Task Force Richardson, greatly expanding the bridgehead. They made contact with Hogan's task force at Rheidt, establishing the new front line. The Erft and its system of locks secured, Spearhead prevented the Germans from flooding the entire battle zone as they had done in the Netherlands in 1944, which greatly slowed down the British in their northern route toward Germany.

Now the route was clear: on to Cologne. Division units moved through the task forces holding open the bridges, then shot up north to the big city's suburbs, through the devastated urban landscape to its massive bridge crossing over the Rhine. Rich Richardson's parent regiment, the Thirty-second Armored, moved through downtown Cologne toward its twin-spired Gothic cathedral and the location of the famous Pershing-versus-Panther duel, filmed by combat cameraman James Bates practically at the church steps.

Though not immortalized on film, Task Force Hogan fought its own duel of the titans in their sector of northeast Cologne. This encounter pitted a Pershing versus a rarely seen Nashorn (Rhinoceros) tank destroyer, on March 6. The German tank destroyer was equipped with an 88-mm cannon, like that of the dreaded FLAK 88 antiaircraft gun, its sixteen-pound armor-piercing shell guided by the usual excellent German optics and gunsights. Its nickname, "Rhino," came from its squat shape with the giant cannon protruding menacingly from its front like a rhino horn.

H Company's T-26 Pershing led the company through the shattered suburban landscape toward the factory district. The landscape of crumbling factory buildings dotted with carcasses of cars and heavy machinery was a hellish vision full of ambush sites. Out of nowhere, the hiding Nashorn fired its 88-mm cannon at only three hundred meters range, impacting the Pershing in the hull. The round entered, barely missing the driver's legs, and crashed into the crew compartment. Private Vernon Sechrist, the fun-loving accordion player from Baltimore, was instantly killed. The rest of the crew bailed out and ran for cover as the ammunition cooked off and burned the turret. Artillery suppressed the ambush position as the remaining H Company tanks took out the German tank destroyer, leaving its open-top compartment cooking like a barbecue pit.[16]

Task Force Hogan's sector of Cologne encompassed not just the Ford factory district but also the famous Cologne Zoo. The approach was eerie as the units advanced in a cautious column, infantry walking briskly beside the tanks, checking every crag and partially collapsed wall. The terrain sloped down to the Rhine and the lead tanks saw the wide brown river two thousand meters ahead. Derelict factories gave way to several gardens and parks. Stray dogs tussled over a filthy, abandoned trench coat. Otherwise, there was eerie silence. Deep, faraway explosions could be heard three miles downriver across from the Cologne Cathedral.

After another thirty minutes of advance, the column arrived at the wrought-iron gates of the Cologne Zoo. The forty-nine-acre compound was all that stood between the column and the banks of the great river. Sam called a halt, climbed down from his tall perch on the turret of his Sherman, and moved forward with a squad of infantry, .45-caliber pistol in hand. The gate opened easily, and the infantry fanned out to check the few buildings on site. Animals bellowed and roared, but no German soldiers remained.

Sam and some of his tankers looked on as recently trucked-in war correspondents gawked at the sights and sounds of a zoo in wartime. A *Stars and Stripes* reporter asked Sam what he planned to do. His soldiers looking on sounded off some ideas: *Use the giraffes as forward observers and the monkeys as snipers! The kangaroos with their pouches will make great messengers.* Sam gave them the side-eye, then flashed his warm grin at the reporter.

"That's right! Everything for the front."[17] The battle ended in a lighthearted moment amid triumphal hoots from the soldiers.

The objective secured, they were on the Rhine at last.

But three kilometers downstream, the massive Hohenzollern Bridge—almost fourteen hundred feet long—lay in ruins, its steel trusses poking up from the waterline. The Germans had succeeded in blowing it up—it was unusable. Crossing the Rhine had to wait.

From March 10 to 19, the battalion moved back to occupy an area north of Cologne. There, they set up roadblocks and awaited replacement tanks for G Company. They also conducted vehicle and weapons training for new replacement personnel.

Sam transferred Tom Magness out of his assault gun platoon and into G Company to lead tanks. He was a proven leader, and G Company was down two officers (Cramer and Lukowski). He also nominated Lieutenant Thomas Cooper for the Silver Star, for his boldness in dealing with the Tiger ambush on G Company. Arnold "Slack" Schlaich, previously decorated for his bravery leading the assault guns at Mortain, accepted a battlefield commission in late December and was now Lieutenant Schlaich, assault gun platoon leader—much to the good-natured heckling of his enlisted soldiers. Among them, recently promoted to sergeant was Tech 5 Herman Rewerts, another old reliable hand who'd seen heavy action from Normandy to the Bulge.

The task force sprang back into action from their assembly area facing the Rhine on March 20. Tanks and infantry brushed aside enemy resistance at Geistingen and Honnef, securing the flank of American units surging through the Remagen bridgehead to the south. TF Hogan crossed the massive Rhine over a pontoon bridge at Honnef shortly after.

It was around this time that Task Force Hogan welcomed a colorful addition into its fold, when an armored column passed by a Luftwaffe stalag abandoned by its German guards. Major Caryl Oliver Imbert Ramsden, Royal Artillery and eighth baronet of his family, was just seven months older than Sam when he found himself liberated by the Hogan tanks after years of German captivity. In classic British understatement he exclaimed, "I say, chaps, you're a welcome sight!" The tall, gaunt British aristocrat, educated at Eton and Oxford, immediately found himself among friends with the rough US tankers. Sam invited him to a repast of canned rations supplemented by a few boiled brussels sprouts and a digestif of scotch whiskey from his flask. "Here's to you and your men, Colonel Hogan," said the blue-blooded British officer as he raised the flask. "The Germans were damned stingy with the prisoner rations." The two hit it off as only soldiers can.

Rejecting an offer for a lift to a repatriation camp, Caryl requested to ride along as part of Sam's command group. It was an unorthodox request, but Sam thought it was safer than leaving him behind until the rear echelons caught up to their forward position. The baronet rode with Task Force Hogan's columns for the next two weeks, thrilled to get a little payback after his long captivity.

His upbeat personality and quick wit were welcome as he navigated the battalion command post, marveling at the speed of the Sherman tank and the prowess and muscle of the US Army artillery. Soldiers and officers got a kick from his heavily accented "Jolly good, old boy" and "Hello, dear chap" as he recounted his life, his captivity, and his plans for a return to good old England.

At the end of his sojourn, he reluctantly accepted a peep ride to the nearest British headquarters, finally returning to his own lines as the allies converged on Germany's industrial heart for the climax. He knew he would return home and not get to participate in the final victory in Berlin, so it was bittersweet for him. Sometime later, he wrote a letter to Sam's family in Texas:

"It is not only your son's kindness that impressed me. After four years in prison camps, one loses touch with war and its methods, and it was therefore a great privilege for me to be able to watch your son commanding his force in action."

Closing his letter with, "After three weeks with the Colonel, I now know exactly what is meant by American hospitality," Sir Caryl Ramsden resumed his life in Great Britain.[18]

April approached and it was time to move on to Germany's industrial heartland, the Ruhr. Sam reported to Colonel Robert Howze's CP near Marburg and was glad to see his friend Walt Richardson.

"Rich, looks like you have some scotch headed your way," Sam prodded as the two commanders closed in for a handshake.

"Well now, Sam, I heard you got your infantry across on that footbridge." Sam had indeed got infantry across on the footbridge on the first day of the crossing, but Rich was the first to cross his tanks at

Pallendorf the following day. Spearhead being an armored division, it sounded like a fifty-fifty split.

"Tell you what: it was a hard fight and we lost some good people. Let's split it and call it a day," said Sam.

Either way, their hardworking staff sections would be able to enjoy a "Kentucky hug" in their coffee during their next rest and refit periods. Both squeezed out a couple of laughs in the middle of their exhaustion, then rose as the leader of the combat command reserve strode in purposefully. Colonel Howze, usually calm and cool, entered the enclosure waving his arms excitedly.

"We'll move! We'll really go!" He took off his steel helmet, striding over to the map board and pointing at a location. "Here, this is Paderborn, home of the SS Tank School—it's Germany's Fort Knox." Sam and Walt looked at each other. That was over one hundred miles away and ninety degrees to the north. Howze knew what they were thinking. "Tomorrow morning you leave for Paderborn. Just go like hell.[19] Get to Paderborn, don't stop!" exclaimed the animated Howze.

The objective was the high ground near the airport. The linkup between Spearhead and the Second Armored Division would encircle all German armies defending the Ruhr—approximately four hundred thousand men, or twenty times the size of each of the US armored divisions. The double envelopment could cripple the German war machine and end the war. Both of the battalion commanders' eyes widened with excitement, fatigue leaving their minds for a bit.

Ninety miles to the north, the heaviest tanks in the German arsenal assembled at Paderborn. The 507th Heavy Tank Battalion (Schwere Panzer Abteilung) was back from the eastern front after attaining six hundred confirmed tank kills. It was being reequipped with the behemoth King Tiger tank.

The beast *looked* deadly. It was ten feet tall and twice as heavy as the thirty-three-ton Sherman. It even outweighed the Pershing. Aggressive lines sloped up its frontal and turret armor (a design that was copied after the war, well into the 1960s, appearing on the US M60 main battle tank), up to a thickness of 185 mm, compared to a Sherman's 100 mm at its thickest. This made it almost immune to the US tank's 76-mm cannon fire.

The turret wrapped around the King Tiger's main armament: the dreaded 88-mm high-velocity cannon, the same one used to shoot down US bombers at altitude. Poking from the elongated turret, the barrel looked more like a telephone pole in thickness and length than a cannon.

Coated in a camouflage scheme of khaki, reddish brown, and green, its fearsome appearance was akin to an enormous Bengal tiger. Thirty factory-fresh King Tigers awaited their crews from the 507th. Another unit, the 512th Panzer Battalion, was in the area armed with the Hunting Tiger tank destroyer, incorporating a huge 128-mm cannon onto a King Tiger chassis. These were experienced and battle-tested units. The 507th alone had six Knight's Cross of the Iron Cross recipients in its ranks.[20] It was the Reich's highest award for bravery.

In addition to these frontline German units, Paderborn and nearby Augustdorf were home to the SS Panzer Reconnaissance Training Center and the SS Panzer Junior Leaders School. Not only were these units part of the fanatically loyal and tenacious SS, seasoned sergeants and officers led them. Master sergeants with years of tank combat experience led the platoons instead of newly minted lieutenants.

Panzer Brigade Westphalen was ordered to hold Paderborn at all costs, to hold a west-to-east defensive line from the edge of Paderborn through Wewer to Scherfede. The brigade's cross-punch, the 507th Panzer Battalion, deployed in front of their command posts at Dörenhagen, Lichtenau, and Kuhlenburg. Tiger tanks and SS infantry emplaced ambushes covering the approaches to Paderborn.

Crushing Paderborn could be the biggest challenge to face Spearhead thus far in the war.[21]

UNDER CLOUDY SKIES PORTENDING RAIN, Task Force Hogan swung north as the leftmost Spearhead unit on March 29, with Paderborn the objective. Sam ordered his long column of tanks forward with a cheery "Up and at 'em!" Inside, though, he felt a deep dread that after all they had been through already, even darker days lay ahead. The armored column moved swiftly through Wunderthausen, and resistance stiffened with each subsequent town. German intelligence was again on point and identified Spearhead's objective as well as the armored column's routes.

Past Cologne and the Rhine, it was flat tank country all the way to Berlin. Thus, the Nazis' "hedgehog" defense strategy made use of fortified towns and villages: strongpoints that, when bypassed by fast-moving US armor, were a deadly trap for the enemy to spring out of and attack the US rear echelons, cutting off the supply of fuel and ammunition. The hedgehogs' teeth were SS troops with antitank guns, Panzerfausts, and the bazooka's heavier and superior counterpart, the Panzerschreck.

Good Friday, March 30, was a black day for the Third Armored Division. Task Force Welborn, on Hogan's right, advanced faster on a route with fewer small towns to slow it down. By 7:00 P.M., the unit approached an old barn with Kuhlenberg to their front. Woods prevented any maneuvering to their right. The lead tank commanders felt uneasy, their experience telling them this was an ideal ambush site. Without warning, from nine hundred yards ahead, eight King Tiger tanks of Third Company, 507th Panzer Battalion, fired upon the lead tank, swiftly destroying it and blocking the column. Then the tail tank shuddered and went up in flames before the column could disperse. In a few seconds, the Germans had immobilized the entire column, cutting the lead elements from the remainder of the task force. German infantry fired volleys from the tree line, further pinning down the American force as the King Tigers continued to fire devastating 88-mm rounds at the rest of the vehicles. Task Force Welborn was trapped in the kill zone. The Americans, silhouetted in the crawling dusk against the fires of the burning Shermans, became easy targets for the experienced German gunners. Another Sherman, one M3 Stuart, and eleven half-tracks of the Thirty-sixth Armored Infantry Regiment were destroyed.

General Rose—leading from the front, as was his custom—was also caught in the ambush. His three-peep element moved out of the kill zone only to run into a King Tiger tank of the 507th Panzer Battalion headquarters, which was moving down from Lichtenau to close the Americans' escape route. The small command group, surrounded, dismounted their jeeps and prepared to surrender. In the dark and confused situation, a trigger-happy King Tiger commander cut down General Rose as he attempted to undo his pistol belt.

Just like that, the towering commander of the Spearhead Division went down in a hail of submachine gun fire.

At the same time to the west, on their approach march to Wewer, Sam heard a tremendous roar of explosions like giant zippers echoing ahead. H Company, in the lead, ran into the defenses of the SS Third "Totenkopf" (Death's Head) Division. Enemy infantry backed by nine 20-mm FLAK guns were putting up a wild firefight. The German FLAK guns, fed by magazines providing a high rate of fire, posed a danger to all—but especially the lightly armored support vehicles, like the half-tracks carrying the mortars and infantry. Sam gripped his throat mike on his tank's intercom: "Elmer, get us moving up to that ridge ahead." Johnson stepped on the gas as the command Sherman crested to where they could view the German position. It looked like a fireworks show, but on a horizontal plane instead of a vertical one.

The German tracers shot forward like multiple bolts of green lighting in streaming rivers of bright phosphorus. The sound reverberated throughout the little valley like a dozen jackhammers pounding all at once. Where a stream of rounds got lucky and hit one of the Sherman tanks, the round deflected off its armor and shot up wildly into the air. Tank gunner Clem Elissondo, excitedly called out over the intercom: "Sir, are you seeing this?!"

"Yes, Clem, we've gotta take those guns out." Sam radioed H Company to his right front. "How Six, flank those positions. Mortars will provide suppression."

Barclay's tanks were already moving, advancing in bounds—as one platoon fired, the other on its right moved up three hundred yards, using the folds of the terrain expertly to avoid receiving a long volley of white-hot 20-mm rounds. For the last one hundred yards, H Company Shermans moved fast, shrugging off 20-mm slugs as three of the antiaircraft gun carriages were turned into piles of junk by coaxial machine gun and cannon fire. Grimes's mortars chimed in with immediate suppression missions that killed or wounded several of the exposed enemy gun crews. Resistance collapsed.

Pulling up in his command tank, Sam saw that H Company was already consolidating on the objective. The task force captured two hundred Germans. Jumping off his command tank to talk to John Barclay, Sam passed a line of prisoners waiting to be searched. Upon interrogation, some informed the Americans that two tanks were posted on the other side of town with orders to shoot up any German infantrymen who retreated.

Walking back past the line of prisoners, Sam's eyes met the hateful gaze of an SS captain. Sam felt a surge of hate in his heart again; he walked up to him and glared into his eyes face-to-face. The lieutenant colonel thought back to the dastardly execution of Lieutenant Modrak's light tank crew. He thought of Jake. Anger, tunnel vision—Sam was seeing red.

Looking at the SS officer's tunic, the American noticed the Iron Cross medal suspended on its ribbon. How many Americans had he killed to "earn" this? Without a word, Sam ripped off the decoration. The German protested, stammering out something about the Geneva Conventions. Sam calmly raised his hand, silencing him: "You're SS. Don't talk to me about the Geneva Conventions. Count yourself lucky to be alive," then strode away.

Meanwhile, seven kilometers away in the Combat Command B sector, Welborn's situation was no better than at the start of the ambush. Darkness engulfed the column as the fires of battle burned out and confused soldiers moved from cover to cover in the darkness. The German commander, Hauptmann (Captain) Wolf Koltermann, moved his Second Company of King Tigers down from Lichtenau to Welborn's rear to close the jaws of the trap. The depleted task force dug in for what was to be a long night and morning. Before sunrise, Task Force Welborn forward elements were relieved to see that the SS had pulled back in anticipation of US air strikes. Koltermann knew the effects US fighter-bomber attacks could have on his tanks. The Germans elected to conserve their combat power for the battles ahead.

Back in front of Task Force Hogan, the weather cleared up enough for air support. With the coming dawn, the Americans needed to shake off the fatigue and drive on. By daybreak, the distress of Task Force Welborn reached their sister units in Combat Command Reserve. After some hasty planning between Sam and John Barclay, they readied to move again to the next enemy position. H Company moved to the front for the attack on Wewer, beginning in the dark hours of March 31.

For the remainder of the day, they battled. The resistance of the remnants of the SS Totenkopf, augmented by Luftwaffe personnel, was stubborn. Doubtless, the SS soldiers threatened to kill any German military personnel who weren't willing to fight to the bitter end. C Company tanks poured 37-mm and machine gun fire into buildings as the attached infantry cleared the area house by house. While attacking Wewer, Task Force Hogan needed to secure the leftmost town around Paderborn, Salzkotten, to open the way for Task Force Welborn's relief.

To this end, Sam detached C Company tanks, several tank destroyers, and I Company, 414th Infantry Regiment, 104th Infantry Division. The rest of the task force held the line against enemy counterattacks and secured Wewer. Upon approaching Salzkotten, the lead tanks heard motor vehicles moving within. Lieutenant Robert Resterer decided to push on. Well-aimed Panzerschreck fire greeted the small C Company tanks and infantry, knocking out an assault gun. A burning enemy vehicle also blocked the main road through town.

The phone rang inside an abandoned factory serving as Resterer's command post. The lieutenant and Shorty Wright looked at each other. Who could possibly be calling?

Resterer picked up the receiver. ". . . Ja?" It was a soldier, speaking German, who happened to be the mayor of Salzkotten, pressed into military service.

"Wer ist das?" came the voice over the receiver.

"Das ist der Soldat auf der hut," Resterer led him on, pretending to be another German.

"Die Amerikaner schreiten kommt, wir haben ausgeraumt." Resterer covered the receiver and translated to Shorty: *The Americans are advancing, so we've cleared out.* Continuing to lead his caller on, Resterer found out that the Germans had cleared out except for dozens of wounded soldiers in the town hospital.

Continuing the conversation, Resterer convinced the bürgermeister to surrender the town and its wounded so they could get medical treatment. It was 2:00 A.M., but Sam was able to radio back to Colonel Howze that Wewer and Salzkotten were secure. On April 3, a tank patrol from H Company made contact with fellow tankers of the Eighth Armored Division—the noose was secured around Paderborn. The results were two hundred prisoners captured and forty German defenders killed in this action.[22]

In the intervening twenty-four hours, Task Force Welborn extricated itself from the ambush site. The Ruhr pocket snapped shut and Spearhead received orders to drive on. Eighteen Allied infantry divisions stayed on to clear the pocket. The Germans within had a choice—surrender or die.

It was a bitter victory, between the heavy casualties and the loss of General Rose, killed in action at the head of his beloved armored columns. His soldiers loved and respected him, and Sam had admired him greatly. Rose had forged the Spearhead—tough but fair, and always leading from the front. Brigadier General Doyle Hickey of Combat Command A assumed command of the division. The Paderborn pocket was renamed the Rose pocket in honor of Spearhead's fallen commanding general.[23]

The Third Armored Division had made history again. But what turned out to be the longest single-day drive against enemy resistance in the history of modern warfare had only felt like another long string of hours "Spearheading" to many of the soldiers. In reality, the bold ninety-mile dash from Marburg to Paderborn and final linkup with the US Seventh Army's units sealed in 376,000 German soldiers, cut off the industrial Ruhr, and eliminated Field Marshal Walther Model's Army Group B as an effective fighting force.

Spearhead and other VII Corps units had dueled with Army Group B beginning in the Normandy hedgerows, through Belgium, and into Germany. The game of cat and mouse was finally up.

Model, staggered by his defeat, marched himself into the woods, pistol in hand.

"In antiquity a defeated general took poison," he had told an aide. But he preferred the quicker death of a bullet to the head. Shuffling slowly into the woods of his shrinking fatherland, the salty, monocled field marshal paused, took a deep breath, placed his service pistol to his temple, and squeezed the trigger.

10

★ ★ ★ ★ ★

NINETY MILES
TO BERLIN

APRIL 6–31, 1945

With Field Marshal Model's Army Group B vanquished, the way was now open to the next objective—Germany's heart. Sam couldn't believe his maps. His armor and infantry were closer to Berlin than they were to Paris. There were a few rivers ahead, the last one being the Elbe. From there on, there was no stopping the Americans from reaching the Reich's capital.

In early April, US intelligence reported that the bridges over the next natural barriers—the Weser, Leine, and Saale Rivers—remained intact. However, the Germans had learned well from their loss of the intact Ludendorff Bridge at Remagen, and likely prepared all of them for demolition. The division issued orders to attack rapidly and take the bridges.

Beyond the first set of bridges was the purported buzz bomb (V-1 rockets) and V-2 ballistic missile factory at Dora. Intelligence was spotty, but it was likely that the factory was heavily guarded. After the British began bombing V-1 and V-2 factories in the west, the Nazi High Command decided to move production farther toward the heart of the Reich, in the faint hopes that these wonder-weapons could turn the tide of the war in Germany's favor.

The Dora-Mittelbau region provided a ready-made facility, dug deep into the Kohnstein Mountain, with two miles of interconnected tunnels dug 640 meters underground. The tunnels had been used previously to store fuel and poisonous gas. With characteristic German efficiency, the move was completed and the factory operational by August 27, 1944.

The Americans did not know the horrors that awaited discovery, as the factory had been using slave labor to crank out rockets and missiles at improbably high rates. Inside the miles of tunnels, the forced laborers strained on assembly lines twelve hours a day, yielding six thousand V-1 rockets and almost five thousand V-2 missiles. The slave labor came from nearby concentration camps, the biggest in the area being at Nordhausen—itself subordinate to Buchenwald concentration camp near Weimar, the former capital and industrial center of Thuringia.[1]

Meanwhile, 120 miles to the west and in conditions described as "general mud," Task Force Hogan rolled out at 5:00 P.M. on April 6 as the northern column of the division's advance. Scattered resistance, felled trees, and mud slowed the advance. One Task Force Hogan dozer tank remained in running condition: Sergeant Emmett Tripp's "Animal." Tripp and his crew worked overtime to clear these obstacles.

Without engineer dozers attached, other felled trees were dealt with manually by two dozen or so infantrymen, who would have to dismount, shoulder arms, and manhandle the trunks off the road, thus exposing themselves to sniper fire and booby traps.

A shot would ring out—a soldier fell, wounded or dead. Angry shouts of "Sniper!" echoed up and down the line as the infantry dove for cover and the tankers sank into their turrets and hatches. Then began the stressful and methodical process of finding the sniper—or snipers. "Did anyone see a flash?!" "The shot came from that copse of trees ahead!" Tank fire or Grimes's trusty mortars then lit up the enemy position and the advance moved on.

The cycle repeated itself with no end in sight. Desperate German "stay-behinders," ordered to slow down and harass the advancing Americans, lashed themselves to trees or dug themselves in to snipe. Mines and grenades booby-trapped enemy corpses and abandoned equipment. The infantry soldiers took one to five casualties for every village they moved through.

Mud was another problem, compounded by the leading tanks, which churned up the muck even worse for the half-tracked and wheeled vehicles trailing the tanks.

Vehicles stuck in the mud were left behind with a security element to await an M32 armored recovery vehicle (ARV) from Service Company—basically a wrecker or tow truck version of the Sherman tank. Ordnance men armed with shovels, cables in hand, knee deep in mud, wrestled to help free tracked and wheeled vehicles from the muck. All the while, the columns ahead kept moving. The expectation was that the stuck vehicles would catch up at the next refueling stop—if they ran into a bypassed pocket of German infantry, they had to fight on through.

The bridge over the Weser River was destroyed on April 7, right in the face of the First Battalion, which was preparing to cross it. Task Force Hogan stopped to refuel and prepare for a forced crossing. Once again, the reliable Twenty-third Engineers put up a long pontoon bridge—at least this time not under direct fire. H Company—in the lead and with infantry support from the Timberwolves—cleared several small towns, capturing twenty-two prisoners. In between towns, columns of dusty but jubilant French, Belgian, and Russian forced laborers moved west, cheering the advancing Americans.

The task force continued advancing as the left wing of CCR, with Task Force Richardson on the right, the two task forces leapfrogging through the next twenty-four hours. The new Third Armored Division commanding general, Doyle Hickey, caught up to the Task Force Hogan CP with a new mission. A polo player in his prior life, Hickey—the pipe-smoking Arkansan—received a quick overview of the situation from Sam and Travis. The general thanked Sam and the operations staff, then issued orders to take Nordhausen. Sam and his command group automatically went into planning and preparation for the attack. This was muscle memory by now, but Sam harped hard on his commanders to stay alert and avoid complacency—no shortcuts due to overconfidence.

This was the home stretch, and it would be a damned shame to lose anyone on it.

After the usual night of map and personal reconnaissance, preparation of equipment, and cross-loading of ammunition and fuel, they rolled out at 8:00 A.M. on April 10. The column headed southeast, skirting the southern edge of the forested Harz Mountains along the open plain north of the Fulda gap—a flat, west-east corridor between the forests and mountains framing the Ruhr. More tree trunks and burnt-out vehicles choked the roads. This slowed the advance as engineers cleared the detritus, sometimes booby-trapped with grenades, or "Bouncing Betty" mines blocking the road. The debris and old vehicle wrecks were then pushed off to the side of the road.

Approaching the noon hour, the column of H, G, and C Companies—rugged foot soldiers of the Thirty-sixth Infantry traveling with the tanks—arrived on the outskirts of Bilshausen. The GIs dismounted as sniper fire cracked from the town. The lead tanks, under Captain Ted Cardon, spotted three German Tigers taking positions two thousand yards away in the wooded area opposite the Americans' line of advance.[2]

Tactical air support was on station, and Cardon guided it in with the VHF radio mounted in his command Sherman. The silver wings of IX Tactical Air Command's P-47s reflected quicksilver beams of sunlight as they roared over the coffee-and-emerald-colored patchwork of fields. They overflew the long olive-drab snake of Task Force Hogan vehicles, dipping their wings. Soldiers, their faces gray with dust, gazed upward with tired smiles and cheered. In two passes, the US fighter-bombers turned the three Tigers into burning hulks as their crews sprinted away into the woods. The pilots reported to Ted that they saw ten more tanks in the vicinity, but they would have to return after loading up on more rockets. The Germans had abandoned one Tiger and withdrawn the rest by the time another flight of P-47s returned. Task Force Hogan pushed on.

A few surrendering Germans seemed very relieved that the war was over for them and reported that ahead were thirteen artillery pieces in the woods between Osterode and Herzberg. Sam wanted more air support so they could destroy any artillery or tanks without having to tangle with them in the woods. G Company, spread out on the left flank, destroyed another Mark IV tank and two large airplanes left behind on improvised airstrips. By 3:00 P.M., dismounted US infantrymen were skirting the woods as the lead tanks pushed on to Gieboldehausen.

The task force scouts identified a strong delaying force of fifty German infantry with half-tracks and at least three tanks six kilometers ahead.

"Roger," came the response from Sam. "Keep to the woods as we secure the area. Break . . . await arrival of air support." The column then advanced farther to get eyes on the enemy force. Task force mortars fired high-explosive rounds four kilometers ahead to keep the German infantry down. Ted Cardon, from his turret position, guided in a flight of Thunderbolts that zoomed in and unleashed their payload of antitank rockets. Smoke rose from the city outskirts as the tanks burned up from the rockets. Two German tanks were destroyed, and the accompanying infantrymen were taken prisoner.[3]

Scouts reported that the next bridge on their route was blown. Sam directed the column to bypass the crossing via a wooded trail the scouts had identified as passable for tanks. The nearest bridge over the little stream looked sturdy enough, but there was no time for the scouts to inspect it. Sam called a halt. Before unplugging his tanker's helmet, he motioned to Clem Elissondo: "Cover me with the .30-caliber, Clem." Clem, wearing aviator sunglasses, rocked back the machine gun's forward assist, gave the Colonel a thumbs up and grimly scanned the tree line ahead. Sam squeezed out of the top hatch, slid down the side of the turret, and stepped down onto a road wheel and then the boggy ground.

He took out his shoulder-holstered .45-caliber pistol and walked up to the bridge. Through the haze of fatigue, Sam admired the thick copses of pines grandly straddling a carpet of reddish pine needles. In a quick lapse of battle focus, he reflected on such beautiful land—what a shame how men turned on each other in war, destroying their own surroundings in the process.

He snapped back to reality. No shots had rung out, and Sam crouched low near the stone base. He then took a knee to look at the sides and bottom. It was sturdy construction—no wires showed on the sides or underneath, as far as he could see. He crossed the short span. Staying low, he repeated his hasty bridge survey on the opposite bank. A short power walk back across and he was waving his Sherman forward, leading it across the bridge. Time to roll on.[4]

Two spearheads converging created another hazard. The route was near Task Force Richardson's area of operations, creating conditions for a possible dangerous friendly fire incident. They took precautions as best they could, with close radio and map coordination. Thankfully, Sam's column continued without incident, securing the fortified villages of Silkerode and Bockelnhagen from enemy infantrymen by 10:00 P.M.

The task force coiled for the night and prepared to move on to Nordhausen at sunrise.[5] For the attack, Task Force Hogan was again supported by the "Old Reliables"—GIs of the Third Battalion, Forty-seventh Infantry, led by their brave commander, the handlebar-mustached Don Clayman. Since last fighting alongside TF Hogan, Don had earned the Distinguished Service Cross and two Purple Hearts. Sam was glad to have this hero back in the fold, though Don's unit arrived into Hogan's lines late on April 11, which delayed their crossing. But they moved on in short, reaching the outskirts of Nordhausen by 9:00 P.M. that night.[6]

THE FOLLOWING DAY, APRIL 12, the morning light revealed the horrors of the concentration camps clustered around Nordhausen, which had provided slave labor for the Dora-Mittelbau underground rocket factory. Task Forces Hogan and Richardson were under orders to move quickly and seize crossings over the Elbe, but as they passed the camps, they stopped to secure the area and render what assistance they could.

As the column approached, they could smell the camp before they even laid eyes on it. Human filth, charred flesh, and smoky ash stung their nostrils as dismal gray and brown forms of people and buildings came into view. Even for these soldiers, who thought they'd already seen every horror that war had to offer, an odd suspension of reality gripped them as they entered the barbed-wire enclosure through torn camp gates. The memory of the concentration camp stuck with Sam for the rest of his life—it made him question his belief in a higher power. What God would allow this kind of cruelty upon his creation?

In one corner of the camp was a stack of human bodies five feet high. The emaciated corpses were lined faceup, half a dozen bodies wide, with firewood interspersed and another layer of corpses on top. The tops of shaved heads and the bottoms of pale, bony feet alternated in each row. The SS guards had fled well before they could hide the evidence of their crimes by setting fire to the stack of bodies. Something in the pile drew the commander's eyes as the tank columns halted. Sam swallowed hard as he thought he saw movement within the stack. Some of the prisoners had been laid in the human piles still alive. For many of them, it was still too late.

Once inside the camp proper, infantry cleared one-story shacks and a few brick buildings clustered within the barbed-wire-topped concrete walls. The American soldiers saw visions rivaling Dante's depiction of hell inside the filthy, dilapidated wooden barracks, their floors covered in dirty straw, with men in pinstripe uniforms here and there too sick to stand. Outside, walking skeletons shambled in the same rough, oversized pinstripe uniforms, milling about in shock, heads crawling with lice and other vermin. Some smiled widely and wept, greeting the Americans with a mix of elation and disbelief.

The tankers radioed back to combat command headquarters requesting urgent medical support and supplies of rations from the division. They stopped long enough to make sure the SS guards had cleared out and to provide some measure of first aid and what rations and water they had with them.

The column had to move on to the next objective. Always the next objective. They rolled on, trying to shake off the shock of what they had just seen. The clean and beautiful countryside through which they drove seemed tainted by the barbarous crimes these woods and pea-green rolling hills had hidden in their bosom for so long.

For Sam and countless others in the column, there was no doubt now what they were fighting for. There was suddenly a new, deeper meaning to what the soldiers had endured over the past years away from home: the hard training, the unpalatable food eaten on the run, the freezing cold endured with little or no shelter, holidays spent sleeping on the frozen hard ground with nothing but a trench coat for shelter—and, of course, the loss of close friends. The column moved on, grimly, with a renewed sense of purpose.

The second tragic event of the day was later that afternoon of the twelfth—the news caught the tanks at a crossroads stop to await fuel trucks. Tankers stood in their turrets, ears to their radios, while infantrymen—perched on hulls or looking up from the ground below—listened intently. President Franklin Delano Roosevelt, who had led the United States for the previous twelve tumultuous years, had died at his convalescent getaway of Warm Springs, Georgia. Commanders observed a moment of silence and prepared for a stiffened resistance from the Germans. The news energized Adolf Hitler and his fanatical entourage as they fantasized that FDR's death could mean a split in the US–UK–Russia alliance. To complete the awful day, Task Force Hogan yet again outran its fuel supply, forcing a halt to await the trucks.

Overnight fueling allowed Task Force Hogan to continue the march by 7:00 A.M. on April 13. Sam, through the veil of exhaustion, marveled at how his body and mind could continue with three to four hours of sleep a night, with occasional catnaps, and a steady diet of cigarettes and black coffee. He vowed never to eat brussels sprouts again, as that seemed to be the only fresh food Sergeant Barclay's cooks were able to get ahold of.

Antitank fire from the front interrupted his ruminations.

A German FLAK 88 dual-purpose cannon fired on the tail of the column from woods to the northeast. Sam worried because Colonel Howze's command post was following his column. The 88 destroyed three half-tracks of the supporting field artillery battalion. Sam radioed out to the tank destroyers guarding his flank to take out the gun. The German crew abandoned it shortly after firing their initial salvo.[7]

The Americans drove on. By noon, the columns had passed Helbra, leaving the CCR command post there and continuing on to Siersleben, where a large prisoner-of-war camp housing British and Soviet soldiers was liberated. By 2:30 P.M., Task Force Hogan captured a nearly intact railroad bridge across the Saale River at Nelben. The German defenders were surprised, and after G Company tankers destroyed their support-ing self-propelled gun, they surrendered. As darkness approached, Task Force Hogan coiled up to rest and fuel near Nelben while engineers pre-pared the bridge to handle the weight of tanks.

Travis Brown reported that the security element of CCR liberated a dozen US paratroopers from another prisoner-of-war camp. The sol-diers, taken prisoner during D-Day, were much relieved to be back behind friendly lines. As the task force refueled and awaited the engi-neers' work, Sam leaned back for a couple of hours of sleep. It was not a dreamless slumber—visions of the walking skeletons of Nordhausen haunted him. He awoke feeling sadness and dread. His usual upbeat personality was taking a hit.

Inside his command tank, the crew made ready to move with radio, ammunition, and oil pressure checks. Still in a daze, the commander looked around his cramped turret space. Sam didn't believe in carry-ing religious amulets or crosses. He thought them crutches, especially now. He did have a photograph of Belle pasted by his commander's periscope to remind him of faith and family. He gazed at it for a mo-ment, but there was an emotional void in his heart. In a quick hand motion, he took it down, folding it into the side pocket of his duffel bag strapped to the outside of the turret. His mother, Mary, would be disappointed in these thoughts. Maybe Belle was right after all to not want children—why bring them into such a barbaric world?

Push these thoughts way down. Keep rolling. Bring these boys back alive.

At daybreak, US infantry crossed to the opposite bank of the Saale to secure it. Hogan's tanks and a battery of artillery followed. Task Force Richardson snaked over and used the same bridge. After the Saale cross-ing, Sam looked out from the turret of his tank as the ground flattened toward the northeast. Well behind his left shoulder, the Harz Moun-tains rose majestically in patches of gray granite surrounded by thick verdant forest as the springtime advanced. The gray reminded Sam of the German uniforms and paint scheme on their tanks. Like the granite, they too refused to yield, except by hammer blows.

Infantry units such as the Ninth and 104th Division needed to mop up within the Harz, so from now on Spearhead relied on its limited number of assigned infantry from the Thirty-sixth Armored Infantry. The plains ahead were dotted with small towns, more "hedgehog" strongpoints. Commanders knew they would be a tough nut to crack with limited infantry if the Germans decided to defend them house to house, Panzerfausts in hand. German defensive positions were set up on the outskirts of each, then inside the towns and on the river itself. Strongpoints, barbed wire, covered foxholes with excellent fields of fire, and mines—including undetectable ones made of glass—awaited the Americans.

Spearhead once again advanced so far that they were too far ahead of their supply line—they lacked fuel again as well as motor oil. Thinning out their ranks even more, the division needed to hold a forty-mile-wide front, including towns and villages, until properly relieved by one of the trailing infantry divisions. Thus, by mid-April, the Third Armored Division was overextended, with its left flank wide open. Sam received orders to close that gap by taking the town of Köthen, then advancing to Aken, on the banks of the Elbe River. The move would protect the division flank while isolating Dessau for the push across the river and on to Berlin. The westernmost task force of the Third Armored Division, Task Force Hogan pushed out in two parallel columns.

Köthen, with a population of twenty thousand, was Berlin's dairy cow. Milk from surrounding farms was gathered and moved on to the German capital via railway. The German military presence was strong, including an important Luftwaffe airfield centered near the Junkers Aircraft Factory. It provided some of the fighter-aircraft cover against Allied bombers targeting Berlin.

Intelligence reported that three new divisions—the Scharnhorst, Potsdam, and Urlich Van Hutten, each six thousand strong—had been cobbled together from the area's air force and naval personnel around a cadre of officer candidates and instructors from the Breslau School of Combat Engineering.[8]

On April 14, the two columns of Task Force Hogan approached Köthen from the south, passing the Luftwaffe airfield, where a large bomber and several Focke-Wulfe 190 fighters remained parked for lack of fuel and pilots. Nazi officials had taken the last serviceable cargo aircraft and fled, leaving the common people to do the fighting and dying.

Of course, soldiers being soldiers, one of Task Force Hogan's mechanically inclined GIs got into the cockpit of an FW 190 as a goof. Egged on by the other soldiers, Tech 4 Leroy Heinz sat wide-eyed and grinning as he cranked the engine, the propeller began to turn, and with a push of the throttle the plane began a slow roll down the runway. The soldiers hollered and clapped. But what to do now? First Sergeant Filyaw's booming voice, jumping, and arm waving imposed some order on the scene as the would-be pilot shut off the fuel switch and clambered off the aircraft to the hoots of his squad members.

Back in the town proper, trouble was brewing. Every small building, barn, or house was a hiding place for the enemy, desperate to slow down the Americans' approach to the river and Berlin. After passing the airfield, Sam heard an explosion as the radio erupted with a request for medics. One of the assault guns had been hit by antitank rocket fire as it moved into position to support the infantry. Sam hung his head as he heard the report. Killed in action while commanding his assault gun was Sergeant Herman Rewerts, a survivor of the Hogan's 400 march. The Minnesotan was only two years younger than his battalion commander.[9]

At the outskirts of Köthen, two battalions' worth of German infantry armed with Panzerfausts blocked the road. Dug in on the sides of the road and around their roadblock, other Germans also moved between the low-lying houses. Simple bypass of this enemy position was not an option—a move like that could trap the US column between the river and the German positions. Rewerts's death also demonstrated the need to clear each and every building and possible ambush site.

A death this late in the war hit Task Force Hogan hard. Everyone could sense that the war in Europe was entering its final phase. Sam Hogan took each combat loss hard, but—over the space of the last three months—to a lesser degree. The losses of Jake, Ed, and so many others had numbed his heart and his faith. Now, with that dreaded ice in his veins, he found worry to be a useless emotion. It's not that he didn't care—he cared too much, and now finally accepted that so much of the ultimate outcome wasn't in his hands to control. Soldiering was a risky business—maybe the riskiest.

A good commander learned to accept some risk and minimize it, through good planning and execution, solid tactics, and overwhelming firepower—but to always know the specter of death was there. Sam desperately wanted to bring the rest of his boys home alive. Maybe they could crack this town's defenses with artillery barrages and a show of armored strength. Maybe he could parlay with the bürgermeister or local party official, as Lieutenant Resterer had done outside Paderborn. But no, that was a pipe dream. The artillery and P-47 bombardment might do the trick. First, however, they had to make sure the town was not full of civilians.

The US tanks pushed forward through the town's outskirts. US infantry strode decisively from cover to cover or crouched low beside the Sherman tanks. They fired a burst of machine gun or well-aimed rifle fire as German infantry popped up to fire their antitank rockets or darted in between narrow streets and alleyways. The going was slow. As the infantry reached each dwelling, the squad split up—sending one fire team to clear the house while the other stayed outside guarding the entryway and its designated tank. This kind of combat was the great equalizer. The Americans were not able to call in artillery or air support on the inhabited dwellings, so close to their forward line of troops.

By 1:00 A.M. on the morning of the fifteenth, G Company and its infantry stalled at a roadblock barring the route through Köthen. Spruce logs and debris anchored on the town's old medieval watchtower kept the US tanks at bay. Sam was in no mood for this. Clem Elissondo had secured a speaker from the psychological operations people at corps and fixed it to the commander's hatch.

"These roadblocks will be removed by dawn or I will destroy this town," Sam bellowed out in his best "Germish." He dropped back into the turret. "Okay, now we wait."

H Company, a few blocks over, reached its objective not quite in the center of town and settled in for a night of pulling guard until daylight so as not to expose its flank as G Company waited to see if Sam's ultimatum would work.

Throughout the night, there was movement to the front, the clanking of metal, the dragging of heavy items across cobblestone. Sam and Tom Cooper squinted through the twilight. *Were the Germans reinforcing?*

The early light of spring dawn revealed the answer. A group of mostly women mixed with a few teenaged boys was dismantling the roadblocks.

At 8:00 A.M., Tom Cooper's G Company roared past the debris of the cleared roadblock, making progress in the daylight. Engineers were pulled up to the front line by the two tank companies to clear out what was left of the roadblocks covering the town's main intersection.[10] Signs showed that, from this intersection, the roads led out to Magdeberg, Leipzig, and Berlin via Dessau.

The engineers—along with Emmett Tripp's dozer—cleared the roads, and G and H Companies advanced, leapfrogging from intersection to intersection with the infantry checking each house. At around noon, a wave of Volkssturm infantry using assault rifles, shotguns, and Panzerfausts hit Task Force Hogan in the left flank. The Germans were using a new tactic of firing their antitank rockets in an arc like a mortar. It wasn't a bad idea, as the gunner could "shoot and scoot" at the tank's weakest spot. A tank's armor is always thinner up top and below—the same principle today makes the US Javelin antitank missile so successful against Russia's best tanks.[11] However, the simple "point and shoot" sights of the Panzerfaust didn't help the Germans' lost cause. The American tanks drove the Germans back with their coaxial machine guns as US infantry added rifle and bazooka fire.

At 1:00 P.M., Sam received the order to clear the rest of Köthen, then move west to link up with Task Force Richardson at a town called Frenz. By late afternoon, the two task forces linked up west of Köthen,

then sent patrols to establish contact with the adjoining Spearhead units from Combat Command A and Task Force Orr (led by Lieutenant Colonel Bill Orr of the Thirty-sixth Armored Infantry Regiment). Thusly, Spearhead's flank was secured.

After the tough fight for Köthen, Task Force Hogan rolled out early on the seventeenth, clearing an initial roadblock and mines at Porst. Along the route, they cleared a chemical plant, another airfield, and an electrical plant. They liberated a hospital that housed several US prisoners of war, including captured VII Corps signal corps wiremen. From there, Sam divided his command into two columns again to envelop Aken. The little town sat right on the bank of the Elbe, four miles from Dessau. It was yet another miniature fortress with about three-quarters of the houses containing infantry armed with Panzerfausts or Panzerschrecks.

As Task Force Hogan closed in around Aken, German artillery fire rained down from the opposite bank of the Elbe. Watching through his binoculars, Sam saw residents hang white flags from balconies and windows in the hopes of sparing their lives and homes. They risked being shot by Gestapo or SS on Heinrich Himmler's standing "no surrender" orders. There was a barricade blocking the road.

"Clem, move forward one hundred meters," Sam barked into his radio.

"Roger, sir." The Easy Eight Sherman roared forward. Flanked by three tanks and infantry squads moving up behind in their half-tracks, Sam's probe got things moving.

"All elements, hold your fire." Through his field glasses, Sam could see doors opening in the stone homes lining the center thoroughfare in front of him. Women, mothers of the Hitler Youth behind the barricades, purposefully strode to the jumble of overturned carts, sandbags, and rubble to take their teenage (sometimes younger) boys away from where they'd been pressed to serve by the local Nazi Party satrap. Sam and his commanders saw some of the drama unfold through their field glasses as they converged on the town at 5:00 P.M.[12] Sam hoped the young enemy soldiers would stand down—the Americans would attack at sunup, regardless.

At 6:00 A.M. the following day, the task force began deliberately clearing Aken. Several roadblocks in the northwestern quadrant of town were covered by fire from FLAK 88s. Sam ordered mortar and artillery fire onto the FLAK gun positions. The mortarmen again saved the blood of their infantry and armored brothers. German artillery and mortars also fired back. These were the last defensive belts protecting Aken city hall, where the German command post sat with its back to the river eight hundred feet behind. It took the remainder of the day to clear out Aken. At 7:00 P.M., a Task Force Hogan patrol established contact with the Eighty-third "Thunderbolt" Infantry Division.

The following morning another body blow struck Spearhead's original founding members. Sam was sipping some coffee, ready for the morning radio call on the regimental net, when Sergeant D'Orio took off his earphones.

"Sir, it sounds like the Germans got Osgood Six," he said grimly.

"What? Let me hear that." The news over the radio was clear, even though Sam started listening in the middle. "Send up a Graves Registration team" . . . break . . . "to pick up Osgood Six." Osgood Six was the Eighty-third Recon Battalion's commander.

During the early morning hours of the eighteenth, Iron Mike Yeomans of Syracuse, New York, was killed in action by enemy artillery fire on the autobahn near the hamlet of Bitterfeld-Wolfen. The Eighty-third Recon Battalion had been called to assist Task Force Lovelady when German infantry attacked their command post as they slogged their way southwest of Dessau. It was one of those harsh ironies of war. Yeomans, an original Spearheader, whose troops were always out front, died in the waning days of the conflict. Sam shook his head and handed back the headphones to D'Orio without a word.

FOR TEXANS LIKE SAM AND Rich Richardson, April 21 held significance as the date of the Battle of San Jacinto. In 1836, near the modern-day city that bears his name, Sam Houston and his ragged army of eight hundred farmers, adventurers, and militiamen destroyed the Mexican army in the field. Amid war cries of "Remember the Alamo!" they captured Mexican general Santa Anna, securing Texas's independence as a republic.

Just as the Texan commanders may have felt observing the tents of the napping Mexican army, a sense of culmination and impending victory pervaded the US ranks. The enemy was not only on the ropes—they were about to fall out of the ring, unconscious. Sam wanted to temper these feelings and ensure nobody got killed or severely wounded in the last days of the war. Never underestimate your enemy. There was still danger ahead. The Germans were hell-bent on preventing a bridgehead across the Elbe at a place where the river horseshoed inside the town of Dessau.

He had had little time to process the events of the last two-hundred-plus days. The shock of seeing close friends die—men like Ben Creamer and Jake Sitzes, for whom Sam had unwittingly developed affection as strong as that of an older brother toward a younger one. What he saw at Nordhausen still confounded him. He didn't want a heart full of hate or distrust for humanity—but how could humans do such things to their fellow humans?

Things were reaching a frenzied climax with no slowdown in pace. The American's combat power dwindled from constant advance, casualties, wear and tear on vehicles, and the need to leave detachments behind to secure their supply lines. The German forces, meanwhile, consolidated within their interior lines. They still had plenty of supplies—Task Force Lovelady had captured a thousand Panzerschrecks in a warehouse along their advance. To add to the chaos, freed prisoners and refugees, as well as civilians in flight from the rampaging Soviets, streamed in the direction of US lines in an emerging humanitarian crisis of historic proportions.

Sam received orders to clear a large factory, and would have to do this with a thinned-out task force. One platoon of infantry, another of light tanks from C Company, and a section of tank destroyers stayed behind guarding Aken. The small force was able to occupy the factory, which turned out to be the Wolfen Film Factory—the site of Germany's first color movie production. Wolfen's 1943 production of *The Adventures of Baron Munchausen* was an oblique criticism of Hitler's propaganda machine and its ability to spin lies and fabrications.[13]

At 6:00 A.M., TF Hogan made its push on Dessau-on-the-Elbe. Artillery boomed to their front and to their back as US preparatory fires peppered the far side, and German mortars and Nebelwerfer rockets responded. Splitting into two weakened columns, they advanced for an hour before a roadblock manned by Panzerfaust-armed infantry and covered by artillery fire stopped their advance.

The drill repeated itself like a never-ending bad dream: Call in artillery and mortars and flank the roadblocks with infantry through the woods as the tanks pin down the defenders with machine gun and tank cannon fire. Roll over the roadblock, make sure all enemy personnel are dead, wounded, or surrendering. Treat your casualties, radio in a report, and move on to the next roadblock. By 2:30 P.M., the outskirts were clear, and the task force pressed on until ordered to halt late in the afternoon so that Combat Command A could come up abreast.[14]

Next, Task Force Hogan, Combat Command A, and Task Force Orr attacked at 5:15 A.M. after a fitful night of probing attacks and exchanges of artillery and machine gun fire. The overcast dawn seemed to stiffen the resistance of the defending German troops, who poured out Panzerfaust and mortar fire. Each house had to be cleared of potential Panzerfaust-armed occupants waiting for an unsuspecting Sherman to get within range.

House-to-house combat continued into the daylight as the US columns reached the center streets of Dessau. Smoke filled the ruined city. Formerly charming medieval buildings with storefront signs in German script reading "Fleischerei" (Butcher), neatly painted over handsome carved wooden doors, stood with half the corner crumbled onto the cobblestone streets and timbers and flooring sticking out of the sides. Follow-on forces would have to demolish what would likely collapse anyway, possibly onto passersby.

Broadcasts over loudspeakers exhorted the German forces to hold out for "Führer and Fatherland." Several corpses swung slowly from lampposts, cardboard signs hanging on their chests identifying them as deserters from the German army. These were more visions of hell—it had been a nonstop nightmare since the Americans set eyes on Nordhausen and drove deeper into Germany.

The US advance ground to a stop in front of a belt of mines placed directly in their path. Engineers moved up under fire to slowly and methodically clear them. While this slow work continued, Sam ordered a patrol consisting of two tanks and infantry to sweep the woods to their west to prevent any flanking attack. A lump was at his throat again—the specter of more loss of life at what was clearly the end of the war for Germany.

The din of battle crescendoed again—a rising action giving the sense of the last act of a play, as the US engineers cleared the mines under the sporadic *POP! POP!* of rifle fire. Ahead was a roadblock—a barricade of cement blocks and destroyed car carcasses of Volkswagens with sandbags piled on top. All the Americans could see were Nazi coal-bucket helmets popping up here and there. Uniformed Hitler Youth were among them. The rest were scared old men and a handful of teenagers looking with doubt through the sights of their bolt-action rifles. At the time, the Americans only knew it was an enemy-held barricade.

Sam couldn't stand the thought of a single additional casualty among his men. One strong volley of tank and mortar fire would wreck the roadblock. He radioed from his turret, "Hawk, this is Six, get ready to blow that roadblock to smithereens." The engineers—crouching down, prodding, digging—were almost finished. Sam waited for the thumbs-up from their sergeant.

"How Six, this is Blue Six—prepare to roll through the roadblock and occupy the far side of town."

"Six, roger," came the reply. Sam squinted as sweat stung his eyes. The dull thud of enemy mortar fire leaving its tubes sounded on the far side of the river—*thoomp, thoomp, thoomp.* He grew impatient—they were sitting ducks waiting for the removal of the mines.

There was a flash of steel behind the enemy barricade. Sam glanced at the engineers, their sergeant crouching down, his SCR radio held against his temple, helmet cocked askew.

"Sir, this is Rock Three—mines are clear."

Sam switched to the Fires net, ready to order a barrage to wreck the enemy barricade. He would then send his tanks crashing through it, the infantry killing or capturing anyone left alive. He hesitated. Why haven't they fired at us yet? Is it a trap?

He stayed on the battalion net: "Guidons, this is Six—no prep fires. Move out to the objective." He glanced down at Elmer Johnson and Clem Elissondo, and Elmer craned his neck and met Sam's grin with his own as he stepped on the Sherman's gas, sending it forward in a slow lurch. The five tanks in the wedge narrowed from an inverted V to a column, with Sam's tank second behind the dozer tank. They expected a hail of Panzerfaust fire at any moment. But suddenly, a white shirt fluttered from behind the barricade.

The tanks rolled closer. Through his periscope, Sam saw German faces, and now hands flying up. The formation halted just one hundred meters from the barricade as the US tank commanders cautiously popped up out of their hatches for a look. The accompanying US infantrymen prudently kept their rifles up, pointed at the heads of the Germans, who began streaming from behind the barricade, hands held high.

Now the tankers could see they were kids, teenagers wearing a hodgepodge of ill-fitting uniforms of field gray or camouflage. Two boys had the Hitler Youth uniform of shorts and brown button-down shirts with a small ceremonial dagger at their waist. Little blond boys, wide-eyed with fear. Tears streamed from their eyes. One or two old men came up behind them with sickly, defeated faces of ash and dust.

Sam breathed a sigh of relief. Standing on top of his turret, he waved for them to come forward. He didn't want to think of what would have happened to these kids if he had ordered the barricade taken by fire. Two US infantrymen moved forward cautiously, their buddies covering them with their rifles, the tankers leveling turret-mounted machine guns at the surrendering Germans—just in case.

This time there was no fanatic faking-a-surrender then detonating a grenade hidden inside a coat pocket. This time there was no sniper fire from the decoy of a white flag of surrender as had happened to other units. Once the German squad was frisked and the barricade cleared, the US infantry gave the younger prisoners a few chocolate bars. Some of the infantrymen flashed tired smiles at the scared German boys to reassure them a bit. Their war was over, and they had survived. Just a bit farther, and maybe the Americans soldiers could say the same for themselves. On to the next objective, the riverbank, to await the arrival of a bridging company to vault them across the Elbe and on to Berlin. Maybe someday they would all get to go home.

Maybe.

AS TASK FORCE HOGAN RUMBLED and clanked to the very eastern edge of Dessau, they looked out on the wide, brown Elbe River. What next? Where was the engineer bridging company?

The river's banks were sandy and stretched out for thirty yards. Sam looked through his field glasses. He estimated it could take seven or eight pontoons to cross it. What if his tanks got bogged down in the soft sand? With German artillery on the far bank, they could destroy the forces bunched up and stuck trying to get on the pontoons. It would be a bloodbath.

Where was the motorcycle dispatch rider with orders to cross and occupy the opposite bank? Sam was alert and impatient. He stared across the river trying to get a sense of what awaited them there.

His recon was interrupted by a radio transmission: "All units, this is Omaha Six—halt and cease all preparations for a river crossing."

Just like that, it was over. Commanders received an additional alert—keep an eye out for contact with the Russian forces.

On the opposite bank, the sounds of the Soviet First Ukrainian Front approaching with a thousand tubes of artillery portended the end of the Third Reich the way the booming notes of horn and timpani bellowed at the end of a Wagner opera. After 220 days of combat, Spearhead columns idled their engines only ninety miles away from Hitler's bunker in Berlin where the dictator would kill himself a week later.

The tired soldiers halted, dismounted their tanks, and looked around in disbelief that it was really over. Mixed feelings of elation and loss filled their hearts. Men were grateful to have survived the tribulations of combat. Hope in their spirits blossomed up slowly for men who, weeks earlier, had tried not to think of what would happen if their life ended on the battlefield.

Now they wondered what it would be like to go back home to a nine-to-five job. What it would be like to start a family with their sweetheart back home.

Their division's exploits would become legend in the US Army. The first division to fire artillery shells into Germany. The first to capture a German town (Stolberg) and breach the Siegfried line. The first to capture a German city after being the first to cross over into Germany since Napoleon in 1810.

But most members of Spearhead just felt lucky to have survived. The fighting had been vicious. Spearhead sustained 2,214 killed in action, 7,451 wounded in action, and 706 missing. Spearhead suffered the loss of 633 Shermans—a staggering loss rate of 272 percent, which excludes tanks that were repaired and put back into service. That means that for every tank Spearhead had at the beginning of the war, 2.7 were destroyed, with replacement tank after replacement tank knocked out by enemy fire.[15]

After April 24, and a few more mopping up operations, for several months the mighty Spearhead Division settled into the routines of an occupying army. There were baseball games, movies, and the occasional marksmanship or field gunnery drill as rumors continued that the division would participate in the invasion of Japan's home island. The entire division passed in review for President Harry S. Truman and General Eisenhower—but, shortly after, on August 6, the atomic bomb ended the Japanese Empire's World War II ambitions and Spearhead's possible role in an invasion. At the command to "fall out," the soldiers gathered into groups. Some let out huzzahs and hollered. Others stood there, somewhat numb. What did this new weapon mean? Would it usher in a new era of deadly aggression between nations? Most chose to focus on the present. When is my number up so I can board that Liberty ship back across the Atlantic?

You could almost hear the collective sigh of relief from the hundreds of soldiers standing at parade rest after the announcement. The news meant they were going home. That they had survived the biggest, bloodiest conflict in world history.

A FEW DAYS LATER, SAM gathered his immediate staff and commanders, all of them dressed smartly in their "pinks and greens" service uniforms. Left shoulders decorated with the red-and-green fourragère cord awarded by the government of Belgium to units that liberated that country from the German war machine. Four combat service stripes on their sleeves. The Silver Star and Bronze Star ribbons adorned many of their coats, attesting to valor on the front lines. Many of them wore the Purple Heart ribbon as well for wounds in combat.

This was goodbye. The battalion commander looked around. The faces were still young, but to look in their eyes revealed that they'd seen it all. Few of the original group who landed in Normandy were still there. But John Barclay, Ted Cardon, Travis Brown, and the ever-faithful Phil D'Orio were about to leave their commander's side for good. There would be reunions in their future. However, Sam realized that he would probably not see these men again. A mixture of survivor's guilt and the discomfort of the memories seeing these good men again would bring to the surface settled the matter for him—he planned to leave the war behind.

The men lined up, saluting, as Sam walked up to each in turn—returning the salute, then warmly shaking their hands. Sam wished them luck in their future endeavors.

"Stewart, I expect to see you as a senator from Louisiana soon."

"Sergeant D'Orio, you take good care, okay? You have your whole life ahead of you. From here on out, it's all gravy."

A hearty shake of the hand with Travis Brown: "Brownie, you come and see me if you ever need anything."

The warm southern accent replied, "Sir, I want you to know you ran a hell of an outfit."

With tears in their eyes, the heroes of Task Force Hogan parted ways. Sam would have cringed at being called a hero. He did not believe himself to be one, but he knew he had served among heroes. The surviving men of the Third Armored Division began returning home aboard crowded troopships and passenger liners, passing back into the United States of America under the welcoming gaze of the Statue of Liberty to continue the rest of their lives, grateful for having survived.

EPILOGUE

★ ★ ★ ★ ★

MARCH 1946

Lieutenant Colonel Samuel Mason Hogan sat impassively under the massive 150-foot vaulted ceilings of the Ludwigsburg Palace throne room, former seat of the dukes and kings of Württemberg, about twenty miles outside of Stuttgart in the US-occupied zone of Germany. Elegant, brownish-pink marble columns trimmed the stucco walls. Towering above him were frescoes reminiscent of the Sistine Chapel in Rome. Blue-painted sky superimposed with white fluffy clouds hosting well-muscled gods who glowered down in judgment on the mortals below.

A *Stars and Stripes* photographer captured Sam—who, three months earlier, had turned thirty years old—sitting at the extreme left of a long oak table looking trim and neat in his pinks and greens. His crew cut, now heavily graying, despite his years, testified to almost a year of nonstop leadership in combat. His visage remained as calm now as it had during battle. Only his left hand, holding up his head in thought, gave any indication of the new burdens he carried.

To his right, under low-hanging, twinkling crystal chandeliers, sat a long bench of US military attorneys from the Judge Advocate General's Corps—or JAGs. Behind them, on naked benches lining the walls, were eight German prisoners, sitting in their drab gray uniforms, devoid of any decoration and with the concerned, dead-eyed looks of men who were about to stand trial for their lives. Through the fifteen-foot windows looking into a magnificent courtyard shone intense sunlight, which only added shadows and grays to the backlit faces of the prisoners.

Perpendicular to the long bench and in front of the fifty-foot marble pillars flanking an ancient throne sat the seven military judges presiding over the Borkum Island war crimes tribunal. Old Glory stood on a pedestal behind them—a reminder that the occupying force held authority and jurisdiction over any proceedings inside the grand throne room.

Sam was part of this tribunal charged with the investigation and prosecution of ten German soldiers and five civilians accused of the August 1944 lynching of a downed B-17 bomber crew—possibly, one of the very same B-17s that had flown over Sam and Task Force Hogan in Normandy during the same month. Sam's job was to be the attorney in charge of the defense of the accused. A strong believer in equality for all under the law, there were few people better for the job.

How did he get there? Sam's upbringing had instilled in him an admiration and respect for the institutions that made the US a beacon of hope and freedom for people across the world. He'd always had an interest in civics, the US Constitution, and the rule of law. Maybe it was in his blood.

He came from a family of not just soldiers and cowboys but several judges—including his father and great-grandfather, Judge John "Law" Miller, who, in the 1860s, dispensed justice from a two-room log cabin to the rough frontiersmen living on the border between Texas and "Comancheria."

Still, he was not one to imitate blindly—he had a rebellious streak for sure. Over the past months, he had pondered his future in the army. A successful, well-known combat commander, Sam could have had his pick of stateside training assignments. After being a division chief of staff or brigade executive officer, he was likely to take command of a tank brigade, a sure step toward general officer rank.

But Sam didn't want that. His marriage had failed, partly due to the rigors of his being away from home. He always did the best job that he could in assignments, never seeking headlines, fame, or military glory. Starred rank was too political, and you lost control over your days. Sam would continue to pick interesting, rewarding assignments over those that might elevate him to flag-officer rank.

The army was short of trained JAGs for the dozens of tribunals needed to bring closure to the war through the prosecution of the most heinous of war crimes. Chief among them were the Nuremburg trials and those in the Pacific theater. A call for highly decorated, college-educated officers to fill the lower-profile tribunals went out, and Sam heeded. He was placed where he was most needed, coordinating the team of German lawyers defending the accused.

Fate led Sam to be caught up in the long chain of events that began in August 1944, when a B-17G bomber with tail number 94–909—so new that it didn't yet have a catchy nickname or nose art—took off on a bombing run over Hamburg that it never completed. After taking ground fire, the pilots—Lieutenants Harvey Walthall and William Meyers—heroically recovered their stricken B-17 from a harrowing inverted dive, and managed to somehow safely land it on a pebble beach on the German garrison island of Borkum.

But a mob of locals, roused by Nazi party officials, lynched the two officers and a majority of the crew as they were paraded through the center of town.

After Victory in Europe (V-E) Day, forced laborers who'd survived Borkum alerted the Allied authorities to the war crime. An investigation, legal process, and trial followed. By midnight on March 23, 1946, the exhausted members of the tribunal awaited the seven judges' decision and sentencing. Sam's team of German defense attorneys had completed their closing arguments earlier that evening.

Finally, the massive wooden doors to the throne room opened, followed by the echoing footfalls of the seven military judges.

Colonel Edward B. Jackson read the verdict in a clear, deliberate monotone: "This military tribunal finds the following defendants guilty . . ." Kurt Goebbel, the ranking officer on Borkum Island; Jacob Seiler, the commander of the antiaircraft battery; Erich Wentzel, the English-speaking officer in charge of the column of prisoners; Johann Schmitz, the sergeant in charge of the prisoners; and Jan Akkermann, the rabid Nazi mayor, were sentenced to a rendezvous with the hangman. Those defendants whose circumstances mitigated their guilt—such as shielding the Americans from mob attack or attempting to render first aid to the wounded—were acquitted. Sam leaned back, not with the arrogance of the victor, but with the satisfaction that he had concluded his final task for World War II. After all these months, after his task force soldiers had already departed Europe, he could begin to leave the war behind and move on with his life.

The last time Sam Hogan had stood on his home soil was August of 1943. His approved leave to return to the United States came through the morning of March 22, 1946. His first action was to purchase a sea ticket from Le Havre and send a cable to his family in South Texas, notifying them of his impending arrival. He closed with a request for "commissary support" on his arrival—barbecued steaks, thick broiled gulf shrimp, oysters, hot biscuits, and plenty of ice cream. He was finally homebound.

ANDEAN HIGHLANDS, ECUADOR, EARLY 1980S

The long-limbed seventy-year-old man climbed the bare ridge with the stride and purpose of a man forty years his junior. His ten-year-old son kept up, and both exhaled white puffs in the thin, cold air of the mountain. Snowcapped glaciers loomed large ahead.

The pair traveled light—two fishing rods and a tackle box. Despite the mountain cold, the man only wore a wool button-down shirt and khaki pants over army-issue leather boots. A tan Stetson cowboy hat protected his fair skin from the equatorial sun.

"We're almost there, son. One foot in front of the other." They searched for a lake full of big trout, untouched by humans, somewhere ahead in the valleys of the Andes. A broad smile crossed the older man's face. Here was a man who loved his family and the freedom of the outdoors.

He seemed to always be in the moment. When he hiked mountains or looked out on the burnt-orange sunset reflecting off the swift, chocolate-colored Amazon, perhaps he thought he needed to take it all in for Ed Wray, for Jake Sitzes, for those young men in his charge who didn't make it, who left this world too early. Too early to have children and grandchildren, destined not to grow old.

In the peace of a clear blue lake, waiting for a fish to bite, the man looked back to the fateful years, through all the unlikely events that had got him to this corner of the earth.

THE LONG SEPARATION OF WARTIME, plus the extended months away supporting the Borkum Island trial, took their final toll on Sam's marriage. Sam and Belle divorced, amicably, in April 1946—the month after the trial had ended. They had grown apart during the war, and the young couple could not overcome her lack of interest in having children.

The war and its horrors didn't ultimately dampen Sam's belief in the inherent goodness of man—he wanted a family of his own. His flirtatious friendship with army nurse Gina Gough, born in a military hospital in Germany, blossomed when they both found themselves stationed near each other on occupation duty. They fell in love, married, and had a boy named Patrick Michael in 1948.

The young family grew to love Germany, and formed strong bonds with their neighbors. Former enemies became good friends and, finally, allies. One neighbor, Frau Nina von Stauffenberg, the widow of the colonel who had led the July 20, 1944, plot to kill Hitler (and paid for it with his life), gifted Sam her husband's cavalry saddle. Sam and his little family showed the widow kindness by helping her with bags of sugar or meat or other commodities that were scarce in postwar Europe.

After his performance in the Borkum trial, Sam was selected to become a judge advocate and attended law school at Columbia University, graduating in 1950.

Life continued with its vicissitudes. Sam lost Gina to cancer in 1963. Patrick and Sam continued on, one foot in front of the other, through postings as varied as the Pentagon and the Republic of Korea. Eventually completing a thirty-year career in the military, Sam retired as a full colonel from his last assignment as defense attaché at the US embassy in Quito, Ecuador. The same year he retired, his son Patrick returned from the Vietnam War, where he had served honorably as a military intelligence combat photographer.

After retirement, Sam and Patrick stayed behind living the expatriate life. He found that his army pension went a lot of farther in South America, plus he loved the unexplored wilds of the continent. Visiting American clients and friends marveled at how the old soldier had reinvented himself as an explorer and environmentalist, leading safaris into the wilderness of South America—from Andean lakes to remote parts of the Amazon basin.

In this new life, he rubbed elbows with a diverse lot, ranging from poor indigenous boatmen to local landed gentry, ex-presidents, and retired generals whom he had met during his diplomatic assignments. One of his safari clients, Duke Franz of Bavaria, belonged to one of Europe's oldest royal families. Sam treated them all with equal warmth and empathy.

He remarried and had two more children. Despite weathering war, and the loss of friends and a wife, he never lost his joy for life or his ability to love. Both younger kids followed his example to successful careers in the US Army. His youngest child, the author of this book, served worldwide, from peacekeeping in the Balkans to humanitarian aid in Haiti and combat in Afghanistan. His final assignment took another Hogan to France, though this time without having to fight his way in. There, he worked daily with the French army on strengthening the two countries' military bonds in the face of Russia's aggression in Ukraine. Sam would have beamed at the thought.

Sam departed for his eternal rest after a boating accident and subsequent fall in 2005, in Corpus Christi, Texas. In the end, he was doing what he loved since his youth—fishing in the Gulf of Mexico. His grandson, Samuel McPeak Hogan, carries on the family tradition as an army chaplain.

THE MEN OF TASK FORCE HOGAN

★ ★ ★ ★ ★

Lieutenant Colonel Walter "Rich" Richardson: Rich went on to a very successful career. Some months after V-E Day, he was placed in charge of General George S. Patton's funeral service—and his deftly handled job did not go unnoticed by the brass. He then served in Europe on occupation duty. Sam and Rich remained good friends, hosting each other's families and going on boar hunts in the Black Forest. Rich's career of thirty years culminated with the two stars of a major general on his collar and overall command of all army forces in and around Saigon during the Vietnam War. He always considered himself an old "Spearheader," and attended reunions in Texas until well into the new millennium when his health began to fail. He passed away at his home in New Braunfels, Texas, in December 2002.

Major Travis Brown: Task Force Hogan's indefatigable operations officer went home to South Carolina after the war. He raised a large family and continued serving his country in the army reserves. He was active in his community and the Third Armored Division Association, bringing the same energy that powered the battalion's high operational tempo in the war. He was the Spearhead Association's vice president and served on its board of governors, attending reunions well into the last years of the millennium. Travis passed away in October 2001, in his native South Carolina, surrounded by his children and grandchildren. On the bottom of his gravestone, under the lines listing his Silver Star and Purple Heart, are the words:

SPEARHEAD 3RD ARMORED DIVISION

Major William "Stewart" Walker: Stewart left the army shortly after the war, having finished his time as executive officer of the First Battalion (Task Force Lovelady). He headed back to his beloved Louisiana and raised three children with his wife, Elizabeth. He remained active in the army reserves and ran for Congress in 1964. Stewart passed away in 1999.

Major Don Clayman: Commanding the Third Battalion, Forty-seventh Infantry, Ninth Infantry Division, Don Clayman finished the war as a lieutenant colonel, eventually retiring as a brigadier general. Watching him take a jeep and light tank to flush out Germans south of Mons, Sam thought he was one of the bravest officers he'd ever seen. The US Army agreed with that assessment—Don received the Distinguished Service Cross, the second-highest award for valor after the Congressional Medal of Honor. He finished the war with an amazing eleven Purple Hearts, for wounds received on eight different occasions: five by small-arms fire and three times by artillery fire. He passed away in 1987, and rests at Arlington National Cemetery.

Captain John Roger Barclay: Barclay finished the war as the H Company commander. He met, then married, Lucetta "Lu" Caudel at Fort Knox in 1946, while attending the Armor Captains Course. He went on to a distinguished career spanning thirty-five years. As a lieutenant colonel, he led a mobile training team in the shah's Iran. He also served in Vietnam, commanded the Third Armored Cavalry "Brave Rifles" Regiment, and became Chief of Armor in 1967. His final assignment took him to the Command and General Staff College at Fort Leavenworth, Kansas, where he served as director of resident instruction. He stayed in Kansas, selling Chevys, playing golf, and serving his community. Lu was by his side when he passed on, at age eighty-nine, in 2007. She followed him four years later. Her gravestone reads: "A soldier's wife."

Captain Carl H. Cramer: After sustaining his third serious combat injury, Captain Cramer was finally sent home to his wife, Juanita. His dream of returning to the noncommissioned officer corps in a peacetime army was happily shelved for a quiet life as a civilian. Carl ultimately disappeared from the history books and the lives of his former soldiers. In the late 1990s, G Company platoon leader Wilburn "Will" Saia attempted to find his old commander. Will was an active member of the Spearhead Association and enjoyed corresponding with his old teammates. Will even contacted the Department of Veterans Affairs to try to get a mailing address or phone number, but with no luck. It's likely that Carl, in common with Sam Hogan, didn't wish to revisit his memories of the war.

Captain Louis Spigelman, MD: Doc became a POW after staying behind with his wounded. He escaped but was recaptured. After VE Day, he moved to Los Angeles to resume his medical practice. He also served as head of orthopedic surgery at Cedars-Sinai Medical Center and taught at UCLA Medical School. In retirement, he became a sculptor. His works were exhibited in juried shows and the homes of private collectors. He passed away on May 6, 1993.

Captain Helaman "Ted" Cardon: After commanding C and H Companies, Ted was reassigned to the Second Battalion, Thirty-third Armored Regiment as its executive officer—filling in the key position when the incumbent became a casualty. He assumed command of the battalion after the war for a brief spell, when Lieutenant Colonel Bill Lovelady returned home. He excelled at his endeavors in business, but his joys were his family—his school sweetheart Virginia (they married in 1940) and their children. He left this earth in September 2011.

Lieutenant Jake Sitzes: Jake was one of Sam's boys who didn't make it back. He was buried on a hillside in what is now the Henri-Chapelle American Cemetery in Belgium. For two years, grateful Belgians placed flowers on his grave. In 1947, his mother, Ann, elected to accept the US government's offer to repatriate his remains stateside (an offer that was made to all surviving family members of soldiers who'd been buried where they fell). Belgians crowded the port of Antwerp to bid farewell to Jake's remains, shipped home next to fifteen hundred of his fellow deceased soldiers. His brother, Bob, named his son after his brave brother, Jake.

Lieutenant Arnold "Slack" Schlaich: After helping save the day with his assault guns at Mortain, Arnold received a battlefield commission during the Battle of the Bulge. After the war, he settled down in his native

Herscher, Illinois. He often reminisced about the "grand friends" he had in the Third Armored Division, lamenting that "no friends like that" could be found today. He passed away in 1977.

Sergeant John Robert Burns Barclay: John returned home to Illinois in the fall of 1945. Waiting for him was his prewar sweetheart, Leila Hoyt, with whom he corresponded during the course of the war. In one of his final letters before returning stateside, John proposed marriage. Leila's reply was an impatient "I thought that was already settled."[1] They were married after his return, and they lived happily for many years, raising two daughters. John attended Spearhead reunions and continued practicing his first love—making large home-cooked meals for others to enjoy—for the rest of his life. He departed in 2020, at the age of 103.

Sergeant John Grimes: Sergeant Grimes stayed on active duty after the war, eventually transferring to the military's newest branch, the US Air Force. He started a family in his native Missouri that included two sons, who both followed his example of service, in the marines and coast guard. His son, James, documented his father's career, and even discovered that Staff Sergeant George Gregan—the mortar platoon sergeant thought fatally wounded at the battle of Mortain after Sergeant Grimes helped put him in an armored ambulance—had survived into old age. Grimes joined his departed comrades on April 13, 2006—just three weeks short of his ninetieth birthday.

Tech 5 Clem Elissondo: Clem returned to his native California to pursue his dream of living on a farm in the Basque tradition of his family. Active in his community, Clem was loved for his storytelling, warm heart, and regard for animals. He was a frequent attendee at Spearhead reunions, including several visits to France and Belgium. In 2005, he followed his beloved commander Sam Hogan into Fiddlers' Green, just two months after Sam's passing. After surviving two direct hits to their tank together, it seems fitting that they parted the earth around the same time.

Staff Sergeant Lee Porter: Sergeant Porter—who saved the "day" that cold Christmas night when he took out a German sentry who was about to discover the escaping Hogan's 400—went on to live a quiet life of devotion to his family in Missouri. At the time of his discharge from the army, Lee requested demotion from staff sergeant to private. The reason he gave the discharging NCO was that he felt that killing men didn't make him a better person. Nevertheless, a good person he was. Lee had all the time in the world for his kids and doted on them. He taught them how to fish and hike through the woods quietly, but he also ingrained in them the values he lived: kindness, integrity, and honor. Lee passed away in October 2005.

MANY OF THE OTHER TASK Force Hogan soldiers who survived the war returned to the US to start families and pick up the pieces of their lives. They brought their "can-do" attitude back to their communities. Taking jobs at the railroad, in banks, on small farms, they helped rebuild the economy into the strongest the world has ever seen.

They stayed in touch with their fellow veterans through the years. The bonds of camaraderie probably helped them cope with the loss and trauma of war in an era before there were understanding, tools, and treatment for PTSD. Talking about events with fellow veterans was therapeutic for many. They and the rest of the division's vets kept alive the legacy of their fallen comrades when they established an association in 1948.

The Third Armored Division Association was another testament to the leadership and esprit de corps of the division. Annual reunions were held throughout the United States, with occasional visits to France and Belgium, where the old soldiers—accompanied often by spouses and grown children—were deservedly greeted like returning heroes. The strong links to the French, Belgian, and German communities they liberated remain today.

They also forged strong links with the new generations of Spearheaders stationed in Germany throughout the Cold War. Until the deactivation of the Third Armored Division, in 1992, the Third Battalion,

Thirty-third Armored Regiment for many years kept up a tradition of a Christmas visit to the triplet villages of Beffe-Hotton-Marcouray. There, they arrived with mobile kitchen trailers to share with young Belgians the thrill of a "camp meal" and a hike through the woods to commemorate Task Force Hogan's daring 1944 escape.

The Belgians, in turn, young and old, remain forever grateful to the World War II US veterans. To this day, Belgians care for graves they have "adopted" at the large US cemetery at Henri-Chapelle. The military cemetery sits on a beautiful country ridge surrounded by green pasture, the plateau of the Ardennes on sentinel duty to the west. Here, most of the Spearheaders killed in Belgium and Germany rest in honor. Oftentimes, the local Belgian people bring flowers and printed photographs or biographies of a deceased soldier on his birthday, or on calendar observances of military service like Memorial Day.

In 2010, as most of the veterans became too sick to travel or began to pass on, the association held its last annual national reunion in Columbus, Georgia. The board, men in their seventies and eighties—veterans from the three combat regiments as well as the division troops and headquarters—agreed to donate the association's physical artifacts, maps, and photographs to the University of Illinois Urbana-Champaign. Until the very last, an efficient, forward-thinking organization. The final mailed newsletter ended with a poignant poem written by one of their own, Cecil Phillips of the Thirty-sixth Infantry Regiment:

> *Whoever you are, Dear Friend, on that last day*
> *Look towards Heaven and you will see*
> *Somewhere beyond the Milky Way*
> *The greatest Reunion we have ever known*
> *Will Already be in progress*
> *All Ranks Complete—Marching on and on and on*

As of 2022, the ranks are almost "complete." To them, this book is dedicated.

ACKNOWLEDGMENTS

★ ★ ★ ★ ★

This book was a labor of love, the bulk of which was completed during the pandemic lockdown of 2020. I could have never finished it without the help and support of many people. Among them are a large group of family, friends, and fans of the Third Armored Division, including my own.

First off, my heartfelt thanks to fellow soldiers and authors who encouraged me to pursue this project and gave me valuable advice to make it a reality: LTC (Ret.) Mark Reardon, LTG (Ret.) Dan Bolger, and MG (Ret.) Brad Gericke.

Through my research, I met up with a devoted group of historians that want to keep alive the memories of these US soldiers and their Belgian cobelligerents. I am indebted to Darren Neely, JD Hobgood, and Bill Warnock, who were always quick to help me answer a question, pass on photographs and unit reports, or point me in the right direction.

In late 2019, I was contacted by François Janssen. He grew up listening to stories of how "Hogan" and his 400 helped liberate his grandparents' Belgian village and then stood fast in the face of the terrible German onslaught of mid-December 1944. He was surprised to hear that Sam Hogan's youngest son was not just writing a book about it but was soon to be posted to Europe with the US Army.

In short, François and his fellow members of the Big Red One reenactment group set up a touching tribute for the seventy-seventh anniversary of Task Force Hogan's breakout from Marcouray. Over the course of three days, more than one hundred reenactors convened from across Europe and the United States. They wore complete and accurate period uniforms sporting the colorful triangular "Spearhead" patches and stencils. They moved about in twenty historical vehicles, including Jeeps, trucks, and an M8 Greyhound scout car, all painted down to the last detail, with accurate company identifiers on their front and rear bumpers.

The group retraced the steps of Task Force Hogan, including the twelve-mile march from Marcouray to the stone barn at Soy. The following day, a ceremony inaugurated a monument in Beffe-Rendeux, near the site of the costly battle against the 116th Panzer Division. My family and I will always be grateful for the warm reception by François and his father and mother, Pascal and Françoise. The same goes for François De Togny, president of the BRO group; Simon Faway; Philippe Dessaucy; Sonny Verkruisse; Ben Schraverus; and all the members of local reenactment groups. Thanks for keeping the memory alive of the World War II veterans and transmitting it to the younger generations.

I am thankful, too, for having met French, Belgian, and German authors who have made it their passion and purpose to research and document the battles fought on their home soil in 1944 and 1945: Jean-Claude Decamps of Maubeuge; Dr. Frank Kreissler, state archivist at Dessau; and Eddy Montfort of the Ardennes. Thank you for your help. It's clear to me that the European unity achieved by the sacrifices of the Greatest Generation will triumph once again over the growing shadows of aggression looming in the east.

German journalist Marcus Michel is another person that contacted me via social media around the time I decided to write this book. Having grown up in eastern Germany, he provided me valuable sources and personal insights into an unreported side of the war—the final battles as TF Hogan approached the Elbe. A hearty *vielen dank* for his assistance and friendship.

Frank Kujat met me in the middle of a snowstorm outside of Henri-Chapelle American Cemetery. We paid tribute to the fallen at the hallowed site where 422 Spearheaders rest in glory. He then showed me the "Slag Pile" battlefield outside of Stolberg. I thank him for sharing his in-depth knowledge: he can recognize the modern-day site from just a glance at an eighty-year-old faded photograph.

Dieter Laes came out from Belgium in the same snowstorm in early 2022 and helped me visualize what took place close to eighty years ago. Dieter is another expert on the area's history and I was deeply impressed by his work documenting the known and less well known characters, events, and locations of the Battle of the Bulge. I look forward to reading his book on the subject.

Henri Rogester for many years honored our World War II vets, hosting them when they visited the battlefields, and kept their memories alive through the research, preservation, and dedication of plaques throughout the numerous battlefields through his association CRIBA (Belgian Ardennes Research Center). My sincere thanks to him as well.

Putting faces to names and telling the story of the soldiers of Task Force Hogan was a primary goal of this book. Many thanks are due to the families of John Barclay, Clem Elissondo, John Grimes, Ray Kuderka, Lee Porter, Jake Sitzes, and Louis Spigelman. Their anecdotes, photographs, and recollections were invaluable in my paying tribute to their memories.

Finally, a big thank-you to Mauro DiPreta, Andrew Yackira, and Don Fehr for helping me realize a dream. A dream of sharing the story of a group of young Americans who left their homes to sail across the Atlantic and literally save the world from tyranny and oppression.

NOTES

★ ★ ★ ★ ★

Chapter 1: First Blood on Hill 91

1. Letter to Next of Kin by Corporal Addison Darbison, US Army Correspondence, National Archives, College Park, MD.
2. "Andrew Jackson Gains His Nicknames," National Park Service, accessed Mar. 22, 2023, www.nps.gov/natr/learn/historyculture/andrew-jackson -gains-his-nicknames.htm.
3. C. Taylor, "St-Lo: XIX Corps Attacks West of Vire," US Army Center for Military History, accessed Mar. 22, 2023, https://history.army.mil/books /wwii/100-13/st-lo_2a.htm.
4. Frank Woolner, *Spearhead in the West 1941–1945: The Third Armored Division* (Frankfurt, Germany: Lucknow Books, 1945), 69.
5. Fred Hadsel, "US Army Interviews in the Field, North of Ranes," Aug. 19, 1944, University of Illinois Archives.
6. Panzer Ace (website), Rick Joshua, accessed Mar. 22, 2023, www.panzerace .net.
7. Will Saia, unpublished correspondence with Mark Reardon, May 1998.
8. C. Taylor, "St-Lo: XIX Corps Attacks West of Vire."
9. Ibid.
10. US Army, "33rd Armored Regiment After Action Report July–August 1944," Aug. 30, 1944, University of Illinois 3AD Archives.

Chapter 2: Preparing to Unleash Hell

1. A. Eaton Roberts, *Five Stars to Victory* (Birmingham, AL: Atlas Printing, 1945), http://www.3ad.com/history/wwll/feature.pages/five.stars.htm.
2. "Schrapnellmine 35 Bounding Mine—S-Mine," *D-Day and Battle of Normandy Encyclopedia,* https://www.dday-overlord.com/en/material /weaponry/schrapnellmine-35, accessed May 2, 2023.
3. Florent Lambert, "The Hogan Task Force," unpublished manuscript in the author's possession, 1978.
4. Will Saia, unpublished correspondence with Mark Reardon, May 1998.
5. James Green, "LT Wray Gets Bronze Star," *Charlotte News,* Sept. 11, 1944.
6. Samuel Hogan, unpublished correspondence with Mark Reardon, May 1998.
7. James Grimes, correspondence with the author, Aug. 2020 to June 2021.
8. Frank Woolner, *Spearhead in the West 1941–1945: The Third Armored Division* (Frankfurt, Germany: Lucknow Books, 1945), 45.
9. Ibid.
10. "US Army Individual Personnel Deceased File, Clarence Creamer," Aug. 17, 1944, National Archives, St Louis, MO.

Chapter 3: Operation Cobra: Breakout from Normandy

1. Russell Hughes, "The Tragedy of Lieutenant General Lesley McNair: The Highest Ranking US Soldier Killed in WWII," War History Online (website), Sept. 11, 2017, www.warhistoryonline.com/world-war-ii/tragey -lieutenant-general-lesley-mcnair-highest-ranking-u-s-soldier-killed-world -war-two.html.
2. Mark J. Reardon, *Victory at Mortain: Stopping Hitler's Panzer Counteroffensive* (Lawrence, KA: University Press of Kansas, 2002), 47.
3. Wilson Whitehead, unpublished correspondence with Mark Reardon, May 1993.
4. Samuel Hogan, unpublished correspondence with Mark Reardon, June 1998.
5. Wilson Whitehead, unpublished correspondence with Mark Reardon, May 1993.
6. Frank Plezia, unpublished correspondence with Mark Reardon, May 1993.
7. Charles Corbin, unpublished interview with Mark Reardon, Jan. 1993.
8. Samuel Hogan, unpublished correspondence with Mark Reardon, May 1998.
9. Reardon, *Victory at Mortain,* 62.
10. Samuel Hogan, "The Death of a Lieutenant," unpublished account in the author's possession, 1978.
11. Reardon, *Victory at Mortain,* 62.
12. Fred Hadsel, US Army Interviews in the Field, North of Ranes, Aug. 19, 1944, University of Illinois Archives.
13. Reardon, *Victory at Mortain,* 81.
14. Will Saia, unpublished correspondence with Mark Reardon, May 1998.
15. Ibid.
16. Ibid.
17. Ibid.
18. Samuel Hogan, unpublished correspondence with Mark Reardon, May 1998.
19. Ibid.
20. "Texans Killed in Action," *Dallas Morning News,* Aug. 12, 1944, accessed through newspapers.com.
21. Hadsel, "US Army Interviews in the Field, North of Ranes."
22. Omar Bradley, "A Tribute to the Infantry," 1944, www.104infdiv.org /tribute.htm.

Chapter 4: Through France Like Butter

1. Frank Woolner, *Spearhead in the West 1941–1945: The Third Armored Division* (Frankfurt, Germany: Lucknow Books, 1945), 75.
2. Ibid.
3. Marcus Schumacher, unpublished interview, May 23, 1993.
4. "Texas Colonel Who Likes Dynamite, Blows Up Enemy," *Rio Grande Valley News,* Aug. 28, 1944.
5. "Attention Texans Section: A Lone Jeep," *Fort Worth Star Telegram,* Sept.10, 1944.

6. Samuel Hogan, "The Death of a Lieutenant," unpublished short account in the author's possession, 1978.
7. Ellis O. Butler, unpublished correspondence with Mark Reardon, Feb. 1993.
8. Woolner, *Spearhead in the West 1941–1945*, 203.
9. "Operation Cobra," Normandy Campaign, D-Day Revisited, accessed May 2, 2023, https://d-dayrevisited.co.uk/d-day-history/normandy -campaign.
10. Ibid., 202.
11. Ibid., 80.
12. Ellis O. Butler, unpublished correspondence with Mark Reardon, February 1993.
13. US Army, "33rd Armored Regiment After Action Report July–August 1944," University of Illinois 3AD archives.
14. Bill Castille, unpublished correspondence in the author's possession, 1998.

Chapter 5: Into Belgium

1. US Army, "33rd Armored Regiment After Action Report July–August 1944."
2. Fred Hadsel, "US Army Interviews in the Field, the Battle of Mons," Sept. 1944, University of Illinois Archives.
3. US Army, "33rd Armored Regiment After Action Report September 1944," Oct. 1, 1944, University of Illinois 3AD archives.
4. Hadsel, "US Army Interviews in the Field, the Battle of Mons."
5. John Barclay, "Interview during 1998 3rd Armored Division Association Reunion," posted May 17, 2019, www.3AD.com.
6. Phil Luciano, "Luciano: Canton veteran served the entirety of World War II," *Journal Star* (Peoria, IL), Nov. 8, 2014, www.pjstar.com/story /news/state/2014/11/08/luciano-canton-veteran-served-entirety/3597 9018007.
7. US Army, "33rd Armored Regiment After Action Report September 1944," University of Illinois 3AD archives.
8. Gerald Astor, *The Bloody Forest: Battle for the Hürtgen September 1944–January 1945* (Novato, CA: Presidio Press, 2000), 67.
9. US Army, "33rd Armored Regiment After Action Report September 1944."

Chapter 6: Attacking the West Wall

1. US Army, "33rd Armored Regiment After Action Report September 1944," Oct. 1, 1944, University of Illinois 3AD archives.
2. Frank Woolner, *Spearhead in the West 1941–1945: The Third Armored Division* (Frankfurt, Germany: Lucknow Books, 1945), 102.
3. Ibid., 99.
4. US Army, "33rd Armored Regiment After Action Report September 1944."
5. Samuel Hogan, "The Death of a Lieutenant," unpublished short account in the author's possession, 1978.

6. "Boys Receive War Trophies from Germany," *The Courier News* (Blytheville, AR), Nov. 23, 1944.
7. "Major Adams in Invasion, on his birthday, anniversary," *The Courier News* (Blytheville, AR), July 10, 1944.
8. *Stolberg,* 26th Infantry Regimental Association (Kansas Press, 1985), 20.
9. Ibid.
10. "Lieutenant Sitzes Killed in Action," *Sikeston [MO] Standard Democrat,* Sept. 22, 1944.
11. "Transcript of Unit Log, 1st Battalion, 26th Infantry Regiment," Oct. 19, 1944, First Division Museum, www.fdmuseum.org.
12. *Stolberg,* 26th Infantry Regimental Association, 24.
13. Hogan, "The Death of a Lieutenant."
14. "Transcript of Unit Log, 1st Battalion, 26th Infantry Regiment."
15. Hogan, "The Death of a Lieutenant."
16. Ibid.
17. Ibid.
18. Ibid.
19. US Army, "After Action Report, Engineers in the Siegfried Line Penetration," Sept. 12–22, 1944, National Archives, College Park, MD.
20. Kenneth Dixon, "Burgomaster Aids Americans," *Dallas Morning News,* Sept. 22, 1944.
21. Woolner, *Spearhead in the West 1941–1945,* 214.
22. US Army, "After Action Reports, 36th Armored Infantry Regiment and Combat Command Reserve," Nov. 1, 1944, University of Illinois Digital Archives.
23. US Army, "33rd Armored Regiment Company Morning Reports," Oct. 1944, National Archives, College Park, MD.
24. Ibid.
25. Marc Spigelman, in discussion with the author, Jan. 22, 2022.
26. Manuel Baker, "My War," unpublished memoir, accessed June 2020, www.3ad.com.
27. J. Dezonia, J. Eatherly, et al., "The Battle of Aachen" (student paper), Combat Studies Institute, Fort Leavenworth, KS: Army Press, 1984, www .armyupress.army.mil/Portals/7/Primer-on-Urban-Operation/Documents /csibattle-Aachen.pdf.
28. "Aachen, Military Operations in Urban Terrain, 4th edition," 26th Infantry Regiment Association, 1999.
29. Ibid.
30. Ibid.
31. Ibid.
32. US Army, "After Action Reports, 36th Armored Infantry Regiment and Combat Command Reserve," Nov. 1, 1944, University of Illinois Digital Archives.
33. "Colonel Passes Up War's Biggest Hangover," *Dallas Morning News,* Nov. 1, 1944, accessed through www.newspapers.com.
34. Woolner, *Spearhead in the West 1941–1945,* 103.
35. Arnold Blumberg, "The Battle of Aachen," *Warfare History Network*

(website), Aug. 2016, warfarehistorynetwork.com/article/the-battle-for
-aachen.

36. "News of Sheffield; Maj Adams Dies," *The Courier News* (Blytheville, AR),
    Nov. 23, 1944.

Chapter 7: Not a Quiet Christmas

1. US Army, "G Company Morning Reports," Dec. 1944, National Archives,
   College Park, MD.
2. "Panzer Brigade 150," Axis History (website), www.axishistory.com
   /various/120-germany-waffen-ss/germany-waffen-ss-brigades/1349-panzer
   -brigade-150.
3. John Prados, *Normandy Crucible: The Decisive Battle That Shaped World
   War II in Europe* (New York: Dutton Caliber, 2012), 33.
4. Video interview of Travis Brown, Clem Elissondo, and Clark Worrell at
   3AD Reunion, 1997, University of Illinois Archives.
5. Samuel Hogan, "Battle of the Bulge," unpublished account in possession of
   the author, 1998.
6. Ibid.
7. Ibid.
8. Ibid.
9. Fred Hadsel, "US Army After Action Interview of LTC Sam Hogan," 1945,
   National Archives, College Park, MD.
10. Video interview of Travis Brown, Clem Elissondo, and Clark Worrell at
    3AD Reunion, 1997, University of Illinois Archives.

Chapter 8: Never Surrender

1. Florent Lambert, "The Hogan Task Force," 1991, unpublished manuscript
   in the author's possession.
2. Frank Woolner, *Spearhead in the West 1941–1945: The Third Armored
   Division* (Frankfurt, Germany: Lucknow Books, 1945), 110.
3. John Barclay, in an interview during the 1998 3rd Armored Division
   Association reunion, posted May 17, 2019, accessed on www.3AD.com.
4. James Grimes, in discussion with the author, Apr. 2020.
5. Lambert, "The Hogan Task Force."
6. Hogan, "Battle of the Bulge."
7. H. Rex Shama, *Pulse and Repulse: Troop Carrier and Airborne Teams in
   Europe During World War II* (Madison, WI: Eakin Press, 1995), 138.
8. Victor Lasky, "A Ringer Tells of Task Force Hogan's 400," *Stars and Stripes*,
   Jan. 4, 1945.
9. Samuel Hogan, "Battle of the Bulge."
10. Hand-drawn map of Marcouray by local historian Albert Hemmer,
    courtesy Dieter Laes.
11. Florent Lambert, "The Story of Hogan's 400," 1991, unpublished
    manuscript in the author's possession.
12. Ibid.

13. US Army, "Company Morning Report, G Co 33rd Armored Regiment," Dec. 28, 1945, National Archives, College Park, MD.
14. Lambert, "The Hogan Task Force."
15. Hogan, "Battle of the Bulge."
16. "Award Recommendation, Witness Statements, SSG Lee B. Porter, 83rd Reconnaissance Battalion," courtesy of Darren Neely.
17. Hogan, "Battle of the Bulge."

Chapter 9: The Scotch Bet and the Rose Pocket

1. Woolner, *Spearhead in the West 1941–1945,* 233.
2. US Army, "33rd Armored Regiment After Action Report," Feb. 1945, University of Illinois 3AD Archives.
3. Hogan, "Battle of the Bulge."
4. John J. Modrak, "Statement of War Crimes," Feb. 1945, University of Illinois 3AD Archives.
5. US Army, "33rd Armored Regiment After Action Report."
6. Cable, Bernard Montgomery to Dwight D. Eisenhower re Conclusion of Ardennes Campaign, January 16, 1945, DDE's Pre-Presidential Papers, Principal File, Box 83, accessed May 3, 2023, www.eisenhowerlibrary.gov /research/online-documents/ardennes-campaign-battle-bulge.
7. Woolner, *Spearhead in the West 1941–1945,* 215.
8. US Army, "HQ Company Morning Reports," January 1945, accessed at the National Archives, College Park, MD.
9. James H. Madison, "Wearing Lipstick to War: An American Woman in World War II England and France," *Prologue Magazine* 39, no. 3 (Fall 2007), accessed Mar. 24, 2023, www.archives.gov/publications/prologue /2007/fall/lipstick.html.
10. Hubert S. Miller, *Roer River Crossing, February 1945, Julich–Germany, Part 2* (Bibliogov, 2013), 32.
11. US Army, "33rd Armored Regiment After Action Report," Feb. 1945, University of Illinois 3AD Archives.
12. US Army, "36th Armored Infantry Regiment, After Action Reports," Mar. 1, 1945, University of Illinois Digital Archives.
13. "James Grimes video interview with John Grimes," 1995, interview in the author's possession.
14. John Welborn, "Commander 33rd Armored Regiment Condolence Letter to Family of John Wolf," 1945, National Archives, St. Louis, MO.
15. US Army, "G Company Morning Reports," Mar. 1945, National Archives, College Park, MD.
16. R. P. Hunnicutt, *Pershing: A History of the Medium Tank T20 Series* (Ryton Publications, 2008), 233.
17. Merry McAllen, "Captured Cologne Zoo Gives Colonel an Idea," *Stars and Stripes*, Mar. 9, 1945.
18. "Mr. and Mrs. DC Hogan Receive News," *Rio Grande Valley News*, Apr. 27, 1945.

19. Jack B. Warden, transcribed interview, accessed Mar. 24, 2023, http://3adspearhead.com/TFRich.html.

20. Haynes Duggan, correspondence with Samuel Hogan, May 13, 1998, in the author's possession.

21. Frank Woolner, *Spearhead in the West 1941–1945: The Third Armored Division* (Frankfurt, Germany: Lucknow Books, 1945), 245.

22. Ibid., 246.

23. Ibid., 145.

Chapter 10: Ninety Miles to Berlin

1. Paul Grigorieff, "The Mittelwerk/Mittelbau/Camp Dora Mittelbaur Gmb—Mittelbau KZ," V2Rocket.com (website), accessed Mar. 24, 2023, www.v2rocket.com/start/chapters/mittel.html.

2. US Army, "33rd Armored Regiment After Action Report," Apr. 1945, University of Illinois 3AD Archives.

3. Ibid.

4. US Army, "36th Armored Infantry Regiment, After Action Reports," Apr. 18, 1945, University of Illinois Digital Archives.

5. Ibid.

6. "Lt. Col. Clayman wounded," *Democrat and Chronicle*, Feb. 20, 1945, accessed through newspapers.com.

7. US Army, "33rd Armored Regiment After Action Report," Apr. 1945.

8. Woolner, *Spearhead in the West 1941–1945,* 151.

9. Darren Neely, in discussion with the author, Jan. 2022.

10. US Army, "33rd Armored Regiment After Action Report," Apr. 1945.

11. US Army, "36th Armored Infantry Regiment, After Action Reports," Apr. 18, 1945, University of Illinois Digital Archives.

12. Ibid.

13. Marcus Michel, in discussion with the author, Aug. 2020.

14. US Army, "36th Armored Infantry Regiment, After Action Reports," Apr. 18, 1945, University of Illinois Digital Archives.

15. Woolner, *Spearhead in the West 1941–1945,* 253.

The Men of Task Force Hogan

1. Phil Luciano, "Luciano: Canton veteran served the entirety of World War II," *Journal Star*, Nov. 8, 2014, www.pjstar.com/story/news/state /2014/11/08/luciano-canton-veteran-served-entirety/35979018007.

INDEX

★ ★ ★ ★ ★

ABOUT THE AUTHOR

★　★　★　★　★

William R. Hogan is a fourth-generation US Army veteran. During his twenty years in the military, he served in armored, airborne, and special operations units. His service took him from peacekeeping in the Balkans and humanitarian assistance operations in Haiti to combat in Afghanistan. Twice he served as a military attaché and most recently as an exchange officer at the French Army headquarters in Paris. Based in Paris and on the US East Coast, Will enjoys travel, skiing, diving, playing guitar, and, of course, military history. He is the son of Samuel Hogan, who was one of the youngest and most colorful tactical-level combat commanders of World War II.